Shopsmith Inc.

3931 Image Drive
Dayton, Ohio 45414-2591

Dear Woodworking Friend,

We hope you enjoy your book, and we'd like to thank you for your interest in Shopsmith. You may already know that Shopsmith is synonymous with Woodworking and the remarkable MARK V woodworking system. But the truth is, you don't have to own a MARK V to take advantage of all that Shopsmith offers.

We do more than sell woodworking equipment — we provide a complete **system** that includes most everything you need to get the most out of woodworking, including project plans, hand tools, hardwoods, finishing products and the instruction you need to develop and expand your woodworking skills. We're your Total Woodworking Company.

From our humble beginning, we have grown and established ourselves as the leader in home woodworking. We have a growing network of more than 30 retail stores conveniently located across the U.S. and Canada. And we're opening more. Our stores are unique in the woodworking industry. They educate woodworkers of all abilities through regularly scheduled classes and seminars taught by our own expert instructors. Plus, our other educational resources — such as books and video training tapes — provide a complete woodworking education. We also keep you abreast of the latest innovations and techniques of interest to woodworking enthusiasts.

In addition to our outstanding educational programs, we also offer our customers the most comprehensive warranty offered by any power tool manufacturer — The Shopsmith Gold Medal Buyer Protection Plan. And our FREE Service Hotline is always just a toll-free phone call away, should you ever have questions or need assistance. Our Customer Services Representatives and store personnel undergo extensive training on woodworking and Shopsmith equipment, so they can provide the answers to your questions.

If you have any questions about woodworking or Shopsmith equipment, please call our toll-free number (1-800-543-7586). We can also direct you to the store nearest you.

All this and more — it's just part of the Shopsmith commitment. So come join the Shopsmith family of woodworkers and find out how fun, safe and rewarding woodworking can be.

Sincerely,

John R. Folkerth
Chairman, Shopsmith, Inc.

Popular Science

WOODWORKING PROJECTS

1988 Yearbook

SHOPSMITH EDITION

Published by **Popular Science Books**
New York, NY

Copyright © 1987 by Popular Science Books

Published by

Popular Science Books
Grolier Book Clubs, Inc.
380 Madison Avenue
New York, NY 10017

Designed by Linda Watts

Produced by Bookworks, Inc.

ISBN: 1-55654-029-9

Second Printing, 1988

Manufactured in the United States of America

Introduction

There's something for everyone in this year's *Popular Science Woodworking Projects Yearbook*. No matter what your woodworking ambitions, you'll find something here to interest you. We carefully chose a broad mix of projects — small and large, classic and contemporary, indoor and outdoor, down to earth and just for fun. Here are a few examples:

The "Country Stuff" chapter includes four quick, easy items that will add a touch of 'down home' to your home: a 'pouting chair', a silhouette 'corner cat', a 'goose basket', and a wooden 'tulip box'. You can make any of these in just a few hours. But if you're looking for a bigger challenge, try the "Pedestal Table" or the "Child's Rolltop Desk".

If you like reproductions of classic furniture, check out the "Lowboy Desk" and the "Chest of Drawers". For something more contemporary, see the "Modular Wall System" or the "Bow-Side Breakfront". Would you rather spend your woodworking time increasing the value of your real estate? Consider building a "Sunshade Gazebo". It's easier than it looks, and it can be built for the same cost as a medium-sized deck!

Some of the projects in this Yearbook are unadorned and just-plain-useful, like the "New Improved Sawhorse" and the "Sawdust Catchers" for your shop. Others are meant to tickle your fancy or your children's imagination. The "Whirligigs" chapter contains the plans for three whimsical wind toys. And the wooden "Toy Steam Train" comes complete with a wooden "Train Whistle".

You won't find many of these projects published anywhere else; most of them have been developed exclusively for this Yearbook. Projects like the ingenious "Library Chair" that turns into a step-stool, or the captivating "Doodle Maker" that draws designs automatically were designed and refined by craftsmen just for publication in this book.

There are more than thirty of these diverse, unique projects, complete with step-by-step instructions, measured drawings and exploded views, and hundreds of illustrations showing you how to safely perform the woodworking techniques you need to build each project.

In putting together these projects, we also brought together woodworkers from all over America and all walks of life. There are professional craftsmen and craftswomen, amateur woodworkers, all with a design or two to share. For those woodworkers who aren't also writers, we helped them to tell their story.

There are a number of heavyweight professionals who have contributed to this Yearbook: *Tom Stender* is a renowned craftsman/designer from Boston, New York, who gives seminars on reproducing classical furniture. This year, he shows off his versatility in two pieces, one contemporary and the other classical. Woodworking author *David Donnelly* of Boise, Idaho, shares some professional secrets with the reader. David Donnelly has published in many woodworking magazines, including "Wood" and "Hands On!".

Popular Science understands that some of the best woodworking is done not for money, but for the love of woodworking. So the editor also included many talented amateurs. *Jim Hasson* of Tempe, Arizona, loves handguns *and* woodworking, as evidenced by the case he built for a rare Colt .45. *Harry Cooper* of Vine Grove, Kentucky, is a retired cabinetmaker who still loves to build things — and loves to give them away. *Vicki Morgan* of Enon, Ohio, is a jet airplane mechanic who loves to work with her hands on and off the job. Currently, she's planning a book of whirligigs with her sister, how-to author Deborah Morgan.

But even though we've managed to include woodworking designs from some very fine people in this Yearbook, please remember that these people are only human. And, as such, they make a few errors now and then.

Please, before you cut up good wood, check and doublecheck the measurements in the Bill of Materials against the dimensions in the plans. It's just good woodworking practice to sit down with a calculator and add up the numbers before you embark on a project. If there is a problem with the measurements, this exercise will save you time and lumber. Even if all the measurements are correct, it will save you time. Checking the numbers, one by one, helps you trace the thoughts of the craftsman who originally designed the piece. This in-depth understanding of the project saves you frustration and helps your work to proceed steadily and smoothly.

With all good wishes,
The Editors

Contributors

Adam Blake ◆ Adam learned his woodworking skills on the job. Several years ago, while he was looking for a part-time job to make money for college, a woodworker hired him to do odd jobs around the shop. He gradually took on more and more responsibility until he was building his own furniture and wooden accessories.

He didn't stop with the small stuff. In that three years, he has also tackled some ambitious remodeling and carpentry jobs. He helped to convert a one-hundred-year-old carriage barn into a modern workshop, remodeled several rooms in an old Victorian mansion near his home town of Tipp City, Ohio, and built the gazebo you see in this volume of the *Woodworking Projects Yearbook*.

Harry Cooper ◆ Harry is not only a fine woodworker, he's a financial wizard. He began woodworking when he retired several years ago. His first tools were a set of carving knives that cost $8.50. Today, his shop in Vine Grove, Kentucky, is equipped with thousands of dollars worth of hand and power tools — and he's paid for them all by making what he calls "scrap box projects".

Harry started out by whittling name plaques from wood he scavenged. "I carved those signs till I ran out of grape crates," Harry recalls. By then he had made enough money to buy a few more tools — but he continued to work with wood that other folks were about to throw away. This has never hindered his craftsmanship. His creations are small, but classy. Today, he admits that once in a while he breaks down and buys a board of real never-been-nailed-up lumber — but not very often.

Chalmer Crowell ◆ Chalmer is a retired machinist who was "always building something", as far back as he can remember. Over forty years ago, he bought a farm near Bradford, Ohio, that needed plenty of work — there was no wiring or plumbing. He remodeled the house, inside and out; put up a garage; and built several outbuildings.

When he retired, he took up woodworking as a hobby and began producing wooden accessories and novelties for his friends, children, and grandchildren. Chalmer converted what was left of an old barn into a shop, and shared it with his children. "Somebody always had some project going on out

there." Today, the shop has been moved to his son's house, and Chalmer has moved into town — but there's still a project or two going on.

David Donnelly ◆ David is a newcomer to woodworking — he just began in 1984. But since then, he's made amazing progress. Not only has he built several pieces of outstanding furniture, he's published articles in *HANDS ON!* and has become a regular contributor to *Wood* magazine.

David began woodworking in his garage in Boise, Idaho, to find some relief from his high pressure endeavors as a producer of instructional and corporate A/V communications. "I took a course in woodworking in a junior college," David explains, "and fell in love with it. This is a means of creative expression where I can set my own standards, fulfill my own expectations. What I do for a living — film and video — is just too expensive to do that. Someone else is always fronting the money, and you're accountable to them."

Nick Engler ◆ Nick founded the woodworking magazine *HANDS ON!*, and managed that publication for several years. During that time, he helped to publish not only the magazine, but over 100 project plans, several books, how-to manuals, and a syndicated newspaper column for woodworkers.

Since then, he's co-authored two new books, *How to Build Outdoor Structures* and *Projects for the Router*. He's also co-owner of Bookworks, Inc., a firm in West Milton, Ohio, that specializes in the production of how-to books. For the last four years, Nick and the staff at Bookworks have put together the *Woodworking Projects Yearbook* for Popular Science Books.

Mary Jane Favorite ◆ Mary Jane grew up around woodworking. She remembers that her family was "always involved in some remodeling project. There was always a nail to pound." Some of her earliest memories are of turning spindles and bowls with her grandfather in his workshop. "I have always liked wood," says Mary Jane, "liked the feel of it, liked working with it."

Later on, Mary Jane began to design things that she needed around the home, things that were "molded to my own needs" — everything from a simple set of shelves to a full-size sofa. Seeking a bigger arena for her designs, she took some commercial art and drafting classes at the College of Art and Design in Columbus, Ohio. Today, she designs wooden furniture and accessories professionally.

Jim Hasson ◆ Jim will tell you that he does furniture repair in Tempe, Arizona. However, that simple statement doesn't begin to describe the magnitude of his job. Jim works in the repair shop that handles all the furniture for the entire Mesa-Tempe school system — 56 schools with over 54,000 students. "We never get caught up," says Jim. Small wonder.

In his off hours, Jim makes finely crafted cases and furniture for friends and relatives. He's also going to school, taking courses in furniture design, cabinetry, and finishing. He's considered opening his own cabinet shop someday, but only on his terms. "I want to make one-of-a-kind pieces for people, no mass-produced stuff". That's another small wonder — he's probably seen one too many of those 54,000 desks.

John H. Mitchell ◆ John is a freelance writer with a talent for carpentry and cabinetry. He's built his own house outside of Coolville, Ohio, as well as helped to remodel some of his friends' homes. He describes his shop as "mobile" and his tools as "straightforward". "I don't do anything fancy; all my woodworking is very down-to-earth".

When he's not building something, he's writing. He's proficient at many different types of writing: John has made a living as a newspaper reporter and a technical writer. He's published fiction and written screenplays. He's even taught writing.

Vicki Morgan ◆ Vicki has "always worked with my hands, ever since I was a kid". The Air Force noticed her talent for tinkering and taught her to be a jet engine mechanic. Today, she's a civilian, but she still maintains aircraft equipment at Wright Patterson Air Force Base, near her home in Enon, Ohio.

When she isn't busy keeping Air Force jets flying, she works with her hands making all sorts of crafts. She builds things not only from wood, but from cloth, ceramics, paper,

"anything I can get my hands on". She builds twenty to thirty projects per year, and gives them away to friends and family.

Thomas Stender ◆ Walk into Tom Stender's house in Boston, New York, and you'll think you've died and gone to woodworker's heaven. Ever since he began woodworking in earnest, Tom has been slowly filling his house with fine hand-crafted furniture. There's a little bit of everything here — Queen Anne, Chippendale, Shaker, Country, Contemporary, you name it. "When I started building things in the barn," he explains, "I thought I'd let the house be the showroom".

Tom began making custom furniture in 1975. At first, he built modern "Studio" pieces, but quickly found that he liked the classical styles much better. Today, he designs and builds elegant furniture in the same tradition as craftsmen from the eighteenth and early nineteenth centuries. He doesn't do many 'reproductions', however. All his designs are original, built along traditional lines.

Phil Stock ◆ Members of Phil's family — his father, grandfather, uncles — always did woodworking, so it was just natural that Phil grew up to do woodworking, too. He considered building furniture and cabinets professionally for a while, but decided against it because he didn't want the enjoyment he got while woodworking to be spoiled by the pressure of a deadline. "Woodworking is such a challenge," he explains. "You need to be free to explore possible solutions to the problems it presents — and free to make mistakes."

When Phil's not woodworking, he's a film producer in Yellow Springs, Ohio. While he does many, many different types of film and audio/visual work, almost three dozen of his films have had to do with woodworking.

And Others…It takes more than a few woodworkers to put together a book of woodworking projects. We'd also like to acknowledge Mary K. Baird, Linda Ball, Karen Callahan, Hue Park, Jean Simmerman, and Denise Wood for their contributions.

And special thanks to Shopsmith, Inc. and *Fine Woodworking* magazine for allowing us to publish some of their materials.

Contents

Techniques

PROJECTS

Designed and built by Nick Engler

Pedestal Table

This classic round table seats up to eight people.

Pedestal tables always seem to offer more flexibility than the rectangular, four-legged variety. The tops are round, so people can sit where they want, all facing one another. If you need to set a place for an extra guest, you don't have to squeeze him in on a corner. Furthermore, there are no table legs to get in the way of the chairs — just one central post in the middle.

The pedestal table you see here was modeled after the classic form that became popular around the turn of the

century. The top is 48″ in diameter, large enough for four to six people. However, the top slides apart, making room for an 18″ leaf — and two more people. (See Figure 1.)

Figure 1. Using special 'equalizer slides', made especially for pedestal tables, the top halves slide apart so that you can install a leaf for more table space.

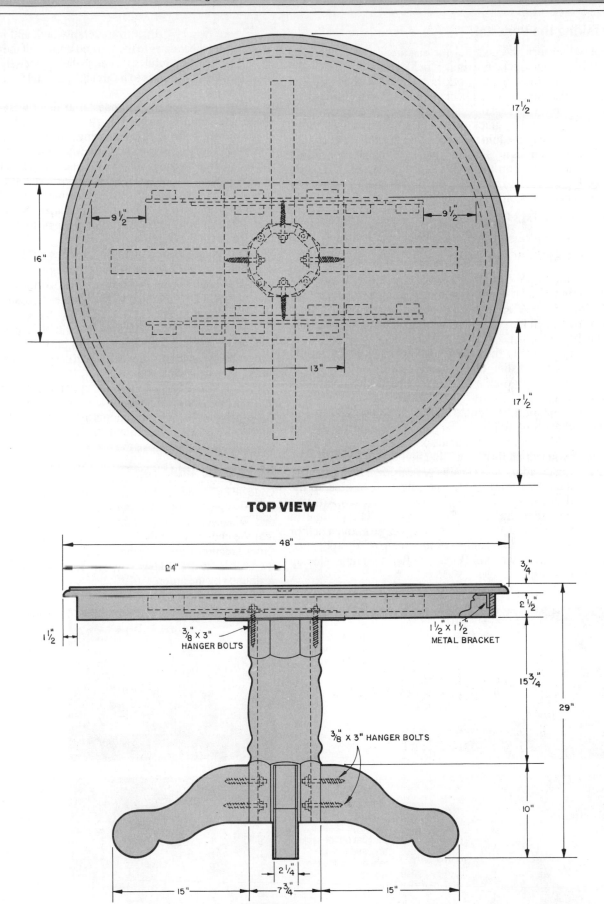

TOP VIEW

SIDE VIEW

Making the Pedestal

You could turn the pedestal for this table from a massive, solid turning block, but that would probably stretch the capacity of most home workshop lathes. A solid pedestal would also be prone to checking and splitting. So instead, make a hollow pedestal.

Rip eight 1½" thick boards at 22½°, as shown in the working drawings. Join the edges, taking care not to change the angle even slightly. When you join the edges of boards at an angle, always tip the jointer fence in towards the work. (See Figure 2.) Dry assemble the boards to make sure they form a perfect octagon.

> **Tip ◆** It's a good idea to rip eight practice boards from scrap stock first, to make sure that you have set the angle of your table saw correctly.

With a dado cutter, cut a ¼" groove down the length of each edge of each board, where they will join together. (See Figure 3.) Rip ¼" splines to fit in these grooves. The splines will strengthen the edge joints between the boards when you glue them together.

Dry assemble the boards and splines to check the fit. When you're satisfied that the parts fit correctly, glue them up. Clamp the pedestal assembly together with band clamps while the glue dries.

Important: It's essential that all the edges of the boards fit together properly. If they don't, this will create a weak spot in the pedestal, and it may come apart after a relatively short time. If you can't adjust your table saw so that it cuts perfect 22½° angles, adjust it as close as you can, then rip the boards. Make the spline grooves and the splines, then glue up the pedestal in two separate halves — four boards each. After the glue dries, sand the edges of the halves flat, so they fit together perfectly. (If you don't have a large enough belt or disc sander, glue 80# sandpaper to a scrap of plywood, and sand the halves by hand.) When you finish sanding, glue up the two halves.

Make two 7¾" discs from scrap wood, and mark the centers. Nail these discs to the top and bottom of the pedestal assembly, being careful to center them precisely on the assembly. Use these discs to mount the pedestal to your lathe. (See Figure 4.)

Turn the shape of the pedestal at the lowest possible speed, and sand it at a speed that's only slightly higher. The shape you see in the working drawings is only a suggestion; if you wish, design your own. However, note that only the middle of the pedestal is shaped; the ends are left octagonal.

When you've finished making the pedestal, saw the legs out on a bandsaw. Sand away any saw marks, and shape the upper edges of the legs with a router or shaper. (See Figure 5.) Screw hanger bolts into the ends of the legs, so that you can attach them to the pedestal.

Drill corresponding holes in the sides or 'panels' of the pedestal, near the bottom. Mount the legs to the pedestal, using the hanger bolts. As shown in the working drawings, the legs should be mounted to every other side, so that they are 90° from each other.

To finish the pedestal, attach the table top mounting plate to the top end. Like the legs, this part is attached with hanger bolts. Later on, this will make it easy for you to detach and re-attach the table top.

Install four hanger bolts in the upper end of the pedestal, in those panels that do not have legs mounted to them. Drill corresponding holes in the mounting plate, and attach the plate to the pedestal. Just thumb-tighten the nuts for now, so that you can easily remove the plate.

Making the Table Top

Glue up 24" wide stock to make the two halves of the table top. Also, glue up 18" wide stock to make the leaf, if you want one. When you glue up the table top and leaf stock, make sure that the end grains of the individual boards all curve in the same direction — towards the top surface. That way, if any of the boards have a tendency to cup, their movement will be restrained by the apron.

Figure 2. Join the edges of the pedestal parts at 22½°. Tilt the jointer fence in, towards the work.

Figure 3. Cut a ¼" groove for splines in the edges of the pedestal parts. Keep the edge of each part flat on the table, and use the rip fence to guide the work.

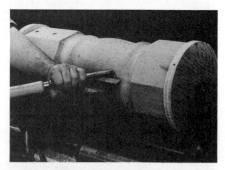

Figure 4. Temporarily, install discs of scrap wood at either end of the pedestal so that you can mount the hollow pedestal to the lathe.

Figure 5. Shape the upper edges of the legs with a router or a shaper.

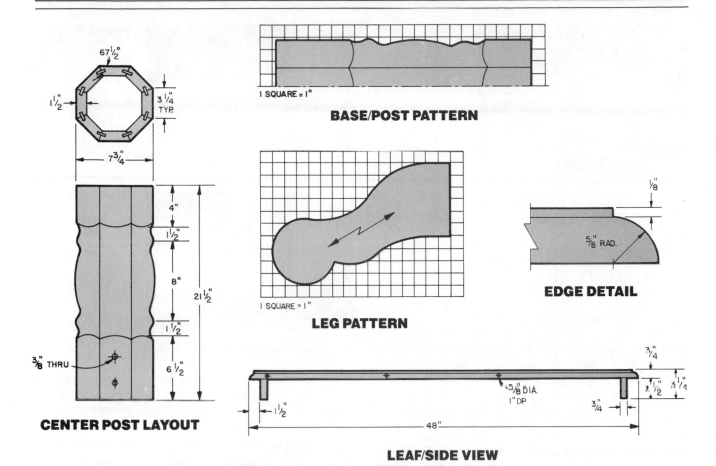

BASE/POST PATTERN

1 SQUARE = 1"

LEG PATTERN

1 SQUARE = 1"

EDGE DETAIL

5/8" RAD.

1/8

67 1/2°

1 1/2"

3 1/4 TYP.

7 3/4"

4"

1 1/2"

8"

21 1/2"

1 1/2"

3/8" THRU

6 1/2"

CENTER POST LAYOUT

LEAF/SIDE VIEW

3/4

2 1/2"

3 1/4

5/8" DIA. 1" DP

1 1/2"

3/4"

48"

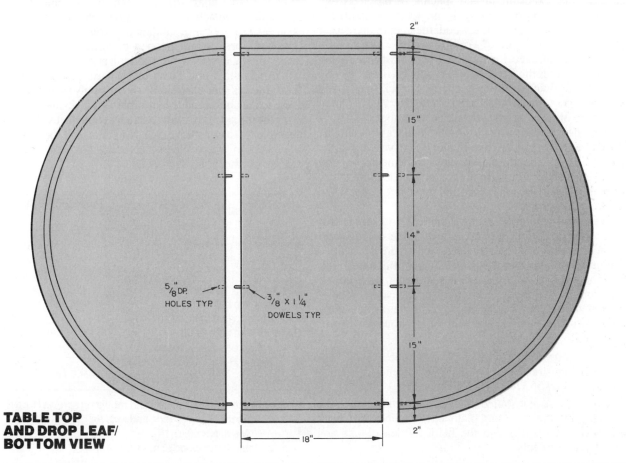

TABLE TOP AND DROP LEAF/ BOTTOM VIEW

2"

15"

14"

15"

2"

5/8" DP. HOLES TYP.

3/8" X 1 1/4" DOWELS TYP.

18"

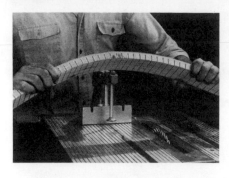

Figure 6. To bend the aprons that attach to the table halves, cut ⅛″ wide kerfs in the back sides of the stock.

Figure 7. To keep the aprons in place, use small angle brackets, screwed to the back side of the aprons and the underside of the top halves, every 8″-12″.

Figure 8. Install equalizer slides to the mounting plate, and then to the top halves.

Rip the leaf to the proper width, and join all the edges of the top stock so they fit together with no gaps. With a string and a pencil, mark the diameter of the table top on the 24″ wide stock. Cut out the semi-circles with a saber saw; then sand the saw marks from the edge. Be careful when you sand that you don't cut too deep. You want to preserve a 'fair' curve. If you cut too deep with the sandpaper, the curve will be irregular. To aid in making an accurate circle, saw a little wide of the line, then sand down to it.

With a horizontal boring machine or a doweling jig, drill holes in the edges of the table top halves and the leaf to dowel them together. These holes must be positioned precisely, so the top will fit together properly with or without the leaf.

Rip stock for the aprons, and cut ⅛″ wide kerfs in the back sides of the aprons that must be curved. These kerfs should go almost through the stock, leaving just ¹⁄₁₆″-⅛″ uncut. They should be spaced close enough together to allow you to bend the wood easily to the curve you need. (See Figure 6.) The exact depth and spacing of the kerfs will depend on the type of wood you use to make the table. Generally, the more brittle the wood, the deeper and closer the kerfs should be. If you're working in oak, which is fairly supple if it hasn't aged for too long, you can probably get away with cutting the kerfs ¼″ apart and ⅝″ deep (leaving ⅛″ uncut). If you're working in cherry or rock maple, you may have to cut the kerfs ⅛″ apart, ¹¹⁄₁₆″ deep. Experiment with a scrap of wood before you cut good lumber.

Attach the aprons to the top halves and leaves with glue and small angle brackets. (See Figure 7.) As you install the aprons, be careful that the ends of one apron line up properly with the ends of the others. To make sure you do things right, temporarily dowel the top halves and the leaf together while you attach the aprons.

When the glue dries, remove the leaf and set the two halves together, bottom side up. Attach a pair of 'equalizer slides' to the bottom of the top halves. (See Figure 8.) Remove the mounting plate from the pedestal, and attach the other side of the slides to the plate. (Some slides are manufactured so that you may have to perform this step in reverse order — plate first, then the top halves.) Equalizer slides are available from most mail-order woodworking supply houses. Here are two sources:

The Woodworker's Store   Constantine
21801 Industrial Blvd.   2050 Eastchester Road
Rogers, MN 55374   Bronx, NY 10461

Once you have installed the slides, attach the top to the pedestal, using the mounting plate and hanger bolts. Check the action of the slides and the fit of the leaf. Make any necessary adjustments.

Once you're satisfied, shape the edge of the top halves and the leaves with a router. Do this with the leaf installed in the table. Make the same shape you cut into the top edge of the legs, so that all the edges match.

Finishing Up

Take the table apart. Remove the top assembly from the pedestal, and detach the slides. Also remove the legs from the pedestal. Do any finish sanding that you still need to do, and (if you're working with an open-grain wood such as oak) fill the grain of the wood with wood filler.

Apply stain and finish to all parts. Use a waterproof finish such as spar varnish. Be sure to apply as many coats of finish to the bottom side of the table top halves and leaf as you do to the top side. This will ensure that both faces of the wood absorb or lose moisture at the same rate, and the top will be less likely to warp. When the finish is dry, rub it out and reassemble the table.

BILL OF MATERIALS — Pedestal Table

Finished Dimensions in Inches

A.	Pedestal panels (8)	1½ x 3¼ x 21½
B.	Splines (8)	¼ x 1 x 21½
C.	Legs (4)	2¼ x 10 x 15
D.	Table top mounting plate	¾ x 13 x 16
E.	Table top halves (2)	¾ x 24 x 48
F.	Table top leaf (optional)	¾ x 18 x 48
G.	Table top aprons (2)	¾ x 2½ x 70¾
H.	Leaf aprons (2 — optional)	¾ x 2½ x 18
J.	Dowels (3-6)	⅜ dia. x 1¼

Hardware

Pedestal table equalizer slides and mounting screws (1 pair)
⅜″ x 3″ Hanger bolts, washers, and nuts (8)
1½″ x 1½″ Metal brackets (14-20)
#6 x ¾″ Roundhead wood screws (28-40)

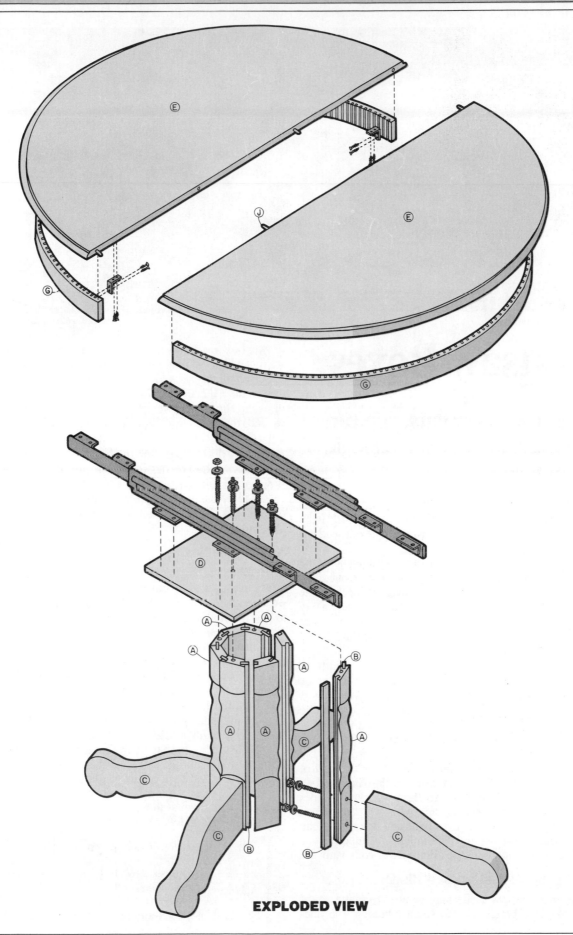

EXPLODED VIEW

Text and photography by David Donnelly   Designed and made by David Donnelly

Bandsaw Boxes

With a few clever cuts, you can make these boxes from a single piece of wood.

Bandsaw boxes are novel, deceptively simple to build, and make ideal gifts. An entire box can be made in an afternoon. The only piece of equipment you need is a bandsaw.

The construction technique guarantees a snug fit for the drawers in the box. The drawers and the box are cut out of the same piece of wood. Naturally, the drawers fit back in the spaces they were cut from. You don't need to worry about any complicated joinery or parts that might be mis-sized. The only gap between the drawer and the surrounding box will be the width of the kerf of the bandsaw blade.

Since you can cut almost any shape on a bandsaw, bandsaw boxes can be made to any design. Drawers can be traditional rectangles, circles, ovals, or any shape that suits your fancy. A box can contain one shape or several; no two boxes will ever look alike. The boxes pictured here were made from scrap wood — the small box from cherry, and the large box from alder.

Although there are no 'plans' as such for this sort of project, I have provided a set of working drawings and an exploded view of the large box to show you how it goes together. *These drawings are only intended as guidelines.* When you get ready to make your own bandsaw boxes, you can change the dimensions — and the shapes — as much as you please. The only limitation is the throat size of your bandsaw.

Choosing and Using Bandsaw Blades

Although any bandsaw blade may be used to make a box, you will obtain a better fit with smaller blades. The one-drawer box was cut with a ¼″ blade, and the two-drawer box was cut with a ³⁄₁₆″ blade. The ³⁄₁₆″ blade turns a tighter radius, makes smaller kerfs, and cuts smoother. Smoother cuts mean less sanding; the less sanding you do, the tighter the fit of the drawers. The two-drawer box measures 5½″ x 5½″ x 4″. This exceeds the 3″ recommended cutting limit of the ³⁄₁₆″ blade, but a sharp, new blade handles the job nicely.

If you decide to stretch the limits of your blades to cut thick stock, observe the following precautions: Cut very slowly, especially on turns; use a fence to guide your straight cuts; and be careful that your blade does not flex. To help prevent flex, adjust the blade tension *slightly* higher than recommended.

Making the Box

In the following text and photos, I've described, step-by-step, how I made the two-drawer box. Remember, the measurements and the sizes given here are *only for this particular box.* When you make your own, they may change slightly. They might also change a lot.

First, prepare the wood. Cut the wood to size, or laminate scraps to get the size you want. Make sure the size of the stock does not exceed the throat capacity of your bandsaw. Round any hard corners or shape the outside contours of the box, then finish sand the outside of the box stock. Do the shaping and sanding at this time, because the stock is easier to handle than it will be after you cut it up.

Once the box is shaped and sanded, cut the sides. Slice off both sides from the stock, as shown in Figure 1. These sides will be glued back on the box later, after you make the drawers. The sides of this particular box are ½″; however, you may safely cut them as thin as ¼″, if you wish. To help guide the cut, attach a rip fence to your bandsaw.

> **Tip ◆** Mark the sides after you cut them, so that you'll be able to glue them back to the same sides of the stock as you cut them from. This way, the grain will match up.

Set the sides aside for a moment. Use a straightedge to

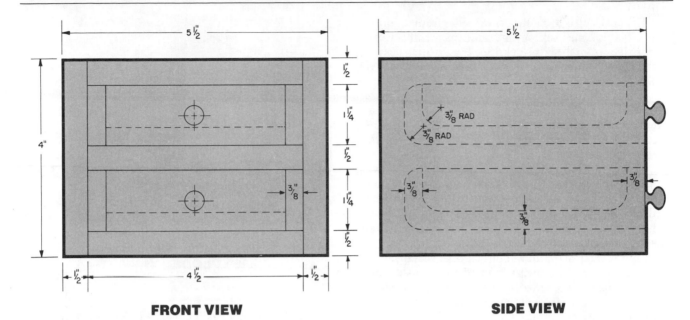

FRONT VIEW

SIDE VIEW

lay out the drawer blank on the side and front of the remaining stock. (See Figure 2.) On this box, I left ½″ of stock between the drawers. The top and the bottom are also ½″ thick, as is the back. Once again, you may want to reduce these measurements to as small as ¼″. When you mark the cutting lines, be sure the corners are rounded and not square. Remember the turning radius of your blade!

At this time, you'll also want to plan out your drawer parts. The bottom and the sides of the drawer should be ¼″-⅜″ thick — mine are ⅜″. The fronts, backs, and sides should be ⅜″-½″ thick. To keep everything uniform, I made mine ⅜″.

Cut the drawer blanks from the stock. If you wish, use a rip fence to help guide the straight cuts. (See Figure 3.) Stop

when you get to the corners, remove the rip fence, and cut the corners and the back of the drawer blank freehand. Accuracy is extremely important when you cut the drawer blank, so work slowly and carefully. When you're finished, carefully mark each drawer blank so that you can identify the top side, and where it fits back into the box. (See Figure 4.)

Note: The drawer blanks for this box are just 1¼″ thick. When you subtract the thickness of the drawer bottoms, that makes each drawer just ⅞″ deep. That's adequate to store small treasures, but it's hardly enough space for anything substantial. If you wanted to store larger items, this same size box could be made with just one drawer. The drawer blank would have been 3″ thick, and the completed drawer 2⅝″ deep.

Figure 1. Using a rip fence as a guide, cut off the sides of the box stock.

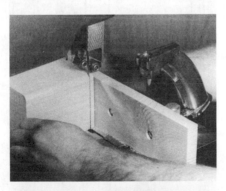

Figure 2. Mark the drawer blanks with a straightedge. Allow ¼″-½″ for the thickness of the box top, bottom, back, and any drawer dividers.

Figure 3. Cut out the drawer blanks, carefully following the lines. Use a rip fence to guide the straight cuts; remove the fence to turn the corners.

Figure 4. Mark the blanks so you can put the drawers back into the same spaces you cut them from.

The next step is to cut the drawer sides from the drawer blanks. This is done in exactly the same manner that you cut the box sides from the box stock. (See Figure 5.) In this case, the thickness of the sides is ⅜″. Mark the drawer sides as you cut them, so you'll be able to glue them back to their proper drawers, on their proper sides.

Mark the cutting lines for the drawer fronts, backs, and bottoms on the remaining drawer blanks. (See Figure 6.) Once again, remember the turning radius of your blade when you mark the corners.

Cut out the insides of the drawers, carefully following the cutting lines. (See Figure 7.) Discard the insides after you've cut them; this is the one portion of the stock you don't need to save. (Of course, if you do save them, you can eventually accumulate enough drawer insides to glue up and make another bandsaw box blank.)

Lightly sand all the drawer pieces. It's easier to sand the inside surfaces of the drawers *before* the drawers are reassembled. Then glue the sides of the drawer back to the drawer bodies. After the glue dries, sand the glue joints. (See Figure 8.)

Lightly sand the inside surfaces of the drawer spaces. As with the drawer, it's easier to reach these spaces before the sides are glued back on. When you've finished with the sanding, glue the sides back on the box; let the glue set up; and sand the glue joints. (See Figure 9.)

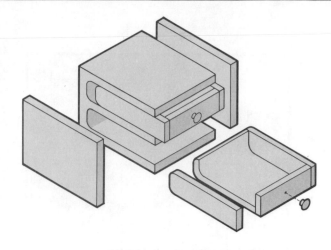

EXPLODED VIEW

Drill in the drawer for pulls, or cut small recesses to make 'finger pulls'. Apply a finish or a stain to the completed box and drawers. You'll find a penetrating oil finish works best; 'building' finishes such as varnish or polyurethane may cause the drawers to stick. After the finish dries, attach the drawer pulls, if you're using them.

Figure 5. Cut the sides off the drawer blanks, in the same manner you cut the box sides.

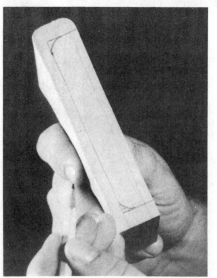

Figure 6. Mark the drawer fronts, backs, and bottoms. When marking the corners, remember to allow for the turning radius of the blade.

Figure 7. Cut out the drawer insides and discard them.

Figure 8. Lightly sand the drawer parts and glue them back together. Be careful to glue each part back to the same place you cut it from.

Figure 9. Sand the parts of the box, then glue them together.

Designed by Nick Engler, made by Adam Blake

TOP AND BOTTOM VIEW

SIDE VIEW

Crumb Catcher

This unique cutting board catches the crumbs when you use it to slice baked goods.

Few cutting boards provide a way to trap the waste when you're slicing food. Some have grooves around the outside edge to catch juices, but there's rarely any other thought given to the problem. This is especially annoying when you're cutting baked goods — the crumbs go everywhere.

The cutting board shown here is *grooved* on one side to catch the crumbs. As you slice the bread, the crumbs fall down into the grooves. These grooves are shallow enough

that they can be cleaned out easily. The other side of the board has a wider groove around the outside edge, to catch juices. Use one side of this board for baked goods, and the other side for meats and vegetables.

Make all the grooves *before* you cut the shape of the board. Cut the grooves on the baked goods side with your saw blade. (See Figure 1.) Each groove is just a shallow saw kerf, 1/8″ wide and 1/8″ deep. Space the grooves 1/4″ apart.

Cut the grooves on the meat and vegetables side with a 1/2″ core box bit mounted in your router. Make a template from a scrap of 1/2″ thick stock. Mount a 5/8″ guide bushing to the base of the router, and adjust the depth of cut to cut a groove 1/4″ deep. Attach the template to the cutting board stock, and rout the groove, keeping the bushing pressed up against the template. (See Figure 2.)

Cut the shape of the board with a bandsaw. Sand away any saw marks, round over the edges, and coat the board with a non-toxic oil finish.

Figure 1. Cut the multiple grooves in the baked goods side with your table saw.

Figure 2. Cut the round-bottom grooves in the meat and vegetables side with your router. Keep the base flat on the surface of the template, and the guide bushing pressed up against the edge of the template.

Designed by Mary Jane Favorite, made by Adam Blake and Nick Engler

Country Stuff

Add a touch of 'down home' to your home with any one of these four simple projects.

Sometimes it's the simple things that you come to love the most. A well-crafted Grandfather Clock or a Philadelphia Highboy will dress up the interior of any house — these are woodworking projects to be admired. But it's the plain, homespun things you build that make your house a home. These are projects to be cherished.

Here are four plain, homespun projects, designed in the down-home 'country' tradition — a 'corner' cat, a goose basket, a 'pouting' chair, and a tulip box. All of them are simple to make; you can build most of them in an evening. You can finish them with a traditional oil finish, or paint them as you see them here. Whatever time you put in them, however you choose to finish them, they'll make your home a bit homier.

CAT PATTERN

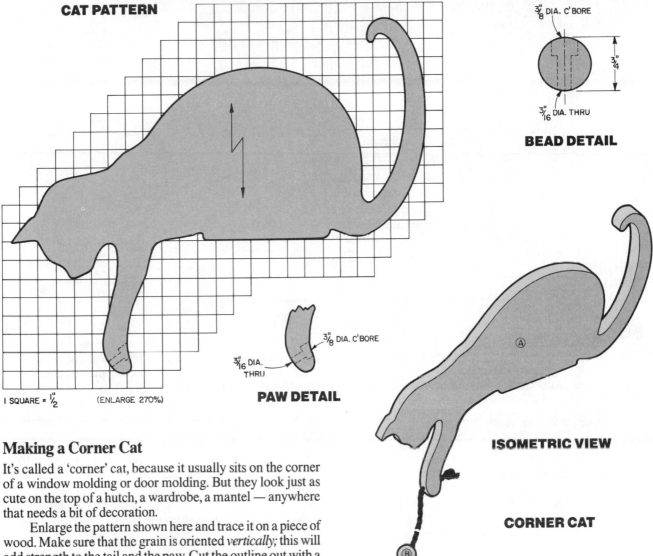

BEAD DETAIL

³⁄₈ DIA. C'BORE

³⁄₄"

³⁄₁₆" DIA. THRU

³⁄₈" DIA. C'BORE

³⁄₁₆ DIA. THRU

PAW DETAIL

I SQUARE = ¹⁄₂"   (ENLARGE 270%)

ISOMETRIC VIEW

CORNER CAT

Making a Corner Cat

It's called a 'corner' cat, because it usually sits on the corner of a window molding or door molding. But they look just as cute on the top of a hutch, a wardrobe, a mantel — anywhere that needs a bit of decoration.

Enlarge the pattern shown here and trace it on a piece of wood. Make sure that the grain is oriented *vertically;* this will add strength to the tail and the paw. Cut the outline out with a jigsaw. Sand the piece, and remove any saw marks from the edge.

> **Tip ◆** The simplest way to enlarge the patterns in this chapter is to take them to an office supply store or a print shop with a variable enlarging/reducing copier. Have the operator use the proper setting, and enlarge each pattern several times. (See Figure 1.)

Figure 1. If you need to enlarge a pattern in this chapter, you can use an enlarging/reducing copier at a print shop. Have the operator enlarge the pattern *several* times, using the proper enlargement setting. This setting is given under each pattern.

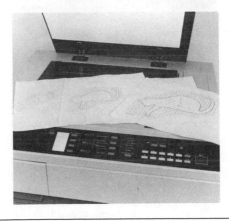

Counterbore a ⅜" hole, ¼" deep in the back of the paw, where shown in the drawings. Then drill a ³⁄₁₆" hole, centered in the counterbore hole, all the way through the paw. Drill a similar hole in a ¾" wooden bead. (You can buy these beads in most crafts supply stores.)

Paint or finish the cat and the bead. Then string a piece of brightly-colored yarn through the paw and the bead. Knot the yarn on both ends so that it won't come out of the ³⁄₁₆" holes. (Hide the knots in the ⅜" counterbores.) Finally, place the cat on some corner with the yarn and the bead hanging down.

BILL OF MATERIALS — Corner Cat	
Finished Dimensions in Inches	
A. Cat body	¾ x 9¾ x 11⅞
B. Bead	¾ dia.
Hardware	
12″ Colored yarn	

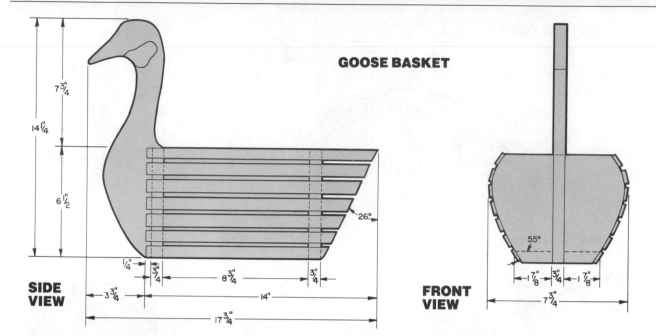

GOOSE BASKET

SIDE VIEW

FRONT VIEW

Making a Goose Basket

Enlarge the patterns for the head and body and trace them on ¾" thick stock. Pay attention to which way the grain runs; the wood grain should be oriented *vertically* to add strength to the goose's neck. Cut these pieces out with a bandsaw or jigsaw.

Rip the wing strips and the bottom from ¾" stock. Bevel the edges of the bottom at 55°, as shown in the drawings. Cut fourteen wing strips, 16" long and ¼" wide.

Attach the head to one of the body pieces with glue and flathead wood screws. After you've attached the head to a body piece, attach the body pieces to either end of the bottom. Countersink and counterbore all the screws, then hide the heads with wooden plugs. You can buy ready-made plugs, or make your own with a plug cutter. (See Figures 2 and 3.)

Carefully mark where each of the wing strips will be located, spacing them evenly over the body. The easiest way to do this is to mark one side of one body piece. Then make a paper 'story tape', using the marked side as a 'master', and use this tape to transfer the marks to the other sides. (See Figure 4.) After you've marked all the sides, fasten the wing strips in place with glue and brads.

After the glue dries, mark the wing strips and cut them off at the proper angle with a saber saw. (See Figure 5.) You may want a helper to hold the assembly while you perform this step. Finally, sand the completed basket and paint or finish the wood. We chose to paint the head, and finish the body, bottom, and wing strips with an oil stain.

Figure 2. To make your own screw plugs, first cut the plugs in a scrap of wood, using a plug cutter. Don't cut all the way through the wood.

Figure 3. Cut the plugs free from the scrap with a bandsaw or jigsaw.

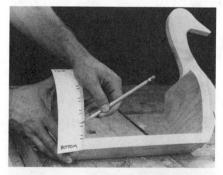

Figure 4. Make a master 'story tape' to locate the positions for the wing strips on each side of the body parts.

Figure 5. After the glue has dried for several hours, cut the wing strip to the proper length and angle with a saber saw. Have a helper hold the assembly while you cut.

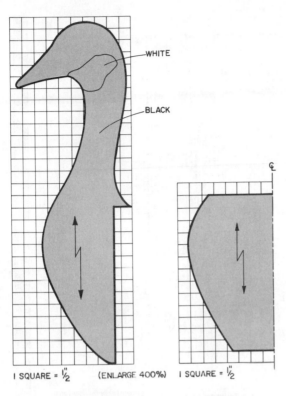

WHITE

BLACK

I SQUARE = ½" (ENLARGE 400%) I SQUARE = ½"

HEAD AND BODY PATTERNS

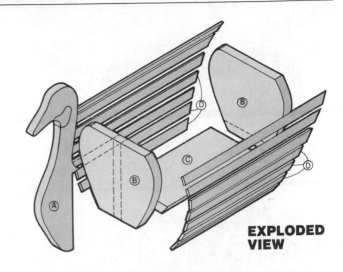

EXPLODED VIEW

BILL OF MATERIALS — Goose Basket	
Finished Dimensions in Inches	
A. Head	¾ x 4¾ x 14¼
B. Front/back (2)	¾ x 6½ x 7¼
C. Bottom	¾ x 4½ x 8¾
D. Side slats (14)	¼ x ¾ x 14

Hardware

#8 x 1¼" Flathead wood screws (6)
1" Brads (28)

Making a Pouting Chair

It's called a 'pouting' chair because it's a child-sized chair that's traditionally kept in a corner. You can sentence your kids to sit on it and pout when they've been naughty. It also makes a great step-stool, to help you reach the uppermost shelves in your cabinets. The long, cut-out back serves as a handle so that you don't have to stoop over to move the chair from place to place.

Cut all parts to size; then enlarge the patterns and trace them on ¾" stock. Cut out the outside shapes on a bandsaw. Use a jigsaw or saber saw to make a 'piercing' cut, and saw the inside shape in the chair back. (See Figure 6.) Notch the chair back and the seat as shown in the working drawings so that they interlock.

Figure 6. Cut out the inside shape of the chair back with a 'piercing' cut. Drill a starting hole, insert the blade, and then cut the shape.

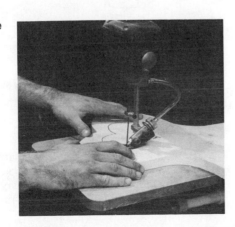

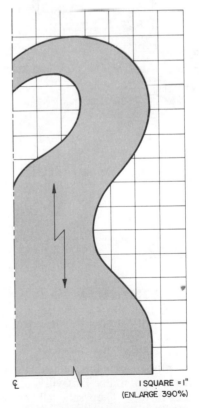

I SQUARE = 1"
(ENLARGE 390%)

CHAIR BACK PATTERN

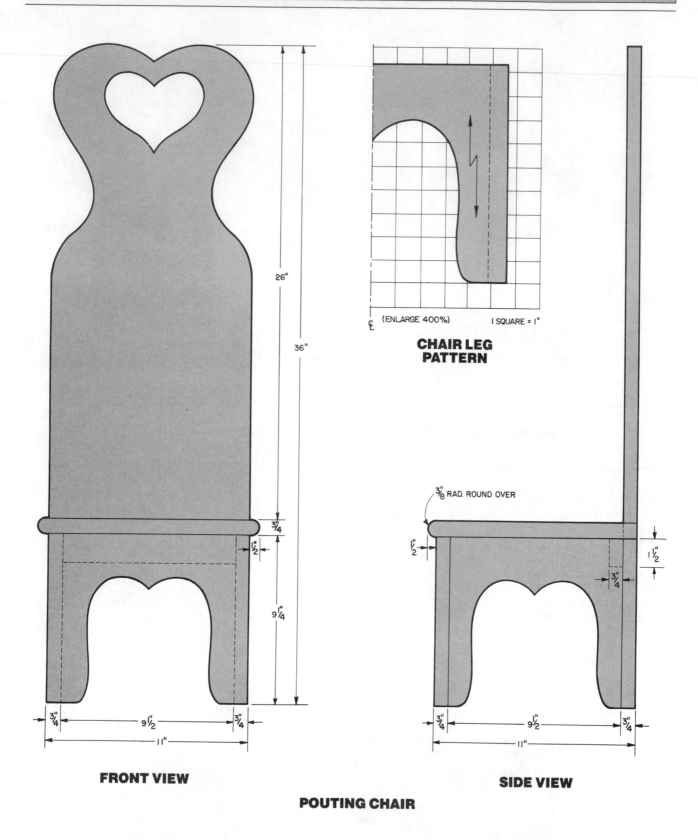

CHAIR LEG PATTERN

(ENLARGE 400%)   I SQUARE = I"

3/8" RAD. ROUND OVER

FRONT VIEW

SIDE VIEW

POUTING CHAIR

Round over the edges of the seat and the front corners of the legs with a shaper or router. This will help prevent scraped shins and stubbed toes. Then sand all the parts smooth, removing any mill marks.

Assemble the parts with glue and flathead wood screws. Countersink and counterbore the pilot holes for the screws so that you can hide the screw heads with wooden plugs. Do the necessary finish sanding; then paint or finish the completed chair.

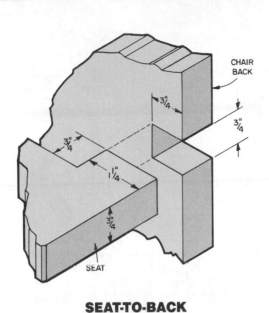

SEAT-TO-BACK JOINERY DETAIL

CHAIR BACK

¾"

¾"

¾"

1¼"

¾"

SEAT

BILL OF MATERIALS — Pouting Chair

Finished Dimensions in Inches

A.	Back	¾ x 11 x 36
B.	Seat	¾ x 11½ x 12
C.	Front leg	¾ x 9¼ x 11
D.	Side legs (2)	¾ x 9¼ x 9½
E.	Brace	¾ x 1½ x 9½

Hardware

#8 x 1¼" Flathead wood screws (18-20)

EXPLODED VIEW

Ⓐ Ⓑ Ⓒ Ⓓ Ⓔ

Making a Tulip Box

This is a traditional 'folk' sculpture — wooden flowers in a wooden planter. The flowers are 'sculpted' using simple techniques on the bandsaw, lathe, and drill press. If you want to try something a little different, make the flowers and the leaves from small scraps of exotic woods — rosewood, teak, zebra wood, purpleheart, burled walnut, etc. Sand the finished pieces till they're smooth as glass; then finish them with oil and wax so they shine like jewels. The effect is stunning.

Start by making the tulip flowers. Saw and rip a 4 x 4 so you have several pieces 3″ x 3″ x 5″. Drill a 1″ hole, 2″ deep in the top end of each piece. Trace the shape of the *top* of the tulip on two adjacent sides of each piece; then cut these shapes on a bandsaw. Cut one side; remove the scrap, turn the piece 90° and cut the second side. (See Figure 7.)

Fill the hole in the top of each tulip with a plug, 1″ in diameter and 2″ long. Mount the plugged stock on a lathe and turn the outside shape of the flowers. (See Figure 8.) Finish the flower tops by drilling a ¼″ hole in the bottom of each piece.

Next cut the leaves, by making 'compound cuts' with a bandsaw. Cut and rip twelve pieces of stock, 1½″ x 2¼″ x 8″.

Figure 7. Cut the shapes of the *tops* of the tulips on a bandsaw. Make two cuts, on two adjacent sides.

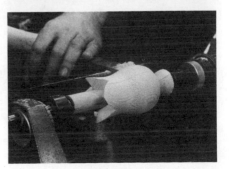

Figure 8. Turn the outside shape of the tulips on a lathe. Plug the tops with a dowel so you can mount the stock on the lathe.

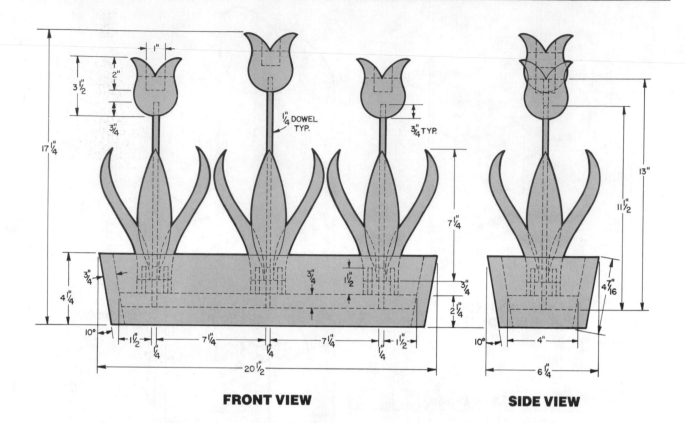

FRONT VIEW

SIDE VIEW

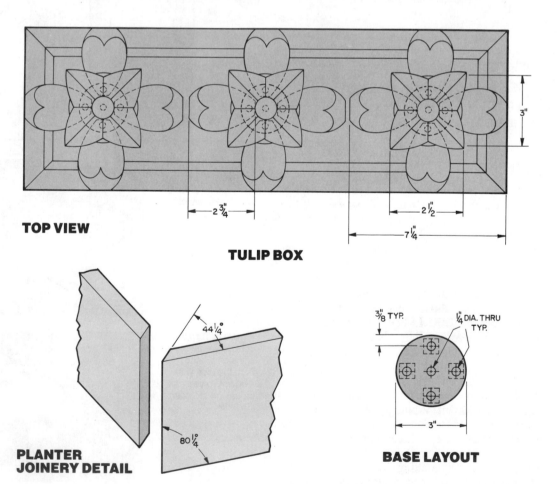

TOP VIEW

TULIP BOX

**PLANTER
JOINERY DETAIL**

BASE LAYOUT

Trace the front pattern of the leaves onto one *face* of each piece, and the side pattern onto one *edge*. Cut the *bottom edge* of the side shapes first, then drill a ¼″ hole in the leaves where shown in the drawings. (See Figure 9.) If you wait until you actually cut the leaves to drill the holes, it will be almost impossible to line up the holes correctly.

After you drill the holes, cut the rest of the side shapes, saving the waste. Then tape the waste back to each piece, and cut the front shapes. (See Figure 10.) Sand away any saw marks; then mount the leaves on round bases using ¼″ dowels. Mount a tulip flower to each base, using a long ¼″ dowel. This long dowel should pass all the way through the base and protrude from the bottom.

Make a long planter from ¾″ stock, beveling the sides at 10° as shown. Drill holes in the bottom of the planter and mount the finished flowers. Do any necessary finish sanding; then paint or finish the planter and the flowers to suit yourself.

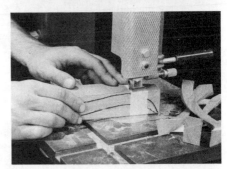

Figure 9. After you cut the bottom edge of the leaves at the proper angle, drill the mounting holes, using a drill press or horizontal boring machine.

Figure 10. Cut the shapes of the leaves on a bandsaw, using the 'compound cutting' technique. Cut the side shape; tape the waste back to the stock; and cut the front shape. When you remove the waste, you'll have a finished leaf.

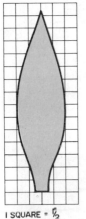
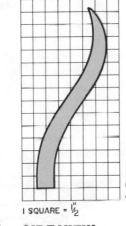

(ENLARGE 400%)

I SQUARE = ½″   I SQUARE = ½″

FRONT VIEW   SIDE VIEW

LEAF PATTERN

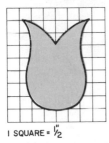

I SQUARE = ½″

TULIP PATTERN

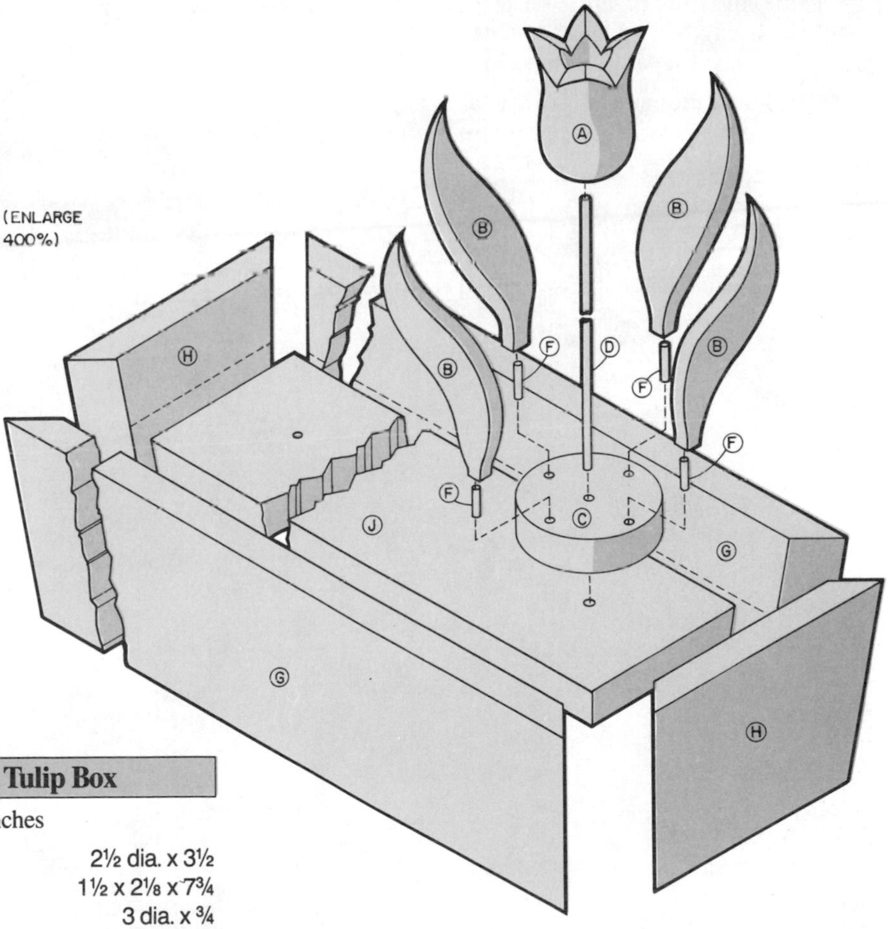

EXPLODED VIEW

BILL OF MATERIALS — Tulip Box

Finished Dimensions in Inches

A.	Tulips (3)	2½ dia. x 3½
B.	Leaves (12)	1½ x 2⅛ x 7¾
C.	Bases (3)	3 dia. x ¾
D.	Short stems (2)	¼ dia. x 11½
E.	Long stem	¼ dia. x 13
F.	Dowels (12)	¼ dia. x 1½
G.	Planter sides (2)	¾ x 4⁷⁄₁₆ x 20½
H.	Planter ends (2)	¾ x 4⁷⁄₁₆ x 6¼
J.	Planter base	¾ x 4 x 18¼

Hardware

4d Finishing nails (12-14)

Stenciling

The Pouting Chair and the Tulip Box in this chapter are decorated using a technique known as stenciling. This is a traditional finishing method that's been around for hundreds of years.

◆ To stencil a project, you first need to make a stencil or *template* of the design. We've provided several designs for you here. Enlarge these to the proper sizes, and lay a sheet of mylar or waxed stenciling paper over the enlarged design. (Mylar is available wherever you buy drafting supplies, and you can get stenciling paper from most craft supply stores.) With a sharp hobby knife, cut out the design in the template. Be careful to leave the 'bridges' in the template. (See Figure A.) These thin strips of material help to strengthen the finished template. Where different colors butt, cut separate stencils for each color.

◆ Choose the paint you want to use to apply the stencil. You can use almost any type of paint if you're careful, but quick-drying, thick pigments work best. Acrylics seem to work best on wood. They're durable, waterproof (after they dry), and you can easily mix up any color you want. Use an old ceramic plate for a palette.

◆ Tape the template to the wooden surface you want to stencil. Dip a stiff brush into the paint and wipe it on the palette so that the brush is fairly 'dry'. Then apply the paint, brushing from the border of the hole in the template toward the center. (See Figure B.) Keep adding coats until the paint is as thick as you want it. Let the paint dry thoroughly, then remove the template.

◆ Allow the stencil to dry for at least 24 hours, then apply an oil finish to the entire project. You can use either Danish oil or tung oil without discoloring the stencil. After the oil finish is dry, you may want to give the stencil some added protection by spraying it with a clear lacquer.

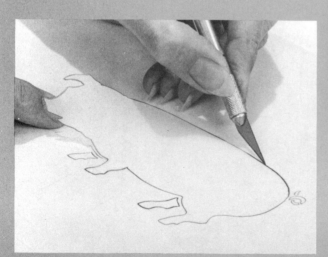

Figure A. The thin 'bridges' in the template help to strengthen it and give the finished design its characteristic 'stenciled' look.

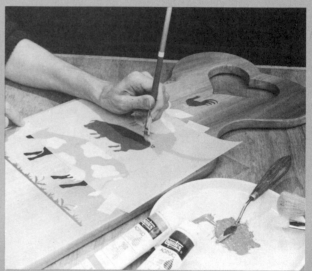

Figure B. Apply the paint with a 'dry' brush, stroking from the border towards the center of the design. If you load too much paint in the brush, it will run under the edges of the template and make your design appear 'fuzzy'.

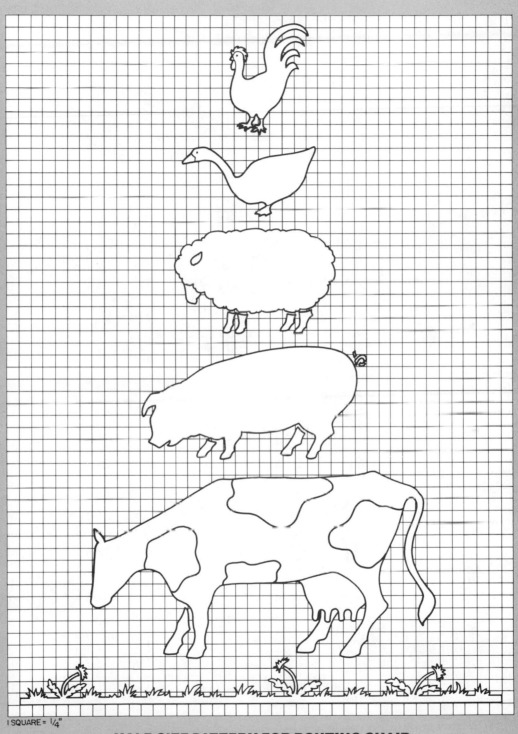

I SQUARE = ¼"

HALF-SIZE PATTERN FOR POUTING CHAIR

I SQUARE = ⅛"

FULL-SIZE PATTERN FOR TULIP BOX

Designed and built by Tom Stender

Bow-Side Breakfront

It's a wonder what you can build with warped lumber.

Tom Stender, a classical cabinetmaker in Boston, New York, had some very pretty curly cherry boards. The trouble was, they were cupped badly. But rather than throw them out or cut them into small strips, Tom decided to

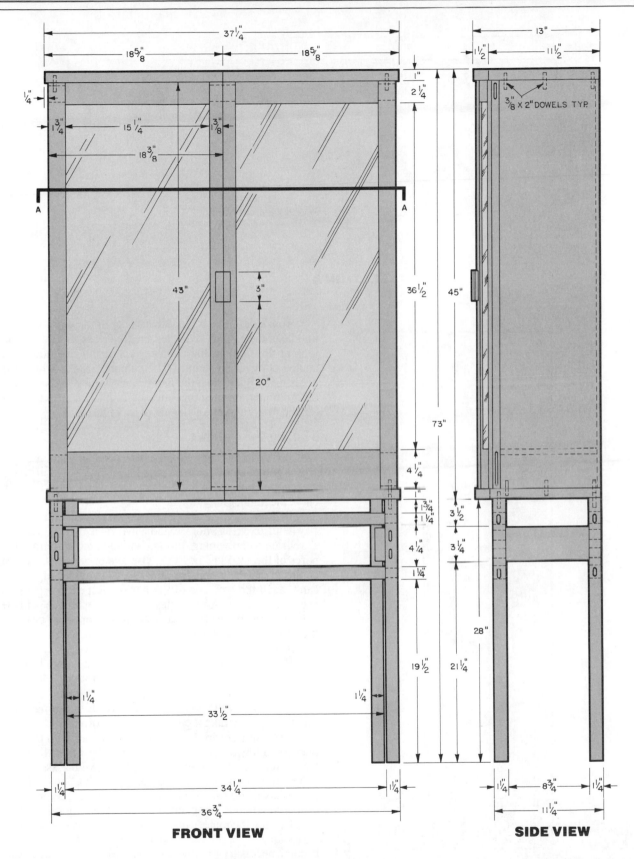

FRONT VIEW

SIDE VIEW

use them as they were for the sides of this contemporary cabinet.

This design represents a departure from Tom's usual woodworking. Tom specializes in reproducing American classical furniture — Queen Anne, Chippendale, and Federal styles. In a classical breakfront, the middle section of the cabinet juts out 2″-4″, so that it's deeper than the side sections. It also has straight sides.

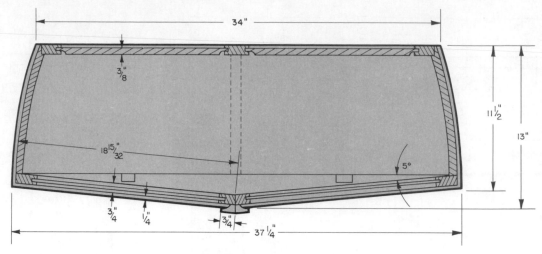

SECTION A

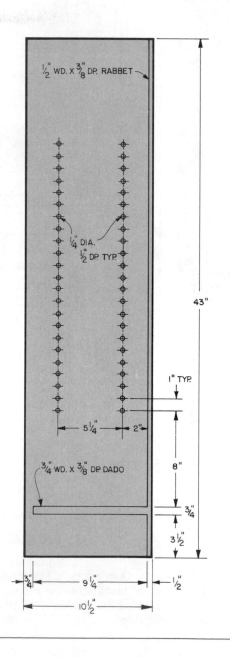

SIDE LAYOUT

Tom's design is a breakfront only in the sense that the middle of the cabinet is deeper than the sides. Take a second look at the front of the cabinet. Notice that the doors are angled out ever so slightly. The cabinet 'breaks' where the doors meet. But even if the name doesn't quite fit the design, this combination of subtle curves (on the sides) and angles (on the front) makes an elegant piece of furniture.

Making the Cabinet

Let's start with the sides. In order to reproduce Tom's design, you're going to need some cupped lumber. If you don't have any cupped boards on hand, there are several ways you can curve the lumber intentionally.

Perhaps the easiest is to take the boards out into the sun. Lay them across sawhorses, and wipe down just *one side* with a wet rag. Keep wiping, forcing as much moisture into the pores of the wood as possible. Use lots of water! If the sun begins to dry the wood, turn the boards over so that the sun can't reach the wet side of the lumber. Repeat this process every few hours. After a day or two, the boards will be cupped. Wrap band clamps around them to preserve this cup, then take them back into your shop and let them dry out for a few weeks.

If you have a large steamer, steam the wood until it's pliable. Then bend it across forms and let it dry. Make the curve of the forms a little more pronounced than you want the final curve of the wood — lumber tends to 'spring back' slightly after you take it out of a bending form.

You can also rip thin strips from a board with the saw blade set a few degrees off square. Joint the strips, then glue them back together so that the angles make the assembled strips curve. Smooth the outside surface with a hand plane or spokeshave, and the inside with a curved scraper, until you have a continuous curve on both sides of the stock.

Cutting the joinery in the sides is an exercise in creative jig-making — and careful handwork. At this point, it may become necessary to draw up a *full scale* set of plans, so that you can accurately gauge angles and measurements. Depending on how your side stock is cupped, your plans may change slightly from those shown here. Carefully transfer the *exact* curve of your boards to your plans, using a flexible curve.

Tip ◆ If you have enough stock, you can transfer the side curves to your full scale drawings by cutting 1″-2″ off one end of *each* side board, and using these short pieces as templates.

Once you've figured out the necessary angles and measurements, rip the side boards to the proper dimensions. Then cut the rabbet in the back edge. To do this, you may have to prop up one edge of the boards on spacer blocks, while you rabbet the other. (See Figure 1.) Make sure the spacer blocks are securely attached to the table saw when you do this.

Cutting the blind dado in the sides is another sticky problem. Perhaps the easiest way to do this is to temporarily 'un-cup' the board by clamping it to thick, strong, straight stock. While the stock is clamped flat, rout the dado; then remove the clamps. (See Figure 2.) With the clamps removed, the stock will spring back to its original cupped shape.

Tip ◆ If your side stock isn't cupped to begin with, you might want to bevel the *back* edge, and make the rabbet and the dado *before* you bend the wood, while you've still got a flat board to work with. However, you'll have to bevel the front edge *after* the board is cupped, when you know for sure just what the curvature will be.

The back is frame-and-panel construction, instead of an ordinary sheet of veneered plywood. (See Figure 3.) Cut the grooves in the stiles and the rails with a saw blade or dado cutter. You can also use this tool to make the tenons on the ends of some of the stiles and rails. (See Figure 4.) To make the raised panels, first cut ³⁄₁₆″ deep, ⅛″ wide rabbets in the edges of the panels. Then cut a cove in the ⅛″ shoulder of the rabbets with a core box router bit. (See Figure 5.) Dry assemble the back to check the fit of all the parts.

Cut the top, bottom, fixed shelf, drawer spacers, and partition. Remember, the edge of the fixed shelf must be curved to match the cup of the sides, and the front corners are notched to fit the blind dadoes. Dowel the top and the base to the sides, and dowel the drawer partition to the base and the fixed shelf. All the dowel joints in this project are blind — you can't see them once the project is assembled. You'll find it helpful to use dowel points to help locate the exact location of the dowel holes on many of the parts.

While you're drilling the dowel holes, also drill holes in the sides to hold the shelf supports. Dry assemble the parts to check the fit. If you're satisfied, disassemble the cabinet and sand the parts. Reassemble the cabinet — top, base, back, fixed shelf, drawer spacers, and partition — with glue. *Do not glue the panels in the back frame, leave these parts free to 'float' in the grooves so they can expand and contract with changes in the weather.*

Figure 3. The back is frame-and-panel construction, with raised panels.

Figure 4. Make the tenons in the ends of the rails and stiles with a dado cutter or saw blade. Use a tenoning jig to help hold the wood square to the blade.

Figure 1. When cutting a rabbet in a cupped board, with a beveled edge to boot, you may find it helps to simplify things if you attach a spacer block to the table saw.

Figure 2. To cut a dado in a cupped board, clamp it flat for as long as it takes to make the cut. When you remove the clamps, the board will spring back to its original contour.

Figure 5. Raise the panels by cutting a rabbet in the edges of the panels, then cut a cove in the shoulder of the rabbet with a core box router bit.

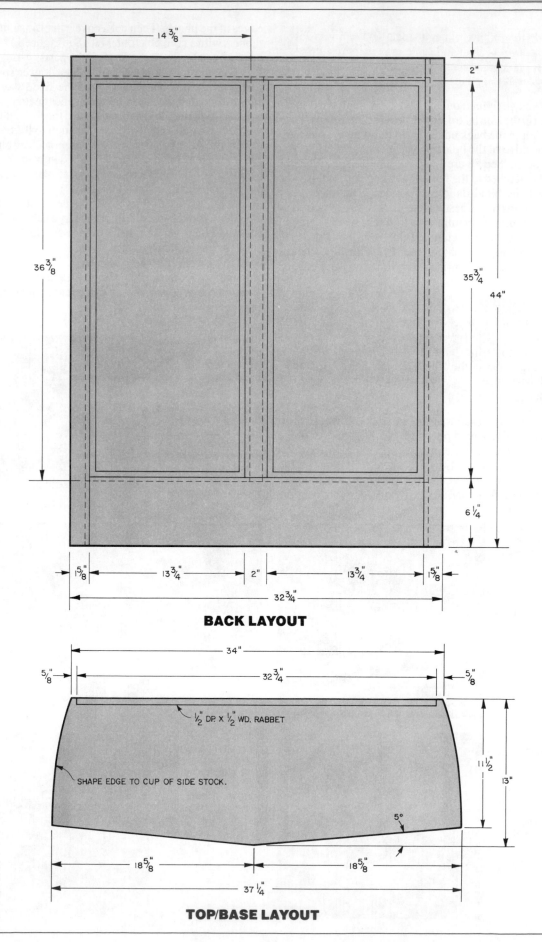

BACK LAYOUT

TOP/BASE LAYOUT

½" DP. X ½" WD. RABBET

SHAPE EDGE TO CUP OF SIDE STOCK.

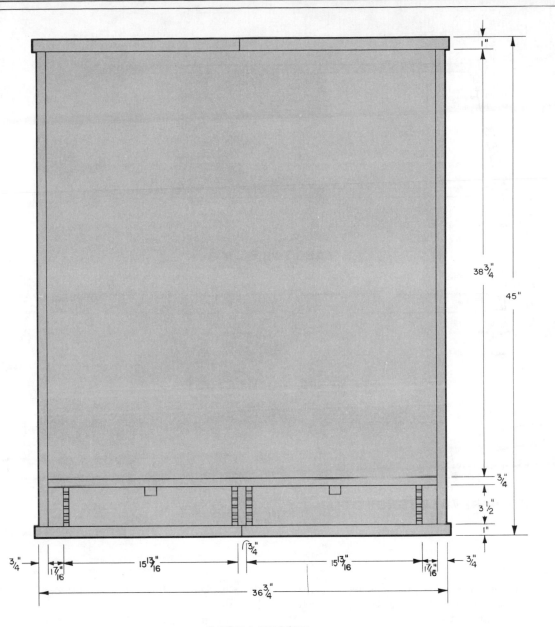

CASE LAYOUT

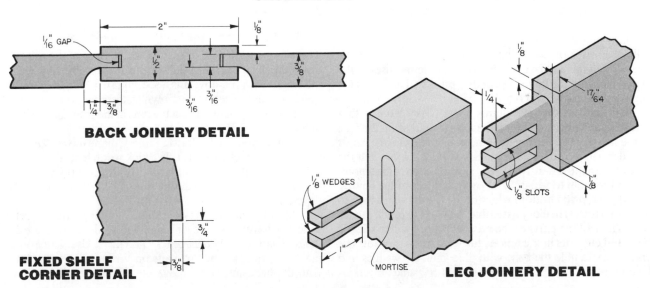

BACK JOINERY DETAIL

**FIXED SHELF
CORNER DETAIL**

LEG JOINERY DETAIL

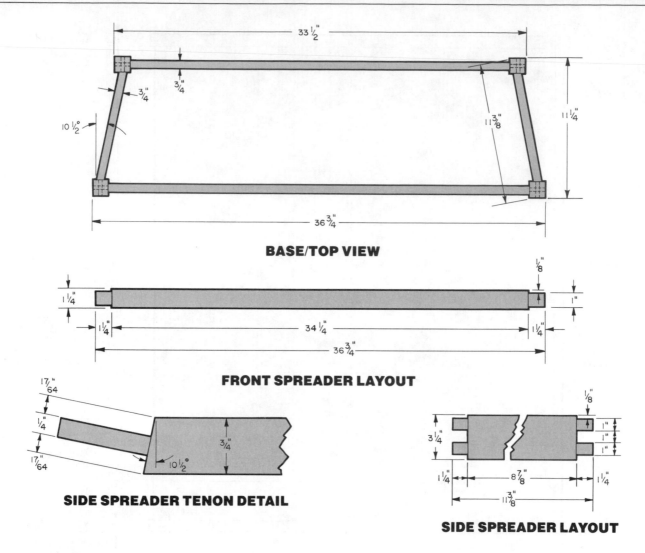

BASE/TOP VIEW

FRONT SPREADER LAYOUT

SIDE SPREADER TENON DETAIL

SIDE SPREADER LAYOUT

Making the Base

Select straight, unfigured wood for the legs and spreaders. The side spreaders are attached to the legs at a slight angle. The angle we show for Tom's base is 10½°; however, that may change slightly in your version of this project. Consult your full scale drawings and carefully calculate the correct angle.

Cut mortises in the legs either by routing slots, or by drilling a series of holes, then cleaning up the sides of the holes with a hand chisel. When you drill the mortises in the angled faces, tilt the table of your drill press so that the angled face is square to the drill bit.

Cutting the tenons requires some tricky work with a bandsaw *and* a backsaw. Saw the long shoulders (in the face of the stock) first, using a bandsaw; then cut the short shoulders (in the edge of the stock) with a backsaw. Tilt the table of the bandsaw at 10½°, and saw the edge of the tenons. Return the table to square, and saw the faces of the tenons. Round the top and bottom edges of the tenons with a rasp to fit the mortises. Then dry assemble the parts to check the fit.

When all the parts of the base fit properly, disassemble them and cut slots in the tenons for wedges — two slots per tenon. Reassemble the base with glue, then tap wedges into the ends of the tenons. When the glue is dry, sand the tenons

and the wedges off flush with the surface of the legs. (See Figure 6.)

Dowel the cabinet to the base. If you want to leave the cabinet detachable from the base for easy transportation, don't glue the dowel joints.

Finishing Up — Doors, Drawers, and Shelves

There are two silverware drawers in the base of the cabinet, under the fixed shelf. The sides of the drawers are attached to the fronts with full dovetails. (See Figure 5.) The layout for these dovetails is left to your own tastes; however, for maximum strength you should cut the pins in the front and the tails in the sides.

Before you cut the drawer joinery, plane the thickness of the sides and back to ½". Use ¾" thick wood for the front, and ¼" for the bottom. You may want to use contrasting hardwoods for the front and the sides. This will accent the dovetails.

Start by making the dovetails. Using a protractor, set a sliding T-bevel to whatever angle you've decided to use for the dovetail (usually between 7° and 12°). Use the bevel to mark the 'tails' of the dovetails on the sides. Saw the lines with the backsaw, and remove the waste between the tails

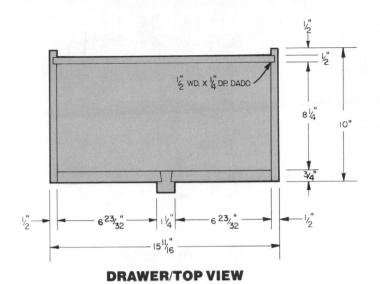

DRAWER/TOP VIEW

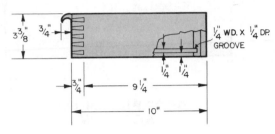

DRAWER/SIDE VIEW

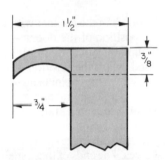

**DRAWER PULL DETAIL
SIDE VIEW**

with a very sharp hand chisel. Then use the tails as a template to mark the mating 'pins' on the front. Once again, saw the lines and chisel out the waste.

The pull is attached to the drawer front by means of a single dovetail. Make this in the same manner as you made the other dovetails: Cut the tail first, then use the tail as a template for marking the slot. With a hand chisel, carefully remove the waste until the slot is ⅜″ deep.

The rest of the drawer joinery is much simpler. Cut a dado in the sides to hold the backs, then put a groove in all four parts — front, back, and sides — to hold the bottoms. Assemble the drawers with glue. If you wish, install a silverware rack in one drawer or both of the drawers.

> **Tip ◆** The drawers will slide in and out of the cabinet easier if you coat the bottom edges of the fronts, backs, and sides with paraffin wax. Do this *after* you have applied a finish to the project.

Cut the door rails and door stiles to size. Rip the outside edge of the inside door stiles at a slight angle, so that they will close properly when they are mounted. If you wish , you can

cut the inside stiles about ¹/₁₆″ wide; then shave them down with a hand plane *after* you've hung the doors. That way, you can get a precise fit.

Assemble the door frames with slot mortises and tenons — the same joints you used to join the legs and the spreaders. Once again, use wedges to secure the tenons in the mortises, then sand the tenons flush with the edge of the stiles. When the glue dries, rout a ⅜″ wide x ⅜″ deep rabbet in the inside back edge of the door to mount the glass. Square the 'corners' of this rabbet with a hand chisel.

Figure 6. Sand the tenons and the wedges off flush with the surfaces of the legs.

Figure 7. The drawers are assembled with full dovetails. Even the finger pulls are dovetailed into the fronts of the drawers.

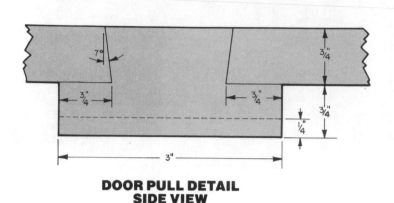

**DOOR PULL DETAIL
SIDE VIEW**

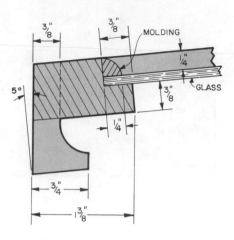

**DOOR PULL DETAIL
TOP VIEW**

Hinge the doors in the cabinet with knife hinges. Carefully adjust the position of the doors — or plane down the inside stiles — until they fit correctly. Install bullet catches to hold them closed. Mark the position of the door pulls, then remove the doors from the cabinet and install the pulls. These pulls are installed in a similar manner to the pulls you used for the drawers. Cut a dovetail 'tail' in the pull, then cut a matching slot in the edge of the door.

Before you reinstall the doors in the cabinet, cut and fit the floating shelves. The ends of these shelves must be curved to follow the contours of the sides. When installed, the shelves rest on movable pins or 'shelving supports'.

Once you're satisfied that the drawer, doors, and shelving all fit and operate properly, disassemble them from the case and remove any hardware. Finish sand all surfaces, then apply a finish to all the parts of the projects. Be sure to finish all surfaces, including the back. And remember to put the

same number of coats of finish on all surfaces, inside and out. This will keep any one part of the cabinet from expanding and contracting faster than other parts, and possibly distorting the finished piece.

Take your time finishing this piece. Carefully sand and smooth the wood between coats. On a project like this, the finish *makes* the piece. A poorly-applied finish will detract from all your hard work. To help ensure success, start sanding with 100# garnet paper. If you need something coarser, use a scraper — it's almost impossible to remove all the scratches left by coarse sandpaper.

When the finish is complete, install glass in the doors. Make or purchase ¼″ x ¼″ 'glazing' molding. Attach the molding to the door frame with small brads. To keep the glass from rattling in the doors, you may want to put a thin strip of felt between the molding and the glass. Finally, reinstall the doors, drawer, and shelves in the completed cabinet.

BILL OF MATERIALS — Bow-Side Breakfront

Finished Dimensions in Inches

A.	Top/Base (2)	1 x 13 x 37¼	**U.**	Drawer spacers (2)	1⁷⁄₁₆ x 3½ x 10
B.	Sides (2)	¾ x 10½* x 43	**V.**	Outside door stiles (2)	¾ x 1¾ x 42⅞
C.	Fixed shelf	¾ x 10 x 36	**W.**	Inside door stiles (2)	¾ x 1⅜ x 42⅞
D.	Partition	¾ x 3½ x 10	**X.**	Top door rails (2)	¾ x 2¼ x 18¹⁵⁄₃₂
E.	Back outside stiles (2)	½ x 1⅝ x 44	**Y.**	Bottom door rails (2)	¾ x 4¼ x 18¹⁵⁄₃₂
F.	Back inside stile	½ x 2 x 36½	**Z.**	Door pulls (2)	¾ x 1½ x 3
G.	Back top rail	½ x 2 x 30¼	**AA.**	Glazing molding (total)	¼ x ¼ x 200
H.	Back bottom rail	½ x 6¼ x 30¼	**BB.**	Adjustable shelves (3)	¾ x 9¼ x 35¼
J.	Back panels (2)	⅜ x 14⅜ x 36⅜	**CC.**	Dowels (22)	⅜ dia. x 2
K.	Legs (4)	1¼ x 1¼ x 28	**DD.**	Wedges (40)	⅛ x ¼ x 1
L.	Front spreaders (2)	¾ x 1¼ x 36¾			
M.	Back spreaders (2)	¾ x 1¼ x 33½			
N.	Side spreaders (2)	¾ x 3¼ x 11⅜			
P.	Drawer fronts (2)	¾ x 3⅜ x 15¹¹⁄₁₆			
Q.	Drawer sides (4)	½ x 3⅜ x 10			
R.	Drawer backs (2)	½ x 3⅜ x 15³⁄₁₆			
S.	Drawer bottoms (2)	¼ x 8¾ x 15³⁄₁₆			
T.	Drawer pulls (2)	⅜ x 1¼ x 1½			

*This dimension may change depending on the 'cup' of the stock.

Hardware

⅜″ x 1⅞″ Knife hinges (2 pair)
½″ Brads (1 box)
⅛″ x 15⅞″ x 35⅛″ Glass (2)
¼″ Pin-style shelving supports (12)

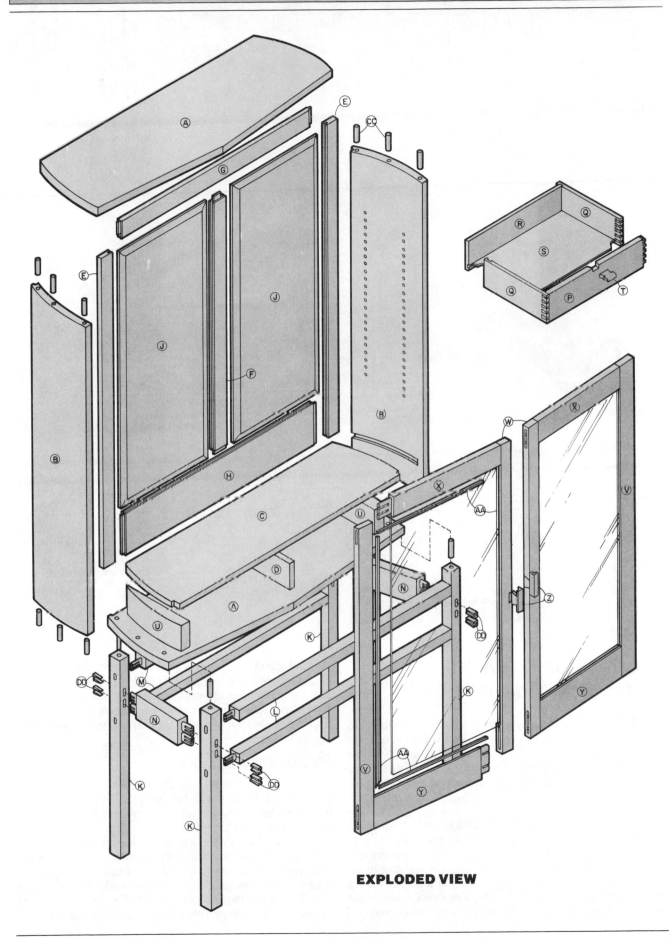

EXPLODED VIEW

Designed and built by Nick Engler

Toy Steam Train

Here's a classic wooden toy from the Age of Steam!

What is it about a steam locomotive that continues to fascinate young and old alike, even though steam power has long been considered 'obsolete' by the nation's railways? Why is it that when you buy or build a toy train for a child, they usually expect a steam locomotive — preferably an old steam locomotive, with a high, fat smokestack?

Perhaps the reason for the fascination lies in the intricate design and the rhythmic motion of a steam locomotive. There is too little poetry about a diesel engine — the shape is too clean, and the motion is monotonous. On the other hand, you can study the exterior of a steam locomotive for a long time without taking it all in. And the syncopated dance that the connecting rods do with the drive wheels is captivating.

Whatever the reason, if you've told your child or grand-child that you're thinking about building them a toy train, they probably have the notion that you meant a toy *steam* train. If you're looking for plans, here's a classic design — a 0-4-2, complete with tender and cars — from the Golden Age of Steam.

Making the Locomotive

Cut the platform parts — upper, middle, and lower — to the proper shape. The upper and middle platforms get notches on both sides, but the lower platform remains a rectangle. Glue these parts up, face to face.

Let the glue cure for *at least* 24 hours, then cut the shape of the cowcatcher. You can make this shape easily by setting your table saw to make a compound cut. (See Figure 1.) Angle the miter gauge at 30°, and tilt the table or the blade at 30°. Then make two cuts, one to form the right hand side of the cowcatcher, and the other to form the left hand side.

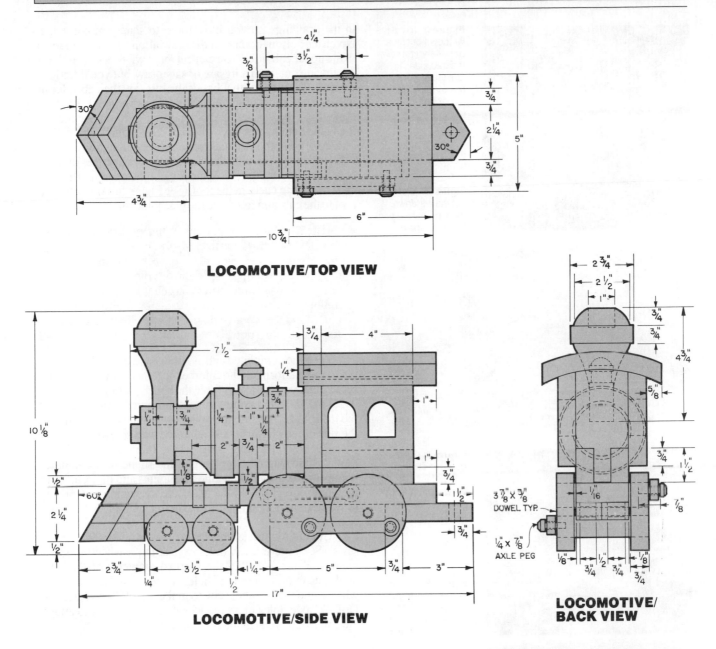

LOCOMOTIVE/TOP VIEW

LOCOMOTIVE/SIDE VIEW

LOCOMOTIVE/BACK VIEW

Set the complete platform aside, and make the turned parts of the locomotive. On your lathe, turn the boiler, smokestack, steam dome, and cylinders. Sand the parts on the lathe. Be careful not to turn or sand the bottom end of the smokestack and steam dome smaller than 1″ in diameter. If you do, these parts won't fit properly when you assemble them to the boiler.

With a bandsaw or saber saw, cut the shapes of the front and back boiler mounts. Glue these to the underside of the boiler, then drill the top of the boiler for the smokestack and the steam dome. Glue the stack and the dome in place.

Tip ◆ If you attach the boiler mounts *before* you drill the boiler, you can use the mounts to keep the boiler from rocking on the drill press.

Cut the parts for the cab — firewall, cab sides, and roof. Cut the upper cab sides and the roof a little longer than shown

Figure 1. Cut the cowcatcher by making compound cuts on your table saw. Angle the miter gauge at 30°, and tilt the blade or table at 30°.

Figure 2. To cut the windows out on a bandsaw, first saw the cab sides in half. Cut the shapes of the windows in the upper half.

Figure 3. After you cut the windows, glue the halves back together again.

Figure 4. Cut the curve in the top edge of the firewall and cab sides *after* you glue up these parts.

Figure 5. Cut the curved roof from thick stock. The curve must match the curve of the cab.

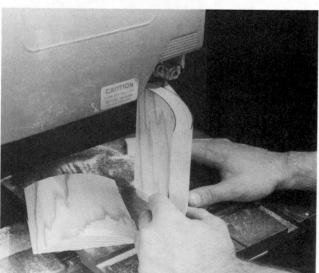

in the drawings, so you have room to shape the top edge. Notch the bottom corners of the firewall, and cut the windows in the upper cab sides. You can cut these windows by making a 'piercing cut' with a jigsaw or saber saw, but you'll find it's easier to cut them with a bandsaw. Just saw the cab sides in half, so that they come apart at the lower edge of the windows. Saw the shapes of the windows in the upper halves, then glue both halves back together. (See Figures 2 and 3.)

Assemble the firewall, upper cab sides, and lower cab sides with glue. Then cut the curve in the upper edges on your bandsaw. (See Figure 4.) After you cut the curve in the cab, cut a matching curve in the roof. (See Figure 5.) Assemble the roof to the cab, and reinforce the glue joint with wood screws.

> **Tip ◆** Many of the joints in this project are reinforced with screws, particularly those joints where end grain is joined to long grain (between the cab and the cab roof, for example), or where the joint will get heavy use. When you reinforce a joint, countersink *and* counterbore the screws, then cover the screw with a wooden plug. Sand the wooden plug off flush with the surface, so it looks like a dowel.

Glue the completed cab assembly and the boiler assembly to the platform, and reinforce the joints with screws. The screws that you use to reinforce the boiler/platform should be 2½″ long — long enough to pass through the platform and the mounts, and up into the boiler. Also, glue the cylinders to the side of the platform, and reinforce with screws.

Cut and drill the drive wheel mounts, truck wheel mounts, and engine coupler. Cut the shape of the coupler with your bandsaw. Then glue the mounts and the coupler to the underside of the platform, where shown in the working drawings. Once again, reinforce these glue joints with wood screws.

Cut out the truck wheels and drive wheels, using holesaws. (See Figure 6.) A holesaw will cut a wheel approximately ¼″ smaller than the marked diameter of the saw. With this in mind, use a 2″ holesaw to make the 1¾″ truck wheels, and the 3½″ holesaw to make the 3¼″ drive wheels. Drill ⅜″ axle holes in all the wheels, and ¼″ holes to attach the connecting rods in the drive wheels.

Figure 6. Cut out the wheels you need with holesaws. Most saws will cut a wheel ¼″ smaller in diameter than the diameter of the saw.

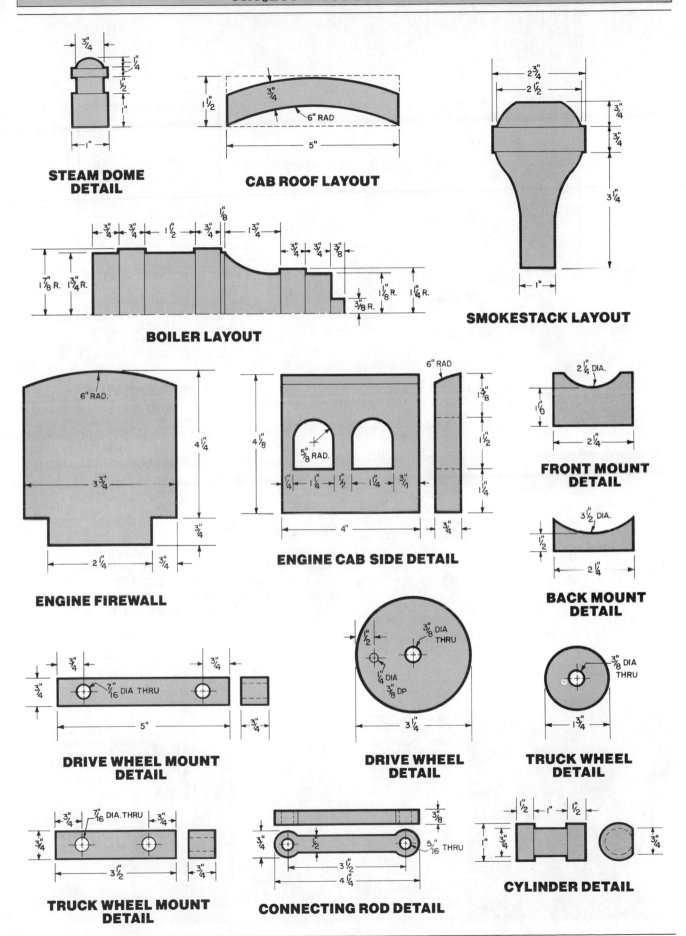

STEAM DOME
DETAIL

CAB ROOF LAYOUT

SMOKESTACK LAYOUT

BOILER LAYOUT

ENGINE FIREWALL

ENGINE CAB SIDE DETAIL

FRONT MOUNT
DETAIL

BACK MOUNT
DETAIL

DRIVE WHEEL MOUNT
DETAIL

DRIVE WHEEL
DETAIL

TRUCK WHEEL
DETAIL

TRUCK WHEEL MOUNT
DETAIL

CONNECTING ROD DETAIL

CYLINDER DETAIL

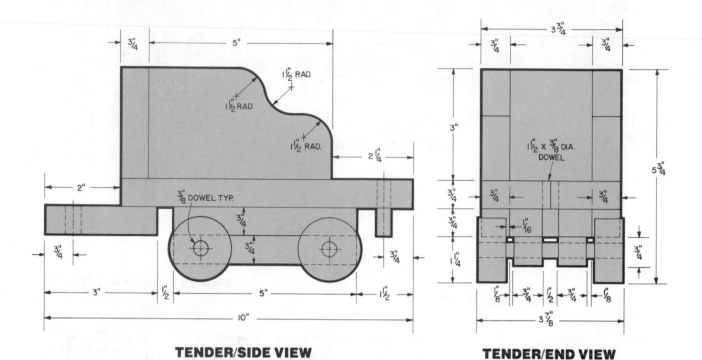

TENDER/SIDE VIEW　　　　**TENDER/END VIEW**

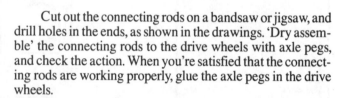

Tip ◆ Sand the wheels by mounting an axle in your drill press, then temporarily mounting the wheels on the axle. Turn off the drill press and lightly touch the sandpaper to the spinning wheel. (See Figure 7.)

Assemble the wheels and the axles to the mounts, gluing the wheels to the axles. Be very careful how you position the drive wheels when you glue them. Refer to the working drawings. When the connecting rod hole on one drive wheel is *up,* the hole in the wheel on the other end of the axle should be *down.* If they aren't positioned properly, the connecting rods won't work.

Tip ◆ To keep the drive wheels properly aligned, even after the glue is dried, drive small brads through the wheels and the axles to keep them in place. (See Figure 8.)

Cut out the connecting rods on a bandsaw or jigsaw, and drill holes in the ends, as shown in the drawings. 'Dry assemble' the connecting rods to the drive wheels with axle pegs, and check the action. When you're satisfied that the connecting rods are working properly, glue the axle pegs in the drive wheels.

Making the Tender

The tender is a good deal shorter — and simpler — than the locomotive. To make this portion of the train, first cut the parts to size. Make four truck wheels with a holesaw, as you did before. Drill the wheels, wheel mounts, coupler, and the platform. Then cut out the shape of the coupler, tender platform, and sides on a bandsaw.

Assemble the tender back and sides to the platform. When the glue dries, glue the coupler, coupler pin, and truck mount to the underside of the platform. Again, wait for the

Figure 7. To sand the wheels, mount an axle in your drill press, then temporarily mount the wheels to the axle.

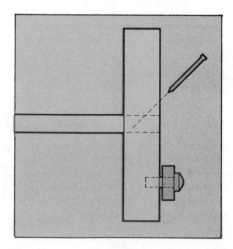

Figure 8. To keep the drive wheels and the connecting rods properly aligned, drive brads through the drive wheels into the axles, as shown.

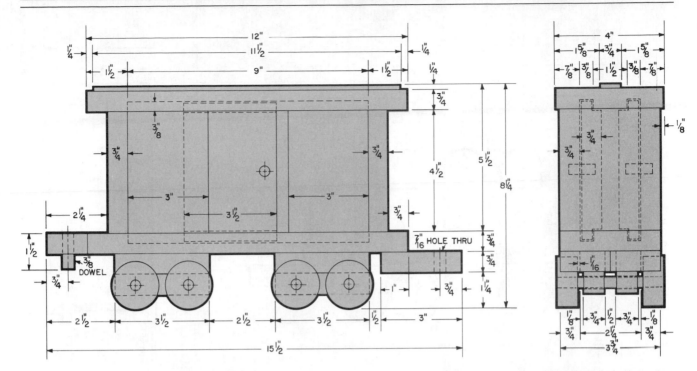

BOXCAR/SIDE VIEW

BOXCAR/END VIEW

glue to dry, then glue the wheel mounts to the truck mounts. Reinforce the glue joints with screws as you assemble the tender — particularly the platform/coupler, platform/truck mount, and truck mount/wheel mount joints.

To complete the tender, insert the axles in the wheel mounts and glue wheels to the axles. Hook the tender to the locomotive by inserting the tender's coupler pin in the locomotive's coupler.

> **Tip ◆** The wheels will turn easier if you rub the axles with paraffin *before* you insert them in the wheel mounts. *Do not* rub paraffin on the ends of the axles, where you intend to glue the wheels.

Making the Cars

The cars that follow the tender all sit on the same basic foundation. This 'foundation' consists of a platform, coupler, and two wheel 'trucks', with four wheels each (or eight wheels per car). We'll show you how to build two different cars in the remainder of this chapter — a boxcar and a caboose — but you can build many other types of cars, if you so desire. On that same basic foundation, you can put a flat car, gondola, tank car, hopper, automobile carrier, even a 'zoo car' with wooden animal shapes.

To make the *boxcar,* first cut the parts to size. Make eight truck wheels with a holesaw, and drill the wheels, wheel mounts, doors, coupler, and the platform. Then cut out the shape of the coupler and platform on a bandsaw.

With a router and a rabbeting bit, cut a rabbet in the top and bottom edge of the doors, as shown in the drawings. With a straight bit, rout two blind grooves in the platform and the boxcar top. (See Figure 9.) These grooves serve as slides for the doors.

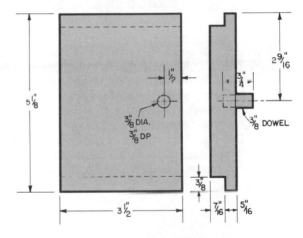

BOXCAR/DOOR DETAIL

Figure 9. With a straight bit, rout two parallel grooves in the boxcar platform and the boxcar roof. These grooves serve as slides for the doors.

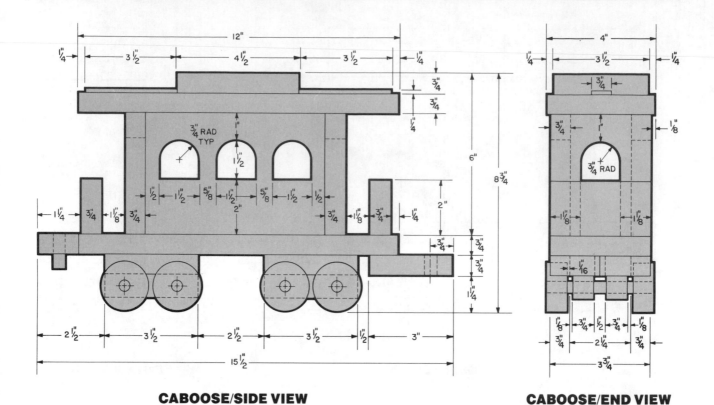

CABOOSE/SIDE VIEW

CABOOSE/END VIEW

Glue the boxcar sides to the ends to make two U-shaped assemblies. Then glue these assemblies to the platform. Glue pulls in the boxcar doors, then put the doors in the platform grooves. Glue the top to the boxcar, being careful not to get any glue in the grooves that could interfere with the action of the doors. Also, glue the top rail to the car top.

When the glue dries on the assembly on top of the platform, glue the other parts to the underside of the platform. Glue the coupler, coupler pin, and truck mounts to the platform, then glue the wheel mounts to the truck mounts. As before, reinforce the glue joints with screws. Finally, insert the axles in the wheel mounts and glue wheels to the axles.

To make the *caboose,* start out like you did with the boxcar. Cut the parts to size, then make eight truck wheels with a holesaw. Drill the wheels, wheel mounts, doors, coupler, and the platform. Then cut out the shape of the coupler and platform on a bandsaw.

Cut the doors in the ends and the windows in the sides with a bandsaw. Make the caboose windows in the same manner you made the windows in the locomotive. Saw the sides in half, so that they come apart at the lower edge of the windows. Saw the shapes of the windows in the upper halves; then glue both halves back together.

Glue the ends and sides together, then glue the assembly to the platform. Glue the car top in place, then the half-roof and the top rails. Complete the car by installing the coupler, coupler pin, and trucks in the same manner you installed them on the boxcar.

Finishing the Train

Carefully sand the completed train with 80# sandpaper, rounding all the sharp corners and edges. If you wish to finish this train, use a non-toxic finish such as mineral oil or salad-bowl dressing. Danish oil is also non-toxic, but only after it sits for thirty days.

If you want to color the train, use latex paint. Latex is not completely non-toxic, but it's a good deal less harmful than oil-base paints. If you want perfectly safe, bright colors, dilute food colors 1:3 with water — 1 part food coloring, 3 parts water. Paint the mixture on the wood, allow it to dry, then seal it in the wood with mineral oil or clear salad bowl dressing.

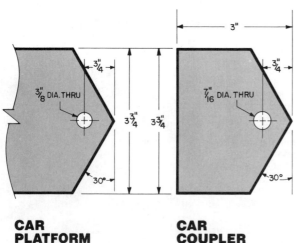

CAR PLATFORM DETAIL

CAR COUPLER DETAIL

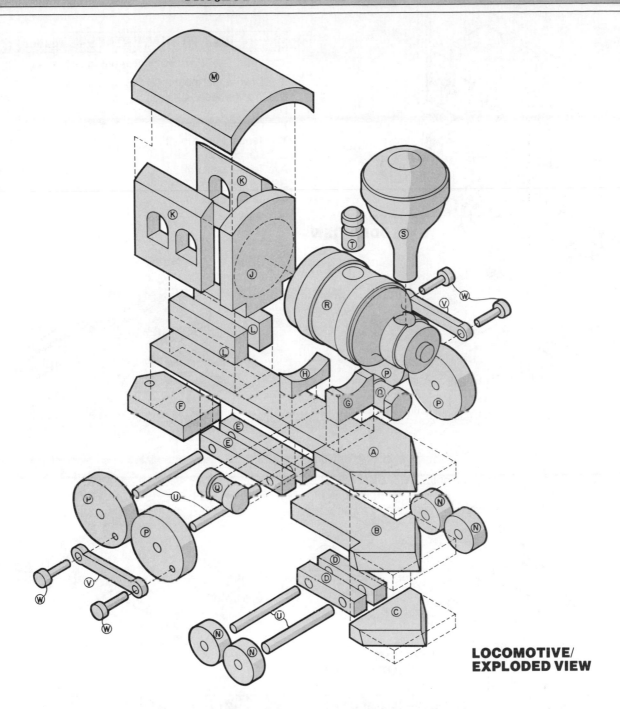

**LOCOMOTIVE/
EXPLODED VIEW**

BILL OF MATERIALS — Locomotive

Finished Dimensions in Inches

A.	Upper platform	¾ x 3¾ x 15½	
B.	Middle Platform	¾ x 3¾ x 7	
C.	Lower platform	¾ x 2¾ x 3¾	
D.	Truck wheel mounts (2)	¾ x ¾ x 3½	
E.	Drive wheel mounts (2)	¾ x ¾ x 5	
F.	Locomotive coupler	¾ x 2¼ x 3	
G.	Front boiler mount	¾ x 1½ x 2¼	
H.	Back boiler mount	¾ x 1 x 2¼	
J.	Firewall	¾ x 3¾ x 5	
K.	Upper cab sides (2)	¾ x 4 x 4⅛	
L.	Lower cab sides (2)	¾ x 1½ x 4	

M.	Cab roof	1½ x 5 x 6
N.	Truck wheels (4)	1¾ dia. x ¾
P.	Drive wheels (4)	3¼ dia. x ¾
Q.	Cylinders (2)	1 dia. x 2
R.	Boiler	3¾ dia. x 7½
S.	Smokestack	2¾ dia. x 4¾
T.	Steam dome	1 dia. x 2
U.	Axles (4)	⅜ dia. x 3⅞
V.	Connecting rods (2)	⅜ x ¾ x 4¼
W.	Axle pegs (4)	¼ dia. x ⅞*

*Measurements of shaft only.

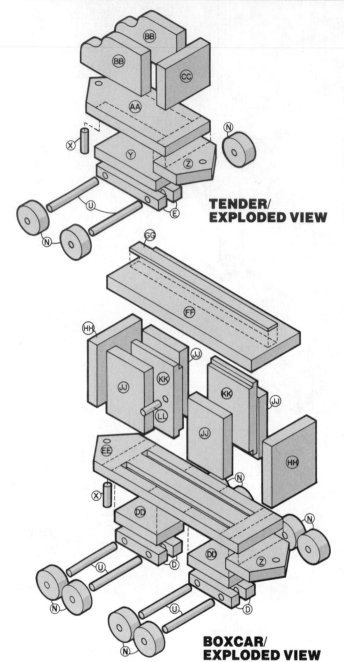

**TENDER/
EXPLODED VIEW**

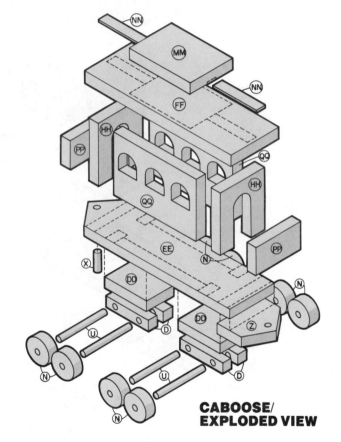

**BOXCAR/
EXPLODED VIEW**

**CABOOSE/
EXPLODED VIEW**

BILL OF MATERIALS — Tender

Finished Dimensions in Inches

E.	Drive wheel mounts (2)	¾ x ¾ x 5
N.	Truck wheels (4)	1¾ dia. x ¾
U.	Axles (2)	⅜ dia. x 3⅞
X.	Coupler pin	⅜ dia x 1½
Y.	Tender truck mount	¾ x 2¼ x 5
Z.	Car coupler	¾ x 3 x 3¾
AA.	Tender platform	¾ x 3¾ x 8
BB.	Tender sides (2)	¾ x 3 x 5
CC.	Tender back	¾ x 3 x 3¾

BILL OF MATERIALS — Boxcar

Finished Dimensions in Inches

D.	Truck wheel mounts (4)	¾ x ¾ x 3½
N.	Truck wheels (8)	1¾ dia. x ¾
U.	Axles (4)	⅜ dia. x 3⅞
X.	Coupler pin	⅜ dia. x 1½
Z.	Car coupler	¾ x 3 x 3¾
DD.	Truck mounts (2)	¾ x 2¼ x 3½
EE.	Car platform	¾ x 3¾ x 13½
FF.	Car top	¾ x 4 x 12
GG.	Top rail	¼ x ¾ x 11½
HH.	Car ends (2)	¾ x 3¾ x 4½
JJ.	Box car sides (4)	¾ x 3 x 4½
KK.	Box car doors (2)	¾ x 3½ x 5⅛
LL.	Door pulls (2)	⅜ dia. x ¾

BILL OF MATERIALS — Caboose

Finished Dimensions in Inches

D.	Truck wheel mounts (4)	¾ x ¾ x 3½
N.	Truck wheels (8)	1¾ dia. x ¾
U.	Axles (4)	⅜ dia. x 3⅞
X.	Coupler pin	⅜ dia. x 1½
Z.	Car coupler	¾ x 3 x 3¾
DD.	Truck mounts (2)	¾ x 2¼ x 3½
EE.	Car platform	¾ x 3¾ x 13½
FF.	Car top	¾ x 4 x 12
HH.	Car ends (2)	¾ x 3¾ x 4½
MM.	Half roof	¾ x 3½ x 4½
NN.	Top rails (2)	¼ x ¾ x 3½
PP.	Railings (2)	¾ x 2 x 3¾
QQ.	Caboose sides (2)	¾ x 4½ x 6¾

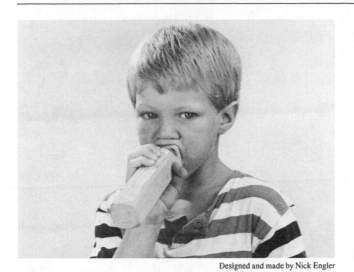

Designed and made by Nick Engler

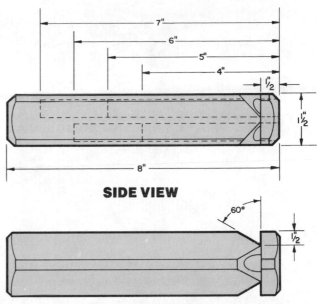

SIDE VIEW

DIAGONAL VIEW

Train Whistle

What good is a train without a whistle?

Once you've finished the toy train in the previous chapter, top it off with a toy train whistle! This wooden whistle sounds four notes at once, in harmony, to recreate sound of an old steam engine whistle — only not quite so loud.

Make the whistle body from a scrap of 2 x 2. Drill four long holes in one end, each hole *precisely* as long as shown in the working drawings. If one or more of the holes aren't the right length, the whistle may sound 'out of tune'. Use a ½" 'aircraft' drill bit to make these holes. (See Figure 1.)

With a bandsaw or a jigsaw, cut four 60° notches in each corner, near the top of the whistle. Each notch should inter-

sect one of the holes. Two simple 'cradles', made of scrap wood, will help you hold the whistle body at the proper angle to cut these notches. (See Figure 2.)

Cut four short pieces of ½" dowel, as shown in the drawings, to partially plug the holes. Glue the plugs in place; then round over all corners and sand the whistle assembly smooth.

Figure 2. Simple 'cradles' made from scrap wood hold the whistle body while you cut the notches.

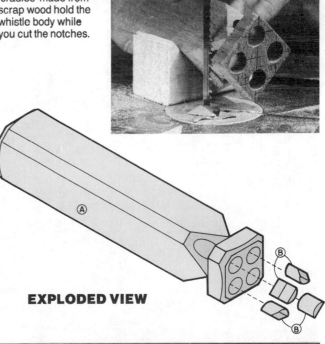

Figure 1. Use a long ½" 'aircraft' drill to make the holes in the whistle body.

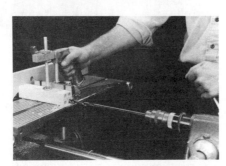

EXPLODED VIEW

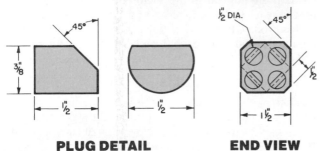

PLUG DETAIL   **END VIEW**

BILL OF MATERIALS — Train Whistle

Finished Dimensions in Inches

A. Whistle Body	1½ x 1½ x 8
B. Plugs (4)	½ dia. x ⁹⁄₁₆

Designed and built by Nick Engler

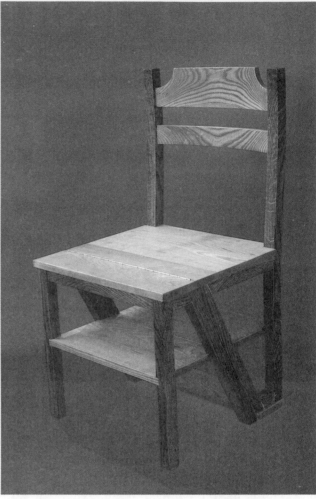

Library Chair

This convertible chair turns into a stepladder.

How many times have you used a chair as a stepladder, despite the warnings that it's unsafe. Well, here's a chair that's *designed* to be used safely as a stepladder. The seat is hinged so that the chair will fold over on itself — and presto! A real stepladder.

This ingenious chair is not a new invention. 'Library chairs' were popular in the Victorian era, when they were used to reach the upper shelves of the high bookcases of the period. Today, they're a useful piece of furniture to keep around the house, to reach the top shelves of your cabinets and closets.

Making the Side Frames

The library chair is made with a 'split frame'; that is, the chair frame is made in two halves: a back half and a front half. These halves are made so that they will mate in not one, but two ways — as a chair, and as a step stool.

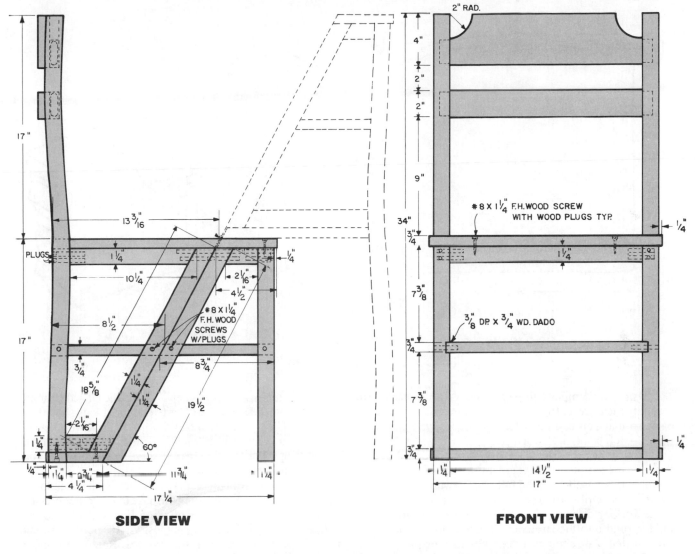

SIDE VIEW

FRONT VIEW

CHAIR LEG PATTERN

1 SQUARE = ½"

Each frame half is further divided into two side frames — right and left. These side frames are mirror images of each other, and are joined by stretchers, slats, steps, and seat halves. Begin this project by building these side frames: right back, left back, right front, left front.

The easiest way to make the side frames — and ensure that each frame is accurate — is to draw the side view of the chair *full size* on a piece of ¾″ thick plywood. Split the plywood where the two frame halves (back and front) come apart. These plywood pieces will serve as back and front *templates* for cutting, drilling, assembling, and gluing up the side frames. (See Figure 1.)

Rip and join all the frame stock to size. The legs are all made from stock 1¼″ square, the stretchers from stock 1″ thick by 1¼″ wide, and the back legs are cut from stock 1¼″ thick by 2″ wide. Trace the back leg pattern on the stock and cut it out on a bandsaw.

Figure 1. Draw the side view of the chair full size on a piece of plywood, then cut the plywood apart where the frame halves separate. Use these pieces of plywood as templates for cutting, drilling, assembling, and gluing up the side frames.

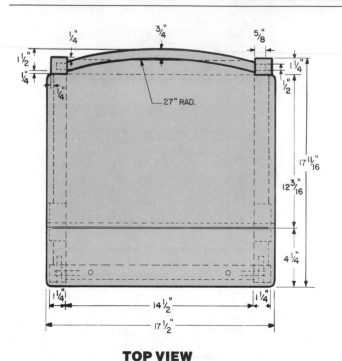

TOP VIEW

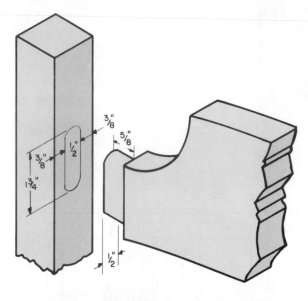

BACK JOINERY DETAIL

Using the template to gauge the length of each part, carefully measure, cut, and miter the frame pieces. Mark the parts so that you can tell which part goes with what side frame — left back, right front, etc.

Clamp the parts for the left back frame and the left front frame in the templates. Be very careful that all the parts are positioned precisely atop the full size drawing you made on the plywood. Drill the corner joints for dowels, where shown in the working drawings. The dowel holes should go through the legs and into the stretchers. Remove the frame pieces from the template and repeat for the remaining pieces.

Remember, the side frames are mirror images of each other. When you clamp the stretchers of the left side frames to the templates, they should be flush with the inside surfaces of the left legs, laying flat against the plywood. When you clamp up the right side frames, however, the inside surfaces will face up, away from the plywood. Use ¼″ spacers in between the right side stretchers and the plywood, so that these stretchers will also be flush with the inside surfaces of the right legs.

Assemble the left side frames with dowels and glue. Cover the holes that show on the outside of the frames with plugs made from the same sort of wood as the legs and stretchers. You can make these plugs with a plug cutter. Before the glue dries, clamp the assembled frames to the templates and make sure that the pieces line up with the drawings on the plywood. Let the glue cure while the pieces are clamped to the templates, then repeat for the right side.

After the glue has dried on all the side frames, sand the plugs flush with the surface of the wood. Finish sand all the frames.

Completing the Front and Back Frames

The next step is to join the side frames to make the front and back frames. To do this, you'll need to cut some joinery in the side frames.

First, cut dadoes for the steps. Clamp the left side frames together, mated as a *chair*. (The two slanted legs should be together.) Clamp the assembled frames to your workbench, with the inside surfaces up. Over the frames, clamp a straightedge. The straightedge will serve as a guide when you make the dadoes.

Mount a ¾″ straight bit in your router. Rout the dado for the steps in the frames, keeping the base of the router pressed firmly against the straightedge. (See Figure 2.) Make the dadoes in several passes, routing just ⅛″-¼″ deeper in each pass. Repeat for the right side frames. Remember, these frames are a mirror image of the left side frames. The frames should be facing in the opposite direction when you rout them.

> **Tip ◆** Feed the router very slowly, especially at the beginning and end of each cut, so that the wood doesn't 'tear out' or chip.

Figure 2. To rout the dadoes in the frames to hold the steps, clamp the side frames to your workbench. Use a straightedge to guide the router.

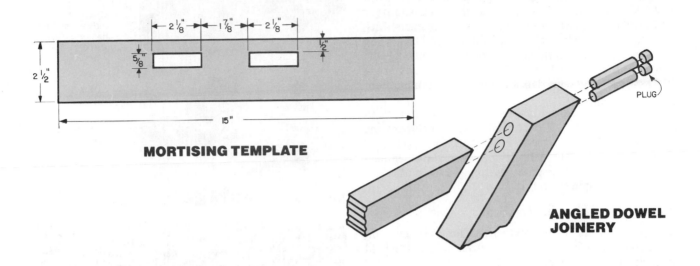

MORTISING TEMPLATE

ANGLED DOWEL JOINERY

Next rout the mortises for the back slats. Mount a ½″ straight bit in your router, and attach a ⅝″ guide bushing to the base. From ½″ thick scrap wood, make a routing template for the slots. The guide bushing will ride in the slots in the template, while the bit cuts the slots.

Clamp the template to the top of the back leg, and rout the mortises. (See Figure 3.) Once again, make these joints in several passes, cutting just ⅛″-¼″ deeper with each pass. Clean out the chips from the mortise after each pass.

With a bandsaw, cut the tenons in the 1½″ thick back slat stock to fit the mortises. Cut these tenons *before* you cut the curved slats from the stock. (See Figure 4.) After you've cut the tenons, cut the scallops in the upper slat, then cut curves of the slats. (See Figure 5.) Finally, hand fit the tenons to the mortises, by rounding the corners and paring them down with chisels and rasps. (See Figure 6.)

Dowel the front and back stretchers to the side frames. First, drill dowel holes in the ends of these stretchers. Then, use dowel centers to mark the positions of the holes on the frames. Drill matching dowel holes in the frames.

Figure 3. Use a template and the guide bushing to rout the mortises for the back slats.

Figure 4. Cut the tenons in the back slat stock *before* you cut the curved shapes of the slats.

Figure 5. Using a bandsaw, cut the curved slats from thick stock.

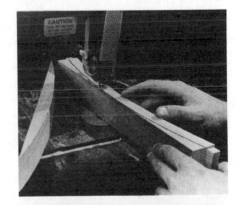

Figure 6. With rasps and chisels, round the corners of the tenons to fit the mortises.

Cut the stock for the steps, beveling the edge as shown in the working drawings. Dry assemble the front and back frames without the seat — just side frames, stretchers, slats, and steps. Check the fit of all the parts and assemblies. When you're satisfied that everything fits correctly, disassemble the frames and finish sand the stretchers, steps, and slats. You'll find it's easiest to sand the slats if you have a pneumatic drum sander. (See Figure 7.)

Reassemble the front and back frames with glue and flathead wood screws. Countersink *and* counterbore the screws, so that you can cover the heads with wooden plugs — the same way you covered the dowels when you assembled the side frames. After the glue sets up, sand the plugs flush with the surface of the wood.

Attaching and Hinging the Seat

Glue up wide stock for the seat parts. The grain must run from *side-to-side*. If it runs front-to-back, the screws that hold the piano hinge in place won't hold.

Bevel the edges of the seat parts as shown in the working drawings. Notch the back corners of the back seat half to fit in between the back legs. Test that both seat halves fit the frames correctly. When you're satisfied that they do, mortise the beveled edges for the piano hinge.

Attach the piano hinge to the seat halves *before* you attach the seat halves to the frames. Clamp the parts together with the top side of the front seat half against the top side of the back seat half. The beveled edges should be flush. It may take some experimenting to get this hinge positioned correctly. You'll be tempted to mount it right in the middle of the two mortises. We found this didn't work well. Ours is mounted 1/16″ from the bottom corner of the front seat half, and 3/16″ from the bottom corner of the back seat half. Yours may have to be positioned differently, depending on the make of the hinge.

> **Tip** ◆ Mount the hinge with just two screws — one top, one bottom — and check the action. If it doesn't work correctly, remove the screws; reposition the hinge, and put two screws in two new holes. Repeat until you get the hinge where you want it. Then remove the hinge and plug all the incorrect screw holes with toothpicks or wood splinters.

Clamp the front and back frame halves together as a chair. Then assemble the hinged seat halves to the frame with glue and wood screws. Once again, countersink and counterbore the screws. When the glue dries, check the pivoting action of the chair. If necessary, plane a little stock from the top ends of the back legs, so that the back frame half sits correctly when it's flipped over in the step ladder position.

You may also want to install 'alignment pins' between the two frame halves, near the bottom of the slanted legs. These pins will keep the frames properly aligned when the project is in the chair position. (See Figure 8.)

Sand any parts that still need it, and round over all hard edges. Then finish the library chair with a hard, scuff-proof finish that repels dirt and can be cleaned easily. We used a combination of tung oil and spar varnish, applied in three coats. First apply straight tung oil, sanding it into the wood with fine wet/dry sandpaper. Let it dry for a day, then apply a second coat of three parts tung oil and one part spar varnish.

Figure 7. A pneumatic sander comes in handy when sanding the curved surfaces of the slats.

Figure 8. If you wish, install alignment pins in the slanting legs to keep the front and back frames halves properly aligned.

Let this dry, then rub it down with coarse steel wool. Finally, apply a coat of tung oil and spar varnish, mixed half and half. Rub it down with fine steel wool and carnauba paste wax.

Warning: *Never* stand above the third step of the ladder. The top board is *not* a step; it's just a shelf to hold tools and other items when you're using the ladder.

BILL OF MATERIALS — Library Chair

Finished Dimensions in Inches

A.	Front legs (2)	1¼ x 1¼ x 16¼
B.	Front side stretchers (2)	1 x 1¼ x 2¹⁄₁₆
C.	Front slanted legs (2)	1¼ x 1¼ x 19½
D.	Back legs (2)	1¼ x 2 x 33¼
E.	Back slanted legs (2)	1¼ x 1¼ x 18⅝
F.	Upper back side stretchers (2)	1 x 1¼ x 10¼
G.	Lower back side stretchers (2)	1 x 1¼ x 2¹⁄₁₆
H.	Front/back stretchers (2)	1 x 1¼ x 14½
J.	Upper back slat	1½ x 4 x 15¾
K.	Lower back slat	1½ x 2 x 15¾
L.	Shelf	¾ x 4½ x 17½
M.	Front step	¾ x 8¾ x 15¼
N.	Back step	¾ x 8½ x 15¼
P.	Front seat half	¾ x 4¼ x 17½
Q.	Back seat half	¾ x 13³⁄₁₆ x 17½
R.	Dowels (32)	⅜ dia. x 2½

Hardware

1½″ x 16½″ Piano hinge and mounting screws

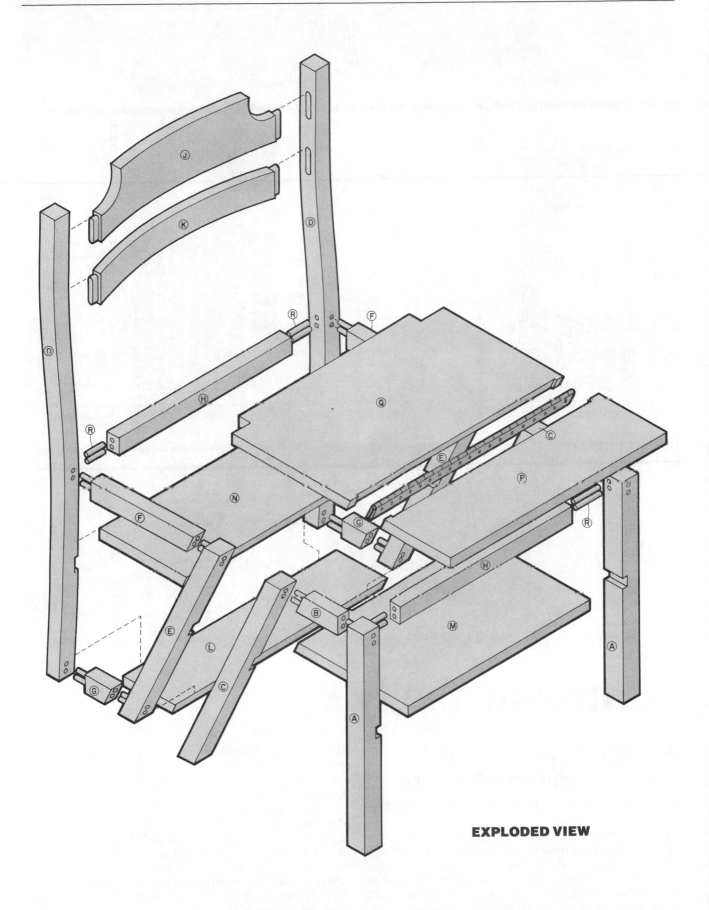

EXPLODED VIEW

Designed by Nick Engler, built by Adam Blake

Bathroom Vanity

A handsome, easy-to-build wooden cabinet creates more storage space in your bathroom.

It has always been something of a mystery to me that, while bathrooms are typically the smallest rooms in the house, people store the most stuff in them. Think about it. The average bathroom contains soaps, shampoos, combs, brushes, hair dryers, hairpins, nail clippers, pills and tonics, band-aids, cotton balls and swabs, gauze, toothpaste, razors, shaving cream, lotions, perfumes, tissue, toilet paper, wash cloths, and towels of all sizes and descriptions. It's a wonder we can cram all of this into a room that's really not much bigger than a closet.

Most bathroom vanities will hold a few of these items — the smaller stuff, like pills and toothpaste. But with a little ingenuity, a vanity could be made to hold them all, making the best possible use of the wall space in a bathroom. The vanity shown here offers an enormous amount of storage. There is a rack for towels, drawers for tiny items, cabinets for larger things, and lots of adjustable shelves for everything in between.

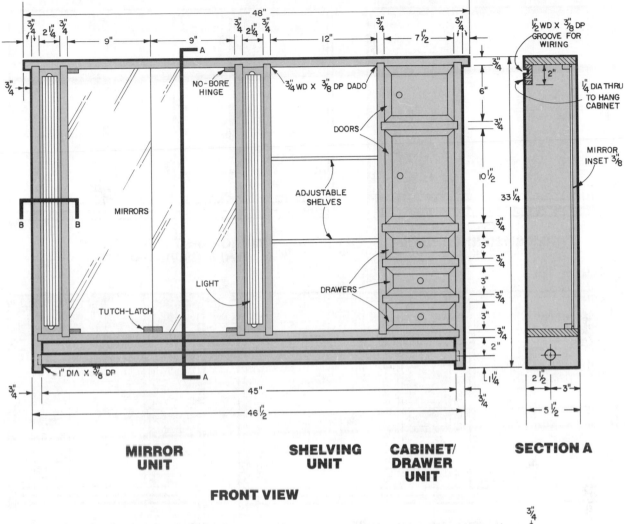

MIRROR UNIT   **SHELVING UNIT**   **CABINET/ DRAWER UNIT**   **SECTION A**

FRONT VIEW

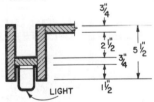

SECTION B

Furthermore, the design of this vanity is easily adaptable to your bathroom. You can expand it or shorten it as needed, to fill the available wall space. There are actually three units in this design: the mirrored cabinet unit, the adjustable shelving unit, and the cabinet/drawer unit. Add or subtract these units to create the vanity you need. Figure 1 shows several possible arrangements of the three units.

Making the Frame

Once you decide on the types of units you want to build, and an arrangement that fits your bathroom, sketch it out on a piece of paper. If you're going to mount lights in your vanity, as I have in mine, make sure that you follow the manufacturer's recommendations for how far you must mount the base or the bulb away from a piece of wood. If you get the lights too close, they could scorch the wood — especially if you use incandescent bulbs.

Cut the frame parts — top, bottom, sides, vertical dividers, and horizontal dividers. Also, cut the towel bar. With a router or dado blade, make dadoes where needed to join the frame parts. Drill 1″ holes partially through the sides to mount the towel bar. Drill ¼″ holes in the dividers where needed to hold shelving supports. Then 'dry assemble' the frame and the bar parts to test the fit of the parts.

When you're satisfied with the fit, finish sand all the frame parts. Reassemble them with glue and screws. Countersink *and* counterbore the screws, so that you can cover the screw heads with wooden plugs. Be careful that the frame goes together absolutely square. If it's the slightest bit cattywampus, the doors or the drawers may not fit correctly.

To finish the frame, attach mounting boards and cleats where needed, with glue and screws. The mounting boards hold the lights. The cleats hold the vanity to the wall. If you can, attach the cleat in the mirrored or the cabinet/drawer units, where they will be hidden by the doors. Note that the cleats have a groove running down their length. This serves as a conduit for electrical wire, so that you can run electricity to the lights. The groove isn't needed if you don't plan to run the wire.

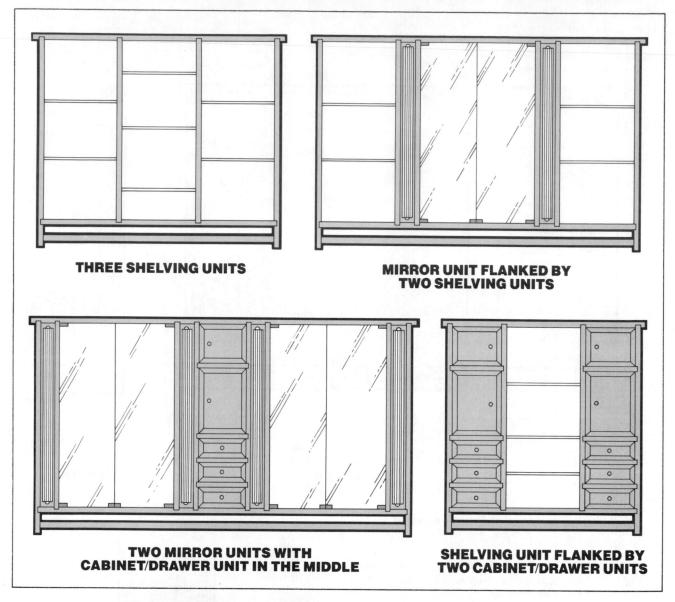

THREE SHELVING UNITS

MIRROR UNIT FLANKED BY TWO SHELVING UNITS

TWO MIRROR UNITS WITH CABINET/DRAWER UNIT IN THE MIDDLE

SHELVING UNIT FLANKED BY TWO CABINET/DRAWER UNITS

Figure 1. There are three 'units' in this design — a mirrored door unit, an adjustable shelving unit, and a cabinet/drawer unit. These units can be arranged in any combination, to create a custom vanity for your bathroom.

Figure 2. Use a no-bore glass door hinge to mount the mirrored doors in the frames.

Making the Doors and Drawers

The doors of the mirror unit are ¼″ thick glass mirrors, hung on special 'no-bore glass' hinges. These hinges hold ¼″ glass doors with no need to drill the glass. The glass simply slips in a special pocket, and is clamped in place by a screw. (See Figure 2.) The hinge itself screws to the inside of the wooden frame.

The door is held closed by a double magnetic 'tutch latch'. Two 'no-bore' magnet strikes fit over the bottom edge of the mirrors. The latch is mounted inside the frame, behind these strikes. (See Figure 3.) To open the door, simply press on the strike, and the tutch latch will automatically pop the door open. To close it, just press the door shut.

These special hinges, magnet strikes, and latches are available from many woodworking supply houses. Here are two mail-order sources:

The Woodworker's Store
21801 Industrial Blvd.
Rogers, MN 55374

Woodworker's Supply
5604 Alameda Pl., NE
Albuquerque, NM 87113

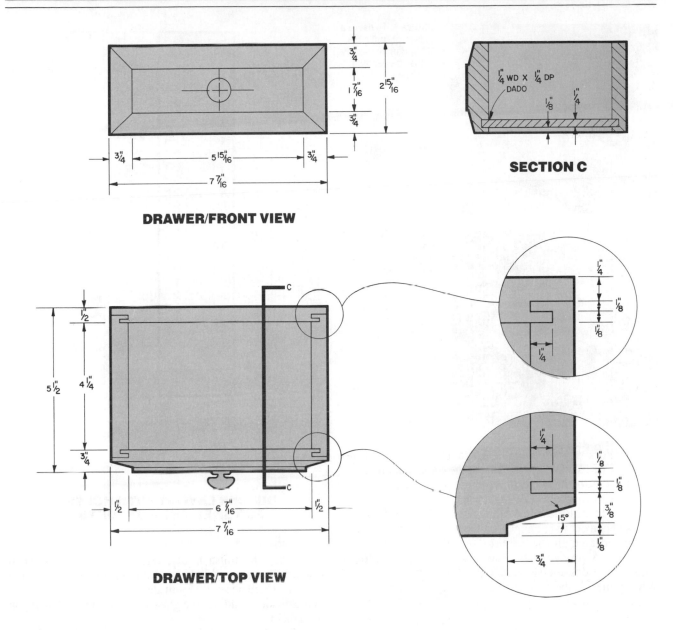

DRAWER/FRONT VIEW

SECTION C

DRAWER/TOP VIEW

The doors in the cabinet/drawer unit are more conventional. They are hung on ordinary butt hinges, and close with ordinary magnetic strikes and latches.

To make the doors, simply cut pieces of ¾″ stock to the proper size. With your table saw tilted at 15°, cut a raised panel all the way around the edge of the doors. (See Figure 4.) Mortise one edge of the doors for hinges; then hang the doors in the frame. The doors should be recessed so that the surface of the raised panel is flush with the front edge of the frame.

Figure 3. A double magnetic tutch latch and no-bore magnetic strikes keep the doors closed and open them automatically.

Figure 4. With your table saw tilted at 15°, cut a raised panel in the cabinet doors.

Figure 5. To make a lock joint, first cut a ⅛″ kerf on the inside of the drawer face, as shown.

Figure 6. Next, cut a matching kerf in the edge of the drawer front or back.

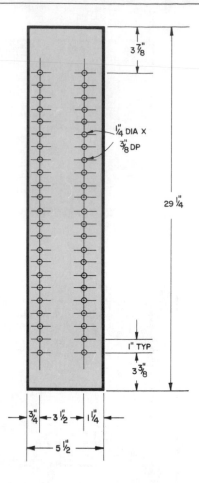

DIVIDER LAYOUT WITH HOLES FOR SHELVING SUPPORTS

The drawers also have raised panels cut into the faces. Cut these raised panels first, then cut the 'lock joints' that hold the drawers together. To make these joints, first cut a ⅛″ groove with your table saw in the edges of the drawer fronts, backs, and the inside faces of the drawer sides. (See Figures 5 and 6.) Then cut the 'tongues' on the drawer front and backs to the proper length. (See Figure 7.) Finish the drawer joinery by cutting ¼″ grooves to hold the drawer bottom in the fronts, backs, and sides; then assemble the drawer parts with glue. When you slide the drawers in place, they should be slightly recessed, so that the raised panels are flush with the frame — just like the doors.

Finishing Up

Remove the mirrored doors from their hinges, and take the hinges out of the frame. Also remove the cabinet door and dismount the hinges. Do any necessary touch-up sanding, then apply a finish to all parts and assemblies.

Since this project will be used in a damp area, I suggest you use a good waterproof finish. I applied a mixture of tung oil and spar varnish. *Don't* use polyurethane; even though the finish is waterproof, it doesn't adhere well to projects that are to be used in wet areas. If you made your vanity out of an open-grain wood (such as oak), be sure to fill the pores with wood filler. This will help keep the wood from absorbing too much moisture.

> **Tip** ◆ Apply as many coats to the *inside* of the vanity as you do to the *outside*. The wood will absorb moisture evenly on all surfaces, and will therefore expand and contract evenly. This prevents the parts from warping or cupping.

When the finish is dry, reassemble the doors. Then install the remaining hardware. Mount pulls on the doors and drawers where needed. Mount shelving supports in the holes in the dividers, and put the glass shelves in place where you need them.

To mount the vanity to the bathroom wall, first locate the studs in the wall. Drill corresponding ¼″ holes in the cleats, then secure the vanity in place with lag screws. These screws must bite into the studs to hold properly.

Figure 7. Finish the lock joint by cutting the 'tongue' in the drawer front or back to the proper length.

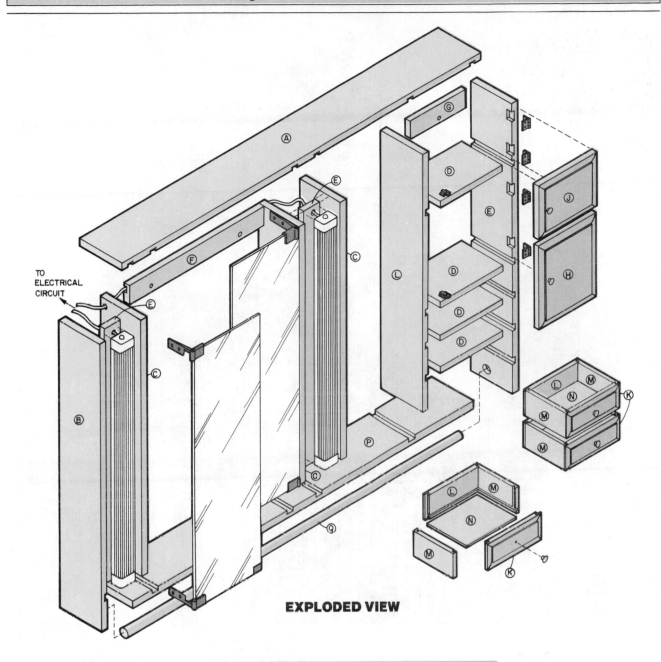

TO ELECTRICAL CIRCUIT

EXPLODED VIEW

BILL OF MATERIALS — Bathroom Vanity

Finished Dimensions in Inches

A.	Top	¾ x 5½ x 48
B.	Sides (2)	¾ x 5½ x 32⅞
C.	Vertical dividers (4)	¾ x 5½ x 29¼
D.	Horizontal dividers (4)	¾ x 5½ x 8¼
E.	Light mounting boards (2)	¾ x 2¼ x 28½
F.	Long cleat	¾ x 2 x 18
G.	Short cleat	¾ x 2 x 7½
H.	Large cabinet door	¾ x 7⁷⁄₁₆ x 10⁷⁄₁₆
J.	Small cabinet door	¾ x 5¹⁵⁄₁₆ x 7⁷⁄₁₆
K.	Drawer fronts (3)	¾ x 2¹⁵⁄₁₆ x 7⁷⁄₁₆
L.	Drawer backs (3)	½ x 2¹⁵⁄₁₆ x 7⁷⁄₁₆
M.	Drawer sides (6)	½ x 2¹⁵⁄₁₆ x 4¾
N.	Drawer bottoms (3)	¼ x 6¹⁵⁄₁₆ x 4¾
P.	Bottom	¾ x 5½ x 45¾
Q.	Towel bar	1 dia. x 45¾

Hardware

¼" Thick mirrors, 8⅞" x 28⅜" (2)
¼" Thick glass shelves, 4¾" x 17⅞" (3-4)
¼" Thick glass shelves, 4¾" x 11⅞" (3-4)
Fluorescent lights, 2" x 28" (2)
Shelving supports (24-32)
No-bore glass hinges and mounting screws (2 pair)
Double magnetic tutch latch and mounting screws
No-bore magnetic strikes (2)
¾" Door/drawer pulls (5)
Magnetic latches, strikes, and mounting screws (2)
1" x 1½" Butt hinges and mounting screws (2 pair)
#8 x 1-14" Flathead wood screws (36-40)
¼" x 3½" Lag screws (2-3)

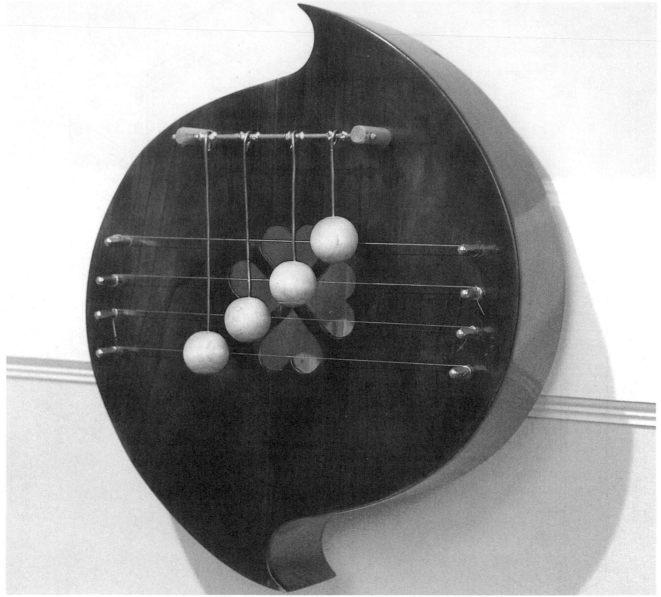

Designed and built by Nick Engler

Door Harp

It makes a little music every time you open the door.

Here's a pleasant way to announce a guest's arrival or departure — a little harp you mount to your door. Every time you open or close the door, the wooden 'strikers' swing away from the harp; then swing back again and hit the strings. The strings are tuned to a chord; and they resonate in harmony, playing a little welcome music or a farewell tune.

This door harp is a true musical instrument, and as such, requires a few materials that you won't find at a lumberyard or woodworking supply store. In particular, you need auto-

harp tuning pegs and banjo strings. (See Figure 1.) These are available at most well-stocked music stores. If the stores don't have them in stock, they can probably order them for you.

Making the Soundbox

A soundbox is simply two sounding boards held apart by side pieces. Together, these parts enclose an air space. The sound is amplified in this enclosed space, and escapes through the soundhole. In making the soundbox, it's important to use thin wood for the sounding boards, approximately ⅛" thick. If you use thicker wood for the sounding boards, the sound of the door harp will be dull and tinny.

Enlarge the pattern for the sides to the proper dimensions, trace it on a piece of stiff cardboard, and cut out a template. Using this template, mark the cutting lines for both sides. *Do not* flop the template when marking the cutting lines. The sides are identical, not mirror images, as you might suspect.

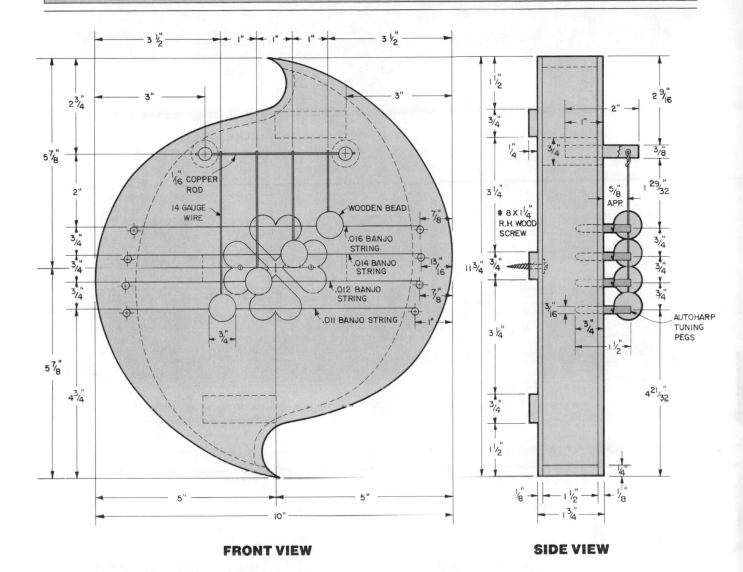

FRONT VIEW

SIDE VIEW

Cut the sides from 1½″ thick stock. Note that the sides get thicker in the middle, so that you can mount the tuning pegs directly in the completed soundbox. Glue the two sides together, 'clamping' them with masking tape.

When the glue sets up, use the assembled sides as a template to mark the sounding boards. Pad saw the sounding boards, cutting them both at once.

Lay out the soundhole in the precise center of the top sounding board. The easiest way to find this center is to measure between the two 'points' at the top and bottom of the piece. The distance should be approximately 11½″. The center of the sounding board is half that distance, or 5¾″.

Once you've laid out the soundhole, drill four ⅜″ holes through the areas you want to open up — this will allow you to insert a jigsaw, scroll saw, or coping saw blade. Saw out the shapes of the soundhole, making four 'piercing' cuts. (See Figure 2.)

Locate the positions of the ¾″ diameter coupling posts on the back side of the top sounding board. These posts serve two purposes. First of all, they 'couple' the top and bottom sounding boards, so that they resonate in unison. (This helps make the sound 'brighter' and 'sustains' the notes longer.) They also provide a place to mount the hanger dowels that hold up the beads. Drill ⅛″ holes in the sounding board,

Figure 1. Purchase the autoharp tuning pegs and banjo strings at a music store.

Figure 2. Cut the soundholes by making 'piercing cuts' with a jigsaw, saber saw, or scroll saw.

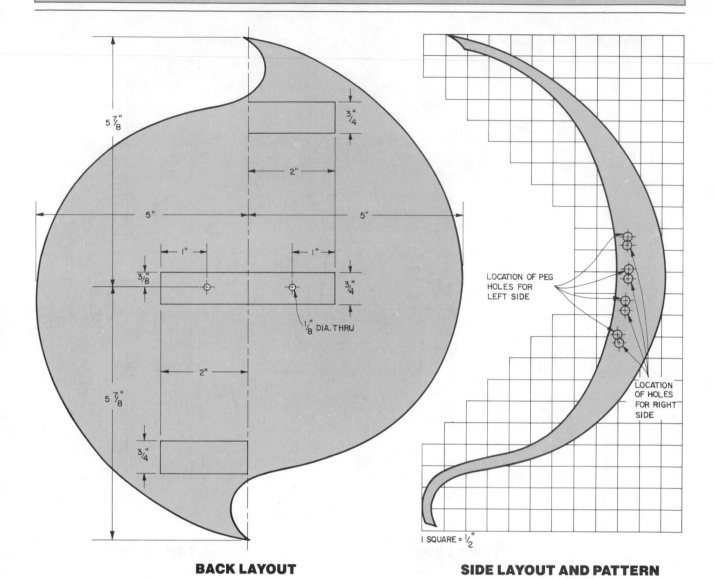

BACK LAYOUT

SIDE LAYOUT AND PATTERN

I SQUARE = 1/2"

LOCATION OF PEG HOLES FOR LEFT SIDE

LOCATION OF HOLES FOR RIGHT SIDE

1/8" DIA. THRU

centered where you want to mount the posts. Also, drill 1/8″ holes centered in the top ends of the posts. Glue the posts to the top sounding board, then hold them in place with #6 x 1/2″ screws. (See Figure 3.) These screws are temporary; you can remove them after the soundbox is complete.

Glue the sounding boards to the side assembly. Be sure to put a drop of glue on the bottom ends of the coupling posts, to attach them to the bottom sounding board. Clamp the parts together, making sure that the joints between the sounding boards and the sides are tight.

Let the glue dry for at least 24 hours, then sand the

completed soundbox to remove any saw marks from the parts, and to make sure that the sounding boards are flush with the sides. Use a disc sander to do most of this work, then switch to a drum sander to get inside the little 'hooks' at the top and bottom of the soundbox. (See Figures 4 and 5.) After this rough sanding, finish sand all outside surfaces of the soundbox.

Remove the screws that kept the coupling posts in position. Then drill 3/8″ holes in the top sounding board, down through the coupling posts. Also, drill holes in the top sounding board, down through the sides, to mount the tuning pegs.

Figure 3. While you assemble the soundbox, hold the coupling posts in place on the top sounding board with small screws. Remove these screws after completing the soundbox.

Figure 4. Sand the sides of the soundbox smooth with a large disc sander.

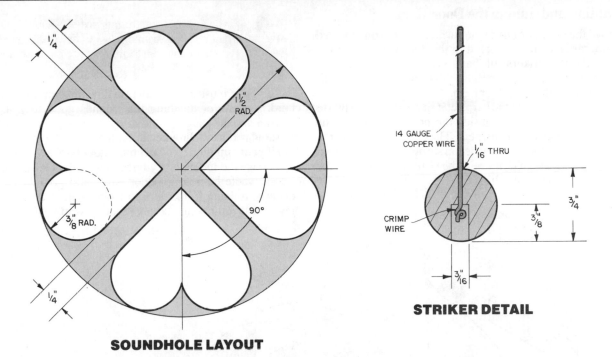

SOUNDHOLE LAYOUT

STRIKER DETAIL

These holes should be 1/64"-1/32" smaller than the diameter of the pegs. For example, if the pegs you purchased are 3/16" in diameter, drill holes 5/32"-11/64" in diameter.

Glue the 1/4" spacers to the back of the soundbox, where shown in the working drawings. After the glue sets up, drill the middle spacer as shown, so that you can use the holes to mount the door harp to a door.

Do any necessary touch-up sanding to the soundbox, and apply a finish. A thin shellac works best. Varnishes and penetrating oils may dull the sound of the harp.

Mounting the Strikers

Insert the tuning pegs in their holes, and screw them down until the 'string holes' (the small holes through the shafts of the pegs) are approximately 1/4" above the surface of the sounding board. Mount banjo string on these pegs, and turn the pegs until the strings are taut. (It's not necessary to tune the strings at this time.) All four stings must be *exactly* the same distance away from the sounding board — *this is important!* Once you've installed the string, temporarily mount the door harp to a vertical surface, using the mounting holes through the middle spacer.

Make the strikers by first drilling 3/16" recesses in wooden beads, then drilling 1/16" holes through the beads as shown in the working drawings. Pass a length of copper wire

through each bead, and crimp the end so the wire won't pull out of the hole. Hide the crimped end in the recess.

Drill 1/16" holes near the ends of the 3/8" hanger dowels, and insert them in their mounting holes. However, *do not* glue them in place just yet. Pass a copper rod through the holes in the hanger dowels — a thin brazing rod works well. Hang the strikers from this rod, looping the wires around it. Position each striker to hit a different string. Then push the hanger dowels in (or pull them out) of their mounting holes until the the strikers hang 1/16"-1/8" away from the strings. If they touch the strings, the striker's will 'dampen' the sound of the harp. If they are too far away, they won't strike the strings properly.

When the hanger dowels are properly positioned, mark them and remove them, along with the rod and strikers. Put a little glue in the mounting holes, and re-insert the dowels, carefully positioning them according to the marks you made. Let the glue set up, then apply a little shellac to the dowels. Finally, reassemble the rod and the strikers.

> **Tip ◆** You can keep the strikers from shifting position on the copper rod by applying little dabs of solder to the rod, one on each side of the striker where it loops around the rod. (See Figure 6.) Also, apply solder to the ends of the rod to keep it from shifting out of the holes in the hanger dowels.

Figure 5. Remove the saw marks from inside the 'hooks' on either end of the soundbox with a small drum sander.

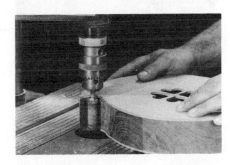

Figure 6. Keep the strikers in place on the rod with little beads of solder.

Mounting and Tuning the Door Harp

Remove the door harp from the surface where you mounted it temporarily, then re-attach it to the door you made it for. Check that the strikers still hang properly. If not, then the door probably isn't plumb. Rather than plumb the door, it's much easier to shim the door harp.

After you've hung the harp, let it sit for an hour or two to adjust to the temperature inside the house. Then tune the strings by turning the tuning pegs. The door harp is meant to be tuned to a 'C' chord: Tune the top string to high C, the next string to E above high C, the next the G above high C, and the bottom string to C above high C.

> **Tip** ◆ Music stores sell 'tuning reeds' — inexpensive harmonica-like instruments — to help guitar and banjo players tune their instruments. You can also use these to help tune a door harp.

If you're musical, you can also tune the harp to a minor chord, seventh, or anything that sounds good to you. By re-arranging the gauges of the strings a little, you can use the old standard mandolin/ukelele tuning, "My dog has fleas." And if your ambition is to become a door harp virtuoso, you can *change* the tuning every once in a while. Or, you could build a whole houseful of door harps and give door harp concerts, running from room to room, slamming doors to play your favorite songs, taking requests from your guests…

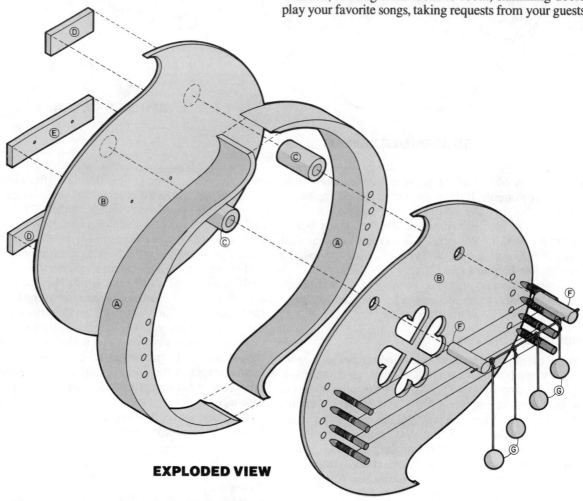

EXPLODED VIEW

BILL OF MATERIALS — Door Harp

Finished Dimensions in Inches

A.	Sides (2)	1½ x 5½ x 11½	.011 Banjo string
B.	Sounding boards (2)	⅛ x 10 x 11¾	.012 Banjo string
C.	Coupling posts (2)	¾ dia. x 1½	.014 Banjo string
D.	Small spacers (2)	¼ x ¾ x 2	.016 Banjo string
E.	Large spacer	¼ x ¾ x 4	¹⁄₁₆″ Copper rod (5″)
F.	Hanger dowels (4)	⅜ dia. x 2	14-Gauge copper wire (12″)
G.	Striker beads (4)	¾ dia.	#6 x ½″ Roundhead wood screws (2)

Hardware

Autoharp tuning pegs (4)

#6 x 1″ Roundhead wood screws (2)
#6 Washers (2)

Designed and built by Vicki Morgan

Whirligigs

All it takes is a little breeze to set these 'gigs a'whirling.

Not so very long ago, it was a common custom that everyone relaxed on the Sabbath — *including* the children. Just as the adults refrained from hard labor, children were expected to avoid boisterous play. Their parents, understanding the need for some sort of amusement, invented 'Sunday toys' — toys that could be enjoyed without a lot of running and jumping. These toys, usually powered by the wind, quickly became known as 'whirligigs'.

Today, whirligigs are more often used to decorate your yard — and keep the birds away from your garden. They can also be displayed inside, where they add a touch of 'country' to your kitchen or living room. Shown here are three traditional whirligig designs for indoors or out: the classic goose, an old biplane, and a colorful paddlewheel.

Making the Paddlewheel Whirligig

The paddlewheel whirligig is, perhaps, the easiest to make; so let's start with it.

First, make a slot-cutting jig that attaches to the miter gauge of your table saw, as shown in the working drawings. This jig will help you space and cut the slots you need to mount the paddles in the wheel. Cut a 10″ diameter wheel from ½″ thick stock and sand away any saw marks from the edge. Drill a ⅛″ hole in the center of the wheel, then divide the wheel into sixteen wedges, each wedge 22½° apart.

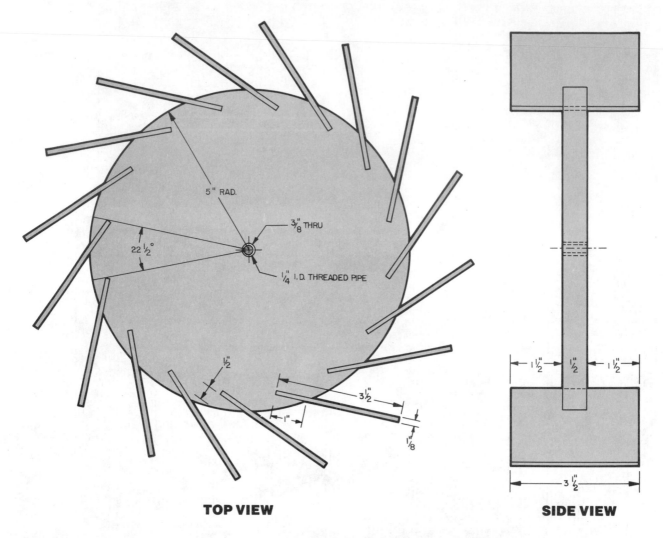

5" RAD.

3/8" THRU

1/4" I.D. THREADED PIPE

22 1/2°

1/2"

3 1/2"

1"

1/8"

TOP VIEW

1 1/2"   1 1/2"   1 1/2"

3 1/2"

SIDE VIEW

PADDLEWHEEL WHIRLIGIG

Adjust the depth of cut on your table saw as high as it will go — you want the slot to be as deep as possible. Mount the wheel to the jig with a #10 machine screw and wing nut, then mount the jig to your miter gauge. Line up one of the wedge marks on the wheel with a mark on the jig. Turn on the table saw, and pass the jig and the wheel over the blade, cutting a slot. Turn off the saw; loosen the wing nut; rotate the wheel to line up the next wedge mark with the mark on the

Figure 1. This simple jig attaches to your miter gauge so that you can cut evenly spaced slots in the whirligig wheel.

Figure 2. A short length of ¼″ I.D. pipe, capped with a nipple and pressed into a hole in the wheel, makes a good pivot bushing for the paddlewheel whirligig.

jig, and repeat the cut. (See Figure 1.) Continue until you have cut sixteen evenly spaced slots in the wheel.

Tighten a nipple onto a short length of ¼″ I.D. threaded iron pipe. With a hacksaw, cut the pipe off ½″ below the nipple. Clean up the edges with a rasp, and ream out the inside of the pipe with a ¼″ twist drill.

Widen the ⅛″ hole in the center of the wheel to ⅜″ — slightly smaller than the outside diameter of the pipe. Then pound the pipe into the hole, until the bottom of the nipple is flush with the surface of the wheel. (See Figure 2.) Cut sixteen square paddles from ⅛″ thick stock. Glue these paddles in the slots in the wheel, using waterproof resorcinol glue.

While the glue is drying, make a mount for the wheel. Rip a 36″-48″ length of 2 x 2 from pressure-treated stock. (You can also use redwood or cedar — any wood that will weather well and can be buried in the ground.) Drill a ¼″ hole, 2″ deep in one end of this post. Cut a length of ¼″ steel rod and sharpen one end with a grinder or belt sander. Press the *blunt* end of this rod into the hole in the end of the post.

Dig a hole 12″-18″ deep somewhere in your yard or garden, where the whirligig will catch the wind. Mount the post in the hole, with the steel rod pointing up. Be very careful to get the post absolutely plumb. Mount the paddle wheel on the steel rod, placing the pipe over the rod so the pointed end of the rod rests against the inside of the pipe nipple.

Tip ◆ A few drops of 10W oil inside the pipe helps the whirligig spin easier, and prevents rust.

If you wish, apply a weatherproof finish to the paddle wheel, or paint it bright colors. We painted ours in a spectrum — each paddle is a slightly different color, ranging from violet to red. This makes a 'rainbow' effect when the wind sets the whirligig spinning.

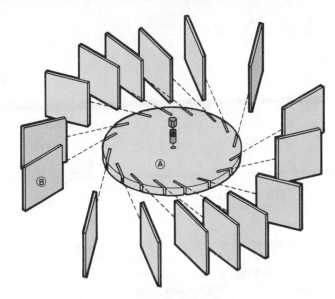

EXPLODED VIEW

BILL OF MATERIALS — Paddlewheel Whirligig	
Finished Dimensions in Inches	
A. Wheel	10 dia. x ½
B. Paddles (16)	⅛ x 3½ x 3½
C. Mounting post	1½ x 1½ x 36-48

Hardware

¼″ I.D. Iron pipe (2″)
¼″ Pipe nipple
¼″ Steel rod (4″)

Making the Goose

Enlarge the body and wing patterns, then trace them onto the appropriate thicknesses of stock. The wings should be ¼″ thick; the body, ¾″ thick. Cut out the shapes with a bandsaw or jigsaw.

Cut two blocks of wood 1¼″ x 1¼″ x 2½″, and drill ⁵⁄₁₆″ holes through the centers of the blocks, as shown in the working drawings. Press ⁵⁄₁₆″ x 1¼″ roll pins into these holes and grind the edges of the pins flush with the wood. These roll pins will serve as 'bushings' for the whirling wings.

Tip ◆ Most hardware stores carry roll pins, but the ⁵⁄₁₆″ pins they usually stock are longer than 1¼″. However, these pins can be easily cut to size with a hacksaw.

Mount a dado cutter on your table saw, with the cutter adjusted to cut a ¼″ slot. Attach an 8″ long miter gauge extension to your miter gauge, just as you attached the slot-cutting jig when you made the paddle wheel. Angle the miter gauge at 45°. Clamp a bushing block to the extension so that the block will pass over the dado knives. Adjust the

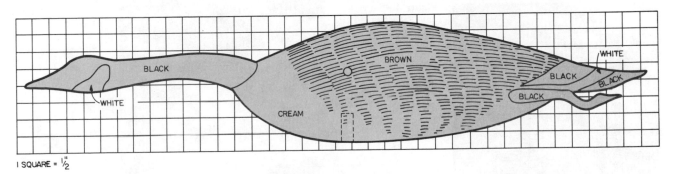

I SQUARE = ½″

GOOSE PATTERN

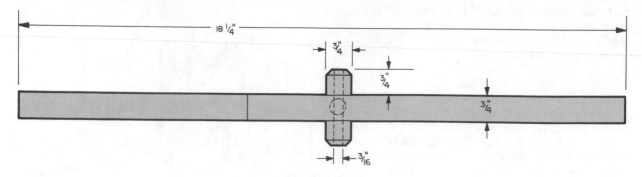

GOOSE/SIDE VIEW

height of the blade so that it will cut a ⅜″ deep slot in the block, from corner to corner. Cut the first slot, then turn the block over and repeat on the other end. (See Figure 3.) The two slots should be at right angles to each other. Do the same for the second block.

Using waterproof resorcinol glue, mount the wings in the slots in the bushing blocks. After the glue dries, 'shape' the hard corners of the bushing blocks with a belt sander, so that they taper down to the flat surfaces of the wings. (See Figure 4.)

Cut two ¾″ lengths of ¾″ diameter dowel, to use as spacers to hold the wings slightly away from the body of the goose. Drill ³⁄₁₆″ holes through the centers of these dowels, and a ³⁄₁₆″ hole through the body where you want to mount the wings. With a hacksaw, cut a 5¼″ length of ³⁄₁₆″ steel rod. Glue the dowel spacers to either side of the body, using this rod to keep the holes aligned.

When the glue dries, drill a ⁵⁄₁₆″ hole, 1¼″ deep in the body of the goose, directly below the hole where you'll mount the wings. Cut the head off a 16d nail and put that in the hole. Then press a ⁵⁄₁₆″ x 1¼″ roll pin in the hole, on top of the nail head. Grind the roll pin flush with the edge of the wood. The roll pin/nail head assembly will serve as a pivot bushing, on which the completed goose will turn into the wind.

Paint the goose body and wing assemblies with waterproof paints. You can follow the color scheme shown in the working drawings, or invent your own. When the paint dries, press the ³⁄₁₆″ x 5¼″ steel rod through the body of the goose so that an equal length of rod sticks out from both sides. Put #10 flat washers on the rod, on both sides of the body. These washers will keep the wings from rubbing on the spacers.

Put the wings on the rods and check the whirling action. They should turn freely. If they bind, there may be a burr on the roll pin bushing. Ream out the inside of the roll pins with a ³⁄₁₆″ twist bit, and check the wing action again.

When you're satisfied with the action, put two more #10 washers, one on either side of the goose, over the ends of the rod. Tap ³⁄₁₆″ cap nuts onto the ends of the rods to keep the wings attached. (See Figure 5.)

Make a mount for the goose similar to the mount you made for the paddle wheel — a 2 x 2 post (made from weatherproof wood), with a sharpened steel rod in the upper end. However, for this project, use a ³⁄₁₆″ rod. Place the goose on the rod and check that it pivots freely. If it doesn't, ream the pivot bushing with a twist drill.

Figure 3. To cut slots to hold the wings in the bushing blocks, clamp the blocks to a miter gauge extension. Pass the blocks over a dado cutter with the miter gauge angled at 45°.

Figure 4. After you glue the wings in the bushing blocks, taper the blocks on a belt sander.

Figure 5. Hold the wings on the rod with cap nuts. These cap nuts are hammered onto the ends of the rods.

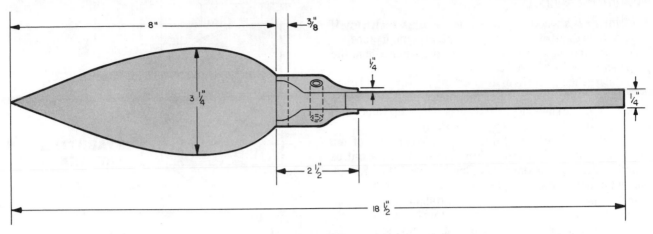

WINGS/SIDE VIEW

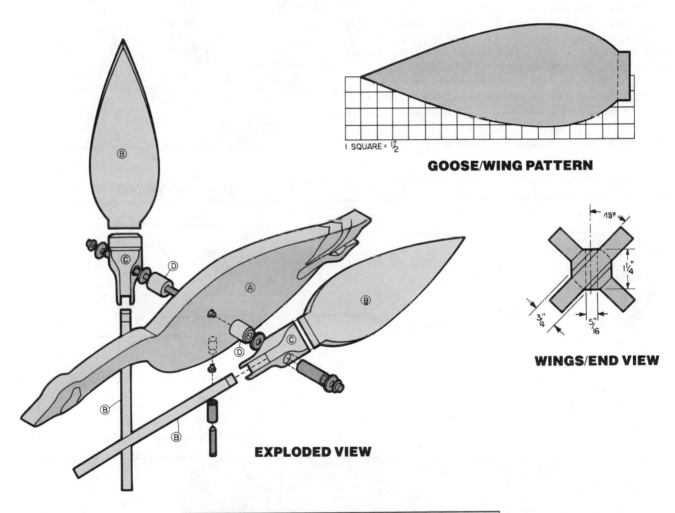

GOOSE/WING PATTERN

1 SQUARE = 1½"

WINGS/END VIEW

EXPLODED VIEW

BILL OF MATERIALS — Goose Whirligig

Finished Dimensions in Inches

A.	Body	¾ x 3¾ x 18¼	
B.	Wings (4)	¼ x 3¼ x 8⅜	
C.	Bushing blocks (2)	1¼ x 1¼ x 2½	
D.	Spacers (2)	¾ dia. x ¾	
E.	Mounting post	1½ x 1½ x 36-48	

Hardware

5/16" x 1¼" Roll pins (3)
16d Nail
#10 Flat washers (4)
3/16" Cap nuts (2)
3/16" Steel rod (9¼")

Making the Biplane

The biplane is a wooden scale model — or a wooden toy, if you prefer to think of it that way — with a spinning propeller. Like a weathervane, it will pivot into the wind so that the propeller faces the breeze head on.

Enlarge the patterns in the working drawings and trace them onto ½″ stock. Cut out all the shaped parts — fuselage middle, fuselage sides, upper and lower wings, elevators, and propeller hub. Sand away any saw marks from the edges.

Drill a ⁵⁄₁₆″ hole, 1¼″ deep, in the lower edge of the fuselage middle, below and slightly in front of the cockpit, as shown in the working drawings. Cut the head off a 16d nail, and put it in this hole, then press a ⁵⁄₁₆″ x 1¼″ roll pin into the hole on top of the nail head. Grind the roll pin flush with the surface of the wood. This arrangement will serve as a pivot bushing, so that the biplane can turn easily into the wind.

Drill the lower wings for the landing gear dowels, and drill both wings for the struts. Note that the strut holes must be drilled at a 10° angle, sloping front to back, as shown in the working drawings. Assemble the upper wing, lower wing, and struts with glue. Also, glue the elevators in the fuselage sides. Once again, use waterproof resorcinol glue.

After the glue dries, assemble the fuselage side to the fuselage middle, and glue the wing assembly in place. Drill holes in the landing gear dowels for the axle pegs, then glue the dowel in place. Be certain that the holes line up with each other, parallel to the wings and at right angles to the fuselage.

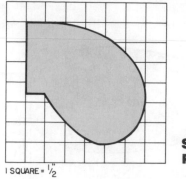

1 SQUARE = ½″

STABILIZER PATTERN

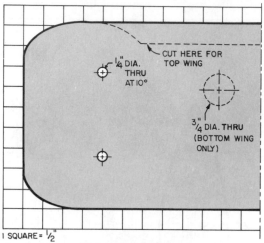

¼″ DIA. THRU AT 10°

CUT HERE FOR TOP WING

¾″ DIA. THRU (BOTTOM WING ONLY)

1 SQUARE = ½″

WING PATTERNS

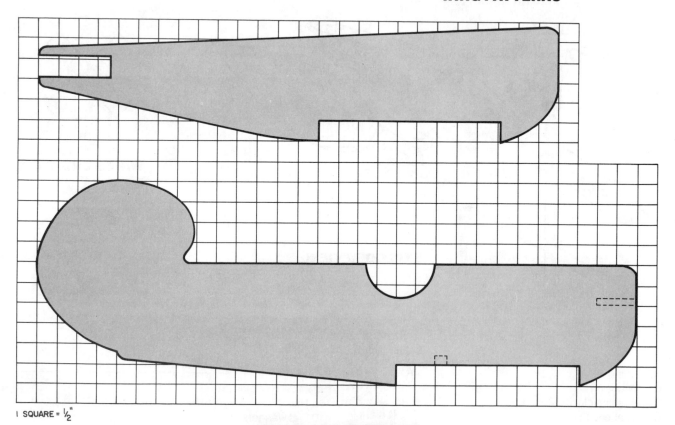

1 SQUARE = ½″

FUSELAGE PATTERNS

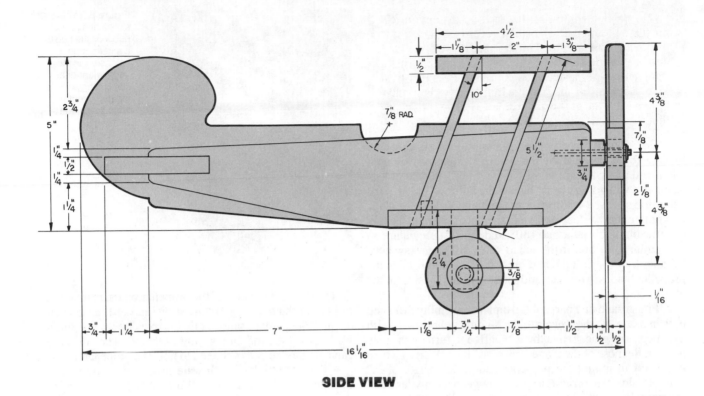

SIDE VIEW

BIPLANE WHIRLIGIG

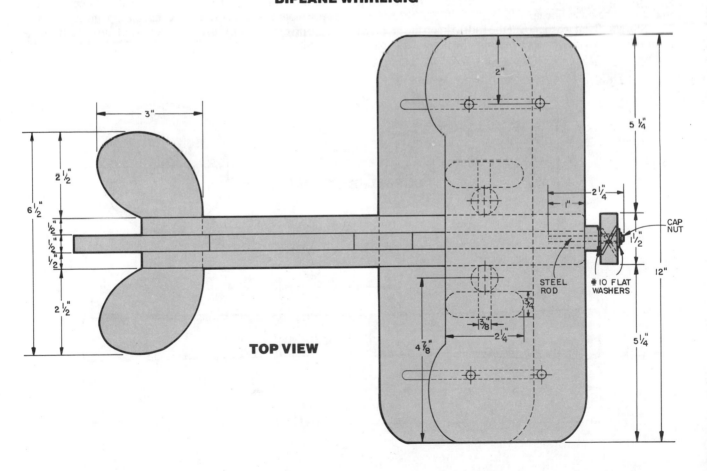

TOP VIEW

Tip ◆ Sometimes, commercial hardwood dowels are just a little smaller than their advertised diameter. If this is the case with the landing gear dowels, coat the ends of the dowels with glue, wrap them in a single thickness of newspaper, and coat the newspaper with glue. Then insert the paper-wrapped dowels in their holes. After the glue dries, trim away any bit of paper that shows.

Cut slots in the propeller hub to mount the propeller blades. To do this, use the miter gauge extension you used when you made the goose. Angle the miter gauge at 30° — as far as it will go. Drill a ⅛″ hole in the hub, and bolt it to the extension so that it will pass over the blade. Adjust the blade height to cut a ⅜″ deep groove in the hub, then pass the hub over the blade. Turn the hub 180°, and repeat. (See Figure 6.)

Enlarge the hole in the hub to 5⁄16″. With a hacksaw, cut a ½″ length of 5⁄16″ roll pin and press it into the hub. Glue the propeller blades in the hub, and set the assembly aside for the glue to cure.

Finish sand any parts of the biplane assembly that need it, then assemble the wheels to the landing gear dowels with axle pegs and glue. Leave the wheel free to turn on the axle pegs. In the nose of the plane, drill a 3⁄16″ hole, 1″ deep where you want to mount the propeller. Cut a ½″ length of ¾″ diameter dowel to serve as a spacer between the fuselage and the propeller, and drill another 3⁄16″ hole in the center of the spacer. With a hacksaw, cut a 2¼″ length of 3⁄16″ steel rod. Glue the spacer to the nose of the biplane, using the rod to make sure the holes line up.

Slip a #10 flat washer over the rod, to keep the propeller from rubbing on the spacer. Then slip the propeller in place.

Figure 6. To cut the slots in the propeller hub, bolt the hub to a miter gauge extension, in the same manner as the slot cutting jig. Pass the hub over the table saw blade at a 30° angle.

Test the spinning action. If the propeller binds, ream out the roll pin bushing with a 3⁄16″ twist bit, and test the propeller again. When you're satisfied that it spins freely, put another washer over the rod on the front of the propeller, then tap a cap nut onto the end of the rod to hold the propeller in place.

Paint the biplane with waterproof paints, using whatever design suits your fancy. World War I aviators painted their planes all sorts of garish colors, so whatever you choose will probably be correct. When the paint dries, mount the biplane on a 2 x 2 post, using a sharpened 3⁄16″ steel rod, just as you mounted the goose. Check that the biplane turns freely on the pivot bushing. If it doesn't, ream out the roll pin with a twist bit.

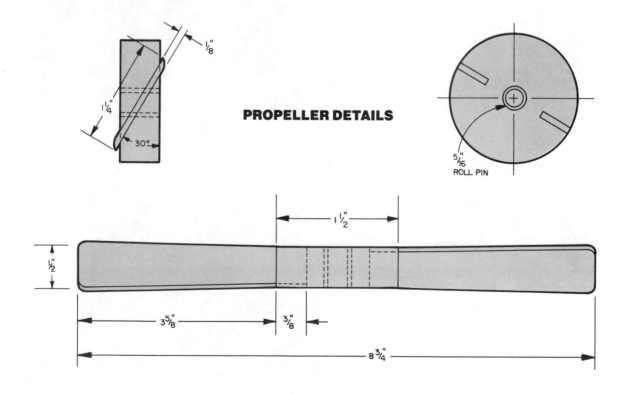

PROPELLER DETAILS

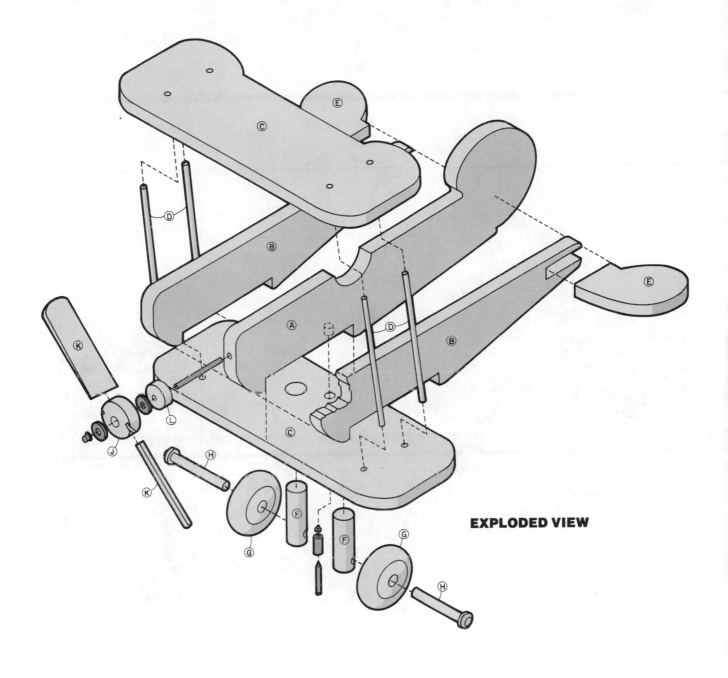

EXPLODED VIEW

BILL OF MATERIALS — Biplane Whirligig

Finished Dimensions in Inches

A.	Fuselage middle	½ x 5 x 15
B.	Fuselage sides (2)	½ x 2¾ x 13
C.	Upper/lower wing	½ x 4½ x 12
D.	Struts (4)	¼ dia. x 5½
E.	Elevators (2)	½ x 3 x 3⅛
F.	Landing gear struts (2)	¾ dia. x 2¼
G.	Wheels (2)	2¼ dia. x ¾
H.	Axle pegs (2)	⅜ dia. x 1⁹⁄₁₆
J.	Propeller hub	1½ dia. x ½
K.	Propeller blades (2)	⅛ x 1¼ x 4
L.	Spacer	¾ dia. x ½

Hardware

⁵⁄₁₆″ x ½″ Roll pin
⁵⁄₁₆″ x 1¼″ Roll pin
#10 Flat washers (2)
³⁄₁₆″ Cap nut
³⁄₁₆″ Steel rod (6¼″)
16d Nail

Designed and built by Nick Engler

Child's Rolltop Desk

This pint-sized rolltop adds a touch of class to the nursery.

Sooner or later every child needs a desk — a place where they can draw, build models, play with miniatures — a place that they can call their very own and let their fantasies take shape. Having your own desk is an important step towards growing up.

Here's a child's desk that is fancier than most: It's a kid-sized rolltop. As designed, it will comfortably accommodate children from three to seven years old. If you wish to build this project for an older child, we suggest you adjust the dimensions somewhat, to make the desk larger.

Making the Desk

The desk itself is a simple table, four legs, aprons, and a top. Cut all the parts to size; then drill screw pockets in the inside faces of the aprons. (See Figure 1.) The pilot holes for these screw pockets should be slightly larger than the shanks of the screws that you intend to use. This will allow the desk top the freedom to expand and contract with the humidity, even after you mount it to the aprons.

With a bandsaw, cut the shape of the front apron. Then drill holes in the ends of the aprons for dowels. Use dowel centers to locate corresponding holes in the legs, and drill these holes in the legs. (See Figure 2.) Also, drill holes for the stabilizing bars in the back legs.

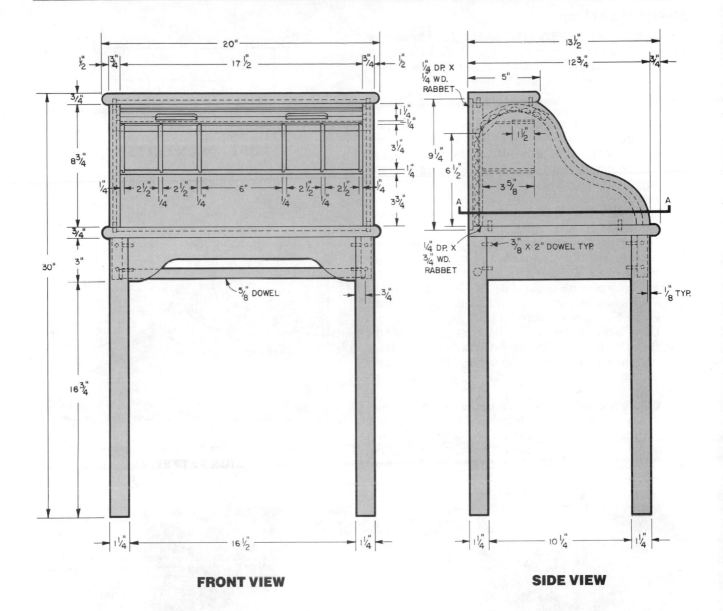

FRONT VIEW   **SIDE VIEW**

Temporarily assemble the legs, aprons, bars, and top to be sure all the parts fit correctly. When you're satisfied that the basic desk assembly fits together properly, disassemble the parts.

Figure 1. Drill screw pockets on the inside edge of the aprons to attach the aprons to the desk top.

Figure 2. After you drill the dowel holes in the aprons, use dowel centers to precisely locate the holes in the legs.

Making the Rolltop

Cut stock for the rolltop sides and top. Using a dado cutter or a router, cut rabbets in the back edge of the desk top, rolltop top, and sides. (See Figure 3.) Note that the rabbets in the desk top and rolltop top are *blind* at both ends. Also notice that there are *two* rabbets in the sides. These rabbets are 'stepped', as shown in the drawings.

Cut the shape of the sides with a bandsaw. Also cut out a template from a scrap of ½" plywood to help you rout the grooves for the tambours in the sides. The size and shape of the template must be *exactly ⅛" smaller* than the grooves you want to cut. Carefully sand the saw marks for the edge of the sides and the template.

To cut the grooves, first clamp the template to the inside face of a side. Mount a ⅜" straight bit in your router, and a ⅝" guide bushing to the router plate. (See Figure 4.) Adjust the depth of cut so that the router will cut a groove ¼" deep in the side. Put the router in place on the template and carefully cut the groove, keeping the router plate flat on the template and the guide bushing pressed up against the edge of the template. (See Figure 5.) Repeat for the other side.

Using dowel centers, as you did when you doweled the aprons and the legs together, drill holes to dowel the sides to the desk top, then the rolltop top to the sides. *Temporarily* assemble these parts to check the fit. Leave the parts assembled for now.

Carefully choose stock to make the rolltop tambours. This stock should be free of defects and have as straight a grain as you can find. With a router or a shaper round over two corners of the tambour stock. Then cut a thin tambour from this rounded edge. (See Figure 6.) Repeat until you have 14 tambours.

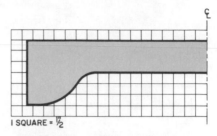

FRONT APRON PATTERN

I SQUARE = ½

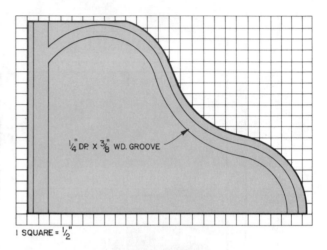

¼" DP. × ⅜" WD. GROOVE

I SQUARE = ½"

SIDE PATTERN

Figure 3. Cut rabbets in the desk top, rolltop top, and sides. The rabbets in the sides are stepped.

Figure 4. To make the tambour grooves, mount a straight bit in your router and a guide bushing to the router plate.

Figure 5. Cut the grooves in the sides with the router, keeping the router plate flat on the template and the guide bushing pressed up against the edge of the template.

Figure 6. Round over the corners of the tambour stock; then rip the tambour from the stock.

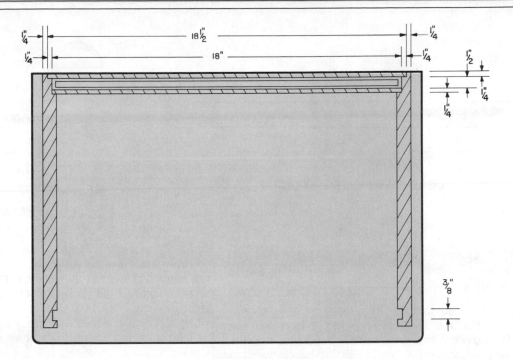

SECTION A

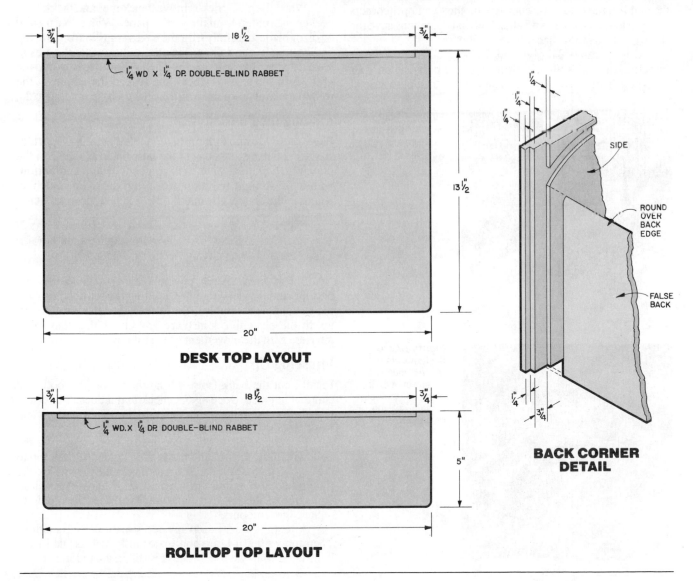

¼" WD × ¼" DP. DOUBLE-BLIND RABBET

DESK TOP LAYOUT

¼" WD.× ¼" DP. DOUBLE-BLIND RABBET

ROLLTOP TOP LAYOUT

SIDE

ROUND OVER BACK EDGE

FALSE BACK

BACK CORNER DETAIL

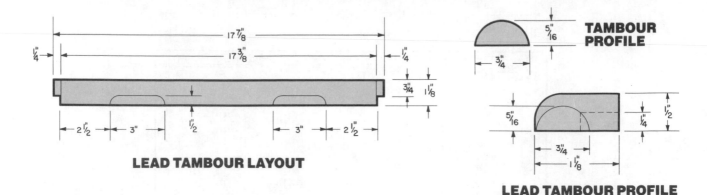

LEAD TAMBOUR LAYOUT

TAMBOUR PROFILE

LEAD TAMBOUR PROFILE

Tip ◆ Don't try to cut the tambours first, and then shape them. The thin stock may come apart when you try to round over the corners.

Make the 'lead' tambour from the same straight, clear stock. Note that this tambour is slightly thicker than the others. Round one corner only, and cut 'handholds' with the router and a ¾″ straight bit. (See Figure 7.) Also, cut tenons in the ends on the lead tambours. Round the two upper corners of these tenons with a hand chisel, so that the tenons have the same profile as the other, thinner tambours.

Cut a scrap of ¾″ plywood, 13″ x 18″ — slightly larger than the finished 'rolltop' will be. Lay the plywood on your workbench and cover it with waxed paper; then put a strip of

Figure 7. Rout the handholds in the lead tambour with a ¾″ straight bit.

Figure 8. Glue the tambours to a piece of muslin. Use scraps of wood to clamp the tambours in place until the glue dries.

muslin, 15″ wide and 14″ long over the waxed paper. Bend the muslin around the edges of the plywood and tack it in place with thumbtacks. Cover the muslin with glue, then arrange the tambours and the lead tambour on top of the muslin. Approximately 1½″ of the tambours should stick out from either side of the muslin. Lay strips of scrap wood on top of the tambours; then clamp them down to the muslin. (See Figure 8.)

When the glue dries, remove the clamps and tacks; then peel up the rolltop from the waxed paper. With a sharp knife or razor blade, carefully trim the excess muslin from the top and bottom of the rolltop. Flex the rolltop several times to loosen up the glue-stiff muslin. Then slide the rolltop into the grooves in the sides to check the fit and the action. If the rolltop sticks at any point, you may have a little sanding to do.

Making the Pigeonholes

Plane down ¼″ stock for the pigeonholes, and cut all parts to size. Round the upper edge of the false back, as shown in the drawings. Cut the dadoes in the pigeonhole top and bottom with a ⅛″ straight bit, mounted in a router. Cut matching tenons in the dividers by making ⅛″ wide, ⅛″ deep rabbets.

Tip ◆ To make small dadoes and tenons accurately, it's best to do the work on a router table. Most dado cutters are too coarse for this sort of fine work.

Finish sand all the pigeonhole parts. Glue the top, bottom, and dividers together; let the glue set up; then glue the pigeonhole assembly to the false back. After the glue sets up, fit the pigeonholes in place and check that they don't interfere with the movement of the rolltop.

Finishing Up

Finally, cut the back from ⅛″ hardboard or plywood, and clamp it in place. Once again, check that it doesn't interfere with the rolltop. When you're satisfied that all the parts fit and work properly, disassemble the rolltop.

Finish sand all the parts that need it; then reassemble the desk with glue, screws, and brads. *Don't* glue the desk top to the aprons; just use the screws. And *don't* glue the back to the rolltop assembly; just fasten it in place with brads. This will let you remove the back, should you ever need to repair or replace the tambours.

After the glue dries, do any necessary touch-up sanding. Then apply a finish. Use a non-toxic finish, such as Danish oil, if the child who will use this desk is still in the toddler stage.

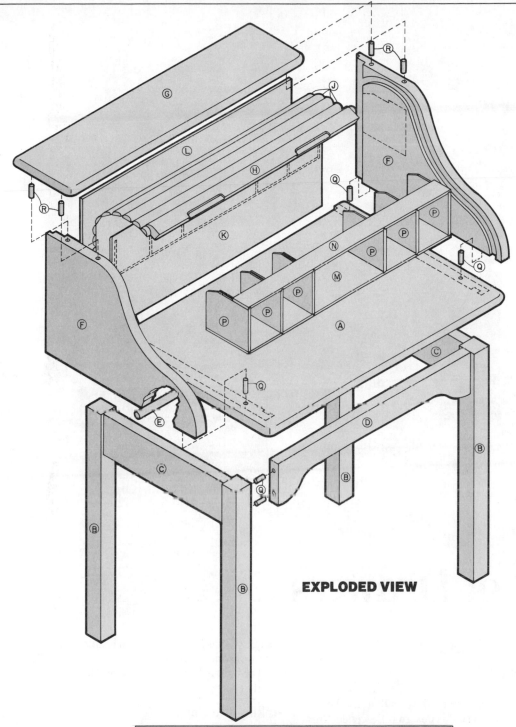

EXPLODED VIEW

BILL OF MATERIALS — Child's Rolltop Desk

Finished Dimensions in Inches

A.	Desk top	¾ x 13½ x 20	L.	Back	¼ x 9¼ x 18½
B.	Legs (4)	1¼ x 1¼ x 19¾	M.	Pigeonhole bottom	¼ x 3⅝ x 17½
C.	Side aprons (2)	¾ x 3 x 10¼	N.	Pigeonhole top	¼ x 1½ x 17½
D.	Front apron	¾ x 3 x 16½	P.	Pigeonhole dividers	¼ x 3½ x 3⅝
E.	Back leg brace	⅝ dia. x 18	Q.	Large dowels (16)	⅜ dia. x 2
F.	Rolltop sides (2)	¾ x 8¾ x 12¾	R.	Small dowels (4)	¼ dia. x 1
G.	Rolltop top	¾ x 5 x 20			

Hardware

H.	Lead tambour	½ x 1⅛ x 17⅞
J.	Tambours (14)	5⁄16 x ¾ x 17⅞
K.	False back	¼ x 6½ x 18

Muslin, 14″ x 15″

1″ Brads (12-18)

Designed and built by Tom Stender

Chest of Drawers

This simple, elegant chest is a true classic.

Do you ever wonder why they call it a 'chest of drawers'? It's because this design is descended from a much older, much simpler piece of furniture — the chest. The chest was the original storage unit, and it served folks well for many, many centuries. However, the chest had one noticeable limitation: It was a real bother to go digging through the contents for something stored near the bottom.

When the science of cabinetry stumbled on the invention of the drawer, craftsmen began building chests with a single drawer at the bottom. This relieved the owner from having to dig quite so far. Soon, craftsmen added another drawer, and then another and another, until they had filled up the whole chest with drawers.

This particular chest of drawers was made by a modern-day craftsman, Tom Stender of Boston, New York. Tom's

specialty is classic furniture, and he adapted the design of this piece from the traditional Queen Anne style. The beautiful wood he built it from is not quite so traditional — it's a rare lot of curly cherry.

Making the Case

It is Tom's practice, when making a piece like this, to cut *all* the parts for the case and 'dry assemble' them *before* gluing any of them up. That way, he can be certain that everything fits properly, and he can easily replace a part that doesn't mate properly with surrounding parts.

This practice has another advantage. When a tree grows, its surrounding environment may impose certain stresses on the living trunk. These stresses remain in the wood long after the tree has been cut down and sawn up into lumber. Sometimes, when you cut or rip a board, you inadvertently relieve some of these stresses. The board may warp or twist immediately after it's cut — or it may wait several days. By dry assembling the major portion of the project, then

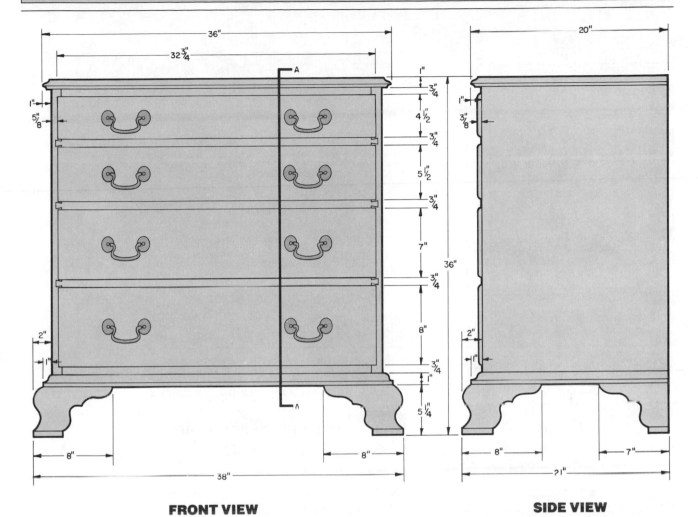

FRONT VIEW

SIDE VIEW

gluing up the parts all at once, you give the wood a chance to get used to the new shapes. Any over-stressed boards that might distort the project will begin to bend *before* it's too late to replace them.

You might object to dry assembling a large project because you think it will require fourteen hands and three times as many clamps. Well, in a properly designed piece, such as Tom's chest of drawers, it requires very few clamps. (In fact, you can dry assemble everything but the back without using a single clamp.) The joinery in this project holds it together quite nicely. The glue simply *reinforces* the joints.

Begin by making the four web frames. These frames support the drawer and keep the case square. Cut all the parts to size. Using a router or a dado cutter, cut ¼″ grooves in one edge of all the parts. (See Figure 1.) The middle web frame stiles require grooves in *both* edges. With the aid of a tenon cutting jig, cut ¼″ matching tenons in the ends of the stiles. (See Figure 2.) The tenons should fit in the grooves snugly, but not tight. Notch the front web frame rails as shown in the working drawings, dry assemble the frames, and set them aside.

The web frames have two parts that must be glued on at a later date: the drawer guides and the kickers. Cut these parts, but it's not necessary to assemble them just yet. However, if you wish, you can screw them in place with *countersunk* flathead wood screws.

Figure 1. Cut the grooves on the insides of the web frame rails and stiles with a router or dado cutter. The middle stiles get grooves on both edges.

Figure 2. Use a tenoning jig to cut tenons in the ends of the web frame stiles.

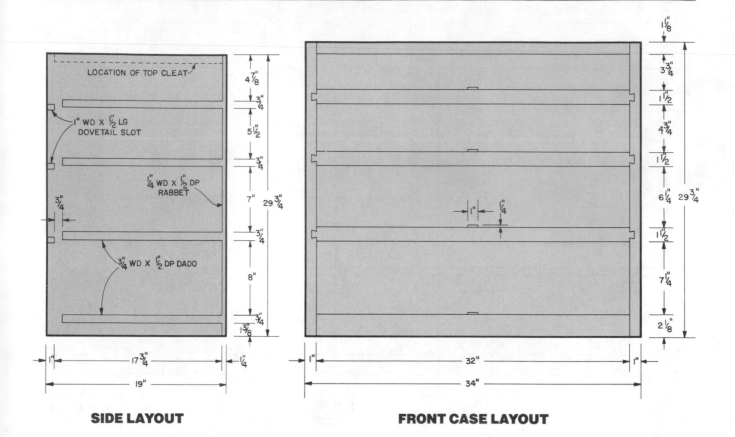

SIDE LAYOUT

FRONT CASE LAYOUT

Next, make the front rails. These parts tie the sides of the case together at the front with french dovetails. Make a hardboard template for the dovetail 'tail', and mark the tails on the three middle front rails. (The reason for the template is that these dovetails should be identical.) Cut the tails with a bandsaw or a backsaw. (See Figure 3.) Drill dowel holes in the ends of the upper and lower front rails.

Glue up wide stock for the sides, taking care that the end grain of all the boards curves in the same direction — preferably *towards* the outside. With a router, cut the rabbet for the back and the blind dadoes for the web frames. Use a straightedge, clamped to the sides, to guide the router as you cut. Square the ends of the dadoes with a hand chisel. (See Figure 4.)

Dry assemble the web frames to the sides. Carefully mark the position of all the front rails, then disassemble the web frames from the sides. Drill matching dowel holes in the sides to attach the upper and lower front rails. To attach the middle front rails, you'll have to cut dovetail slots. Mark these slots using the tails of the front rails as templates. Then, using a Forstner bit, carefully drill out as much waste as you can. (See Figure 5.) With a *very sharp* hand chisel, remove the rest of the waste. (See Figure 6.) Keep testing the fit of the tail in the slot as you work, and stop when the fit is snug, but not too tight.

Cut the back from ¼" thick plywood. Cut the cleats from ¾" thick solid stock, and drill *and* counterbore the cleats for roundhead wood screws. Notice on the working drawings

Figure 3. Cut the 'tails' of the dovetails in the front rails with a bandsaw.

Figure 4. After routing the blind dadoes in the sides, square the ends with a hand chisel.

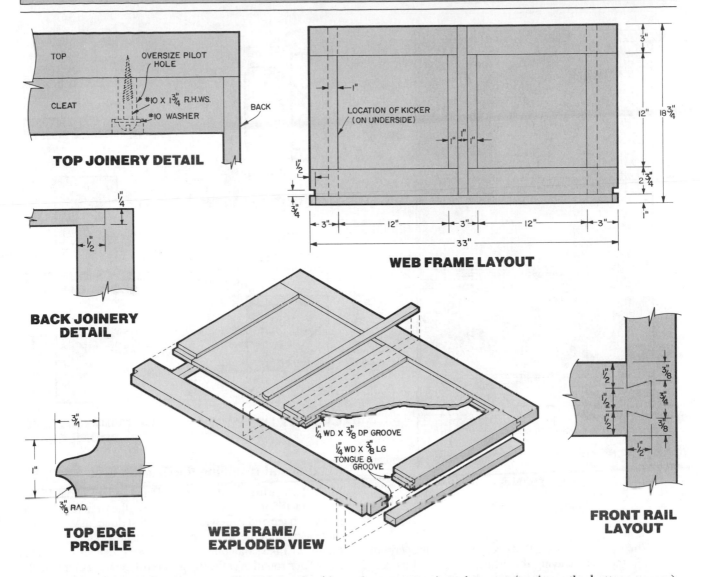

TOP JOINERY DETAIL

TOP

OVERSIZE PILOT HOLE

CLEAT

#10 X 1¾" R.H.WS.

#10 WASHER

BACK

BACK JOINERY DETAIL

1/4"

1/2"

WEB FRAME LAYOUT

1"

LOCATION OF KICKER (ON UNDERSIDE)

1" 1" 1"

3"

12"

18¾"

2¾"

1"

1/2"

3/4"

3"   12"   3"   12"   3"

33"

TOP EDGE PROFILE

3/4"

1"

3/8" RAD.

WEB FRAME/ EXPLODED VIEW

¼" WD X 3/8" DP GROOVE

¼" WD X 3/8" LG TONGUE & GROOVE

FRONT RAIL LAYOUT

1/2"
1/2"
1/2"

3/8"
3/4"
3/8"

1/2"

that the pilot holes in the cleats are oversize. This lets the sides and the top — which the cleats join — expand and contract with changes in humidity. For this same reason, the cleats will *not* be glued to the sides or the top, when it comes time to assemble the case with glue.

Cut the top and shape the front and side edges as shown in the working drawings. This shape requires two passes with two separate shaper cutters or router bits — an ogee (to shape the top corner), and a cove (to shape the bottom corner). When you've completed the top, finish sand all parts.

Now you're ready for the dry assembly. Screw the cleats to the sides, then assemble the sides with the upper and lower front rails in place. Put the middle front rails in their slots, and slide the web frames in their dadoes. Attach the top to the cleats with screws, and attach the back with band clamps.

Figure 5. To make a dovetail slot, first drill as much of the waste as you can from the slot with a flat-bottom drill bit.

Figure 6. Then remove the rest of the waste with a hand chisel.

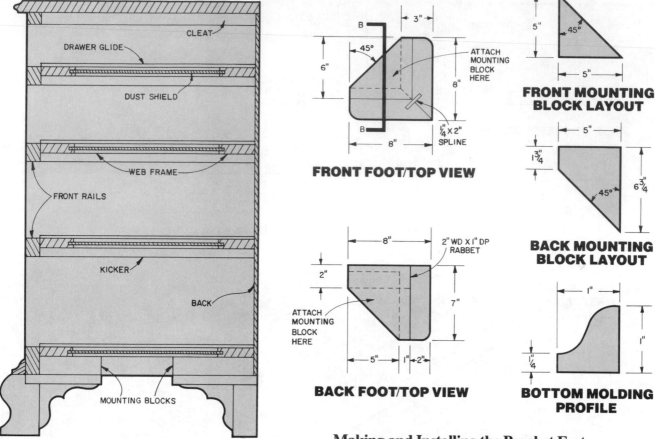

FRONT FOOT/TOP VIEW

BACK FOOT/TOP VIEW

FRONT MOUNTING BLOCK LAYOUT

BACK MOUNTING BLOCK LAYOUT

BOTTOM MOLDING PROFILE

SECTION A

When you're satisfied that everything fits properly, disassemble the case, leaving the cleats attached to the sides. Glue up the web frames, and glue the drawer guides and kickers in place. Note that the bottom web frame does not get kickers. (The purpose of the kickers is to keep the drawer below the frame from tipping when you pull it out. Since there's no drawer below the bottom web frame, it doesn't need kickers.) *Do not* glue the dust shields in their grooves, let them float freely so that they can expand and contract. As you clamp up the frames, take care that they are absolutely square.

Next assemble the sides, upper front rail, and lower front rail with dowels and glue. Then glue the tails of the middle front rails in the dovetail slots in the sides. Slide the web frames into their dadoes and glue the front edge of the web frame front rail to the back side of the front rails. However, *do not* glue the frames in the dadoes. They must be allowed to float, like the dust shields, so that the sides can expand and contract.

Screw the top to the cleats. Once again, *do not* glue it in place. Glue the back in place in the rabbets, and wrap several band clamps around the case to hold it while the glue dries. Make sure that the case is absolutely square as you tighten the bands. Reinforce the back-to-side rabbet joint with small brads. *Do not* glue or nail the back to the back edge of the web frames.

Making and Installing the Bracket Feet

Make the legs from 3″ thick stock. Plane and rip a board 5¼″ wide and 48″ or more long. Cut a cove in the front face of this stock 1″ deep and 2½″ wide. This is best done on your table saw, by passing the wood across the blade at an angle. (See Figure 7.) Take small bites, cutting just ⅛″ deeper with each pass. Then round over the top portion of the front of the stock with a hand plane. (See Figure 8.) This will form the classic cyma or S-curve.

Cut a 1″ deep, ¾″ wide rabbet in the top back edge of the stock, then cut the stock into four 8″ lengths and two 7″ lengths. Miter one end of the 8″ front leg pieces, where they will join. The back leg pieces (7″) should be cut square, then cut a second 2″ wide, 1″ deep rabbet on the back, to join the back pieces.

Figure 7. To shape the bracket feet, first cut a cove in the front face of the stock by passing the board across your table saw at an angle to the blade.

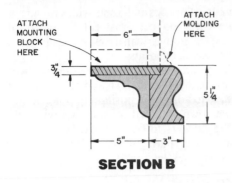

SECTION B

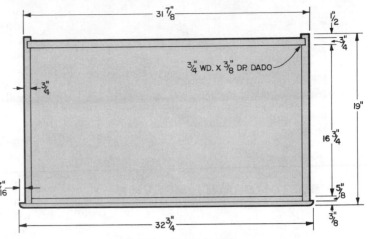

DRAWER/TOP VIEW

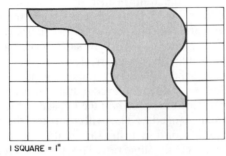

I SQUARE = I"

FOOT PATTERN

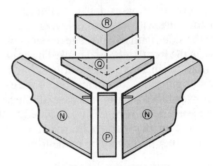

FRONT FOOT/EXPLODED VIEW

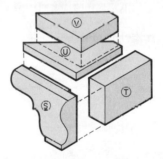

BACK FOOT/EXPLODED VIEW

To finish the front feet, cut ¼″ spline grooves in the mitered faces. Glue the leg parts together with reinforcing splines. Cut 6″ x 6″ triangular-shaped brackets to fit in the rabbets, and glue them to the bracket feet. Then cut 5″ x 5″ triangular mounting blocks, and glue those on top of the brackets. If you wish, reinforce the glue joints by screwing the brackets to the feet, and the mounting blocks to the brackets, with flathead wood screws.

The back feet are made in a different manner. Glue 2″ thick blocks in the rabbets in the back side of the feet, then glue triangular brackets to the top of this assembly. These brackets should be 1″ longer on one of the sides than the bracket you made for the front feet. Glue mounting blocks to the tops of the brackets. These blocks, too, should be longer than the front feet mounting blocks. Reinforce the glue joints with screws.

Attach the feet to the case with glue. Reinforce these joints by driving flathead wood screws through the case into

Figure 8. Then round the top portion of the front face with a hand plane, completing the classic cyma curve.

the mounting blocks. Don't worry about the screws showing — the base molding will cover them up.

Select 1″ thick stock for the base molding and shape the edge. Then cut the molding free from the stock. Don't try to do it the other way around — don't cut the molding free, then shape it. Smaller pieces of stock can't be safely shaped.

Cut the molding to size and miter the end. Attach the front molding to the front of the case and the feet with glue. Reinforce this joint by driving screws through the case from the *inside* and into the back of the molding. That way, you won't be able to see the screws.

Glue the side moldings to the feet, but *don't* glue them to the sides of the case. The grain of the parts is opposed to each other, and a glue joint will someday pop. Instead, screw the molding to the sides with roundhead wood screws from the inside of the case. Drill oversize pilot holes for the screws in the sides, just as you did in the cleats, so that the sides can expand and contract.

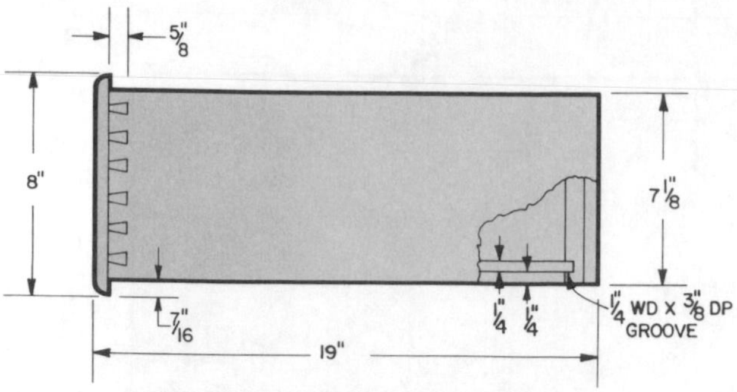

BOTTOM DRAWER/SIDE VIEW

Making and Installing the Drawers

The drawer construction is fairly standard. The front is attached to the sides with half-blind dovetails, and the back is attached to the sides with a dado. The drawer bottom rests in a ¼″ groove in the front, sides, and back. The drawer guide on the web frames fits in a notch in the drawer back. This keeps the drawer straight as it slides in and out of the case.

The drawer faces overlap the case all the way around. These faces are made from ⅜″ stock glued to the drawer fronts. Only the faces need to be made from expensive hardwood; the other parts may be made from less expensive lumber.

> **Tip ◆** Consider making the drawer fronts, sides, back, and bottoms from cedar. Cedar repels insects, helps discourage mildew, and imparts a fresh scent to the things that you store in the drawers.

Cut the dovetails in the sides and fronts with a router and a dovetail template. Or, if you're a purist, cut them by hand. Make the dadoes and the grooves with a router or dado cutter, then notch the backs with a bandsaw.

Dry assemble the drawers, omitting the drawer faces. Check the action to see that they slide in and out of the case easily. You may have to adjust the position of a notch on a drawer back, or file down the heads of some screws in the cleats to get all the drawers to fit properly. When you're satisfied, glue the drawer parts together. *Don't* glue the drawer bottom in its grooves; let it float.

Finishing the Project

Finish sand all the parts that still need it. When you sand, start with 100# sandpaper and work your way up into the finer grits. Never use coarse paper on hardwood — you'll never get the scratch out, no matter how hard you sand. If you have to remove a lot of stock to smooth a part, use a scraper.

Once you've sanded the entire project, wipe it down with a tack cloth to remove the excess dust. Then apply a finish. Be sure to coat the inside *and* the outside of the case with the same number of coats. That will ensure that the parts absorb and release moisture at the same rate so that they expand and contract at the same rate. This, in turn, will help keep the case square.

Don't finish the drawers, except for the drawer faces. The wood on the side of the drawers should be left bare to absorb moisture and odors that might otherwise affect the things you have stored in the drawers.

When the finish is complete, rub paraffin on the bottom of the drawers and the drawer glide to help them slide in and out of the case more easily. Install Chippendale drawer pulls on the front of the drawers, to match the style of the feet and moldings.

BILL OF MATERIALS — Chest of Drawers

Finished Dimensions in Inches

A. Top	1 x 20 x 36
B. Sides (2)	1 x 19 x 29¾
C. Front top rail	1 x 1⅛ x 33
D. Front middle rails (3)	1 x 1½ x 33
E. Front bottom rail	1 x 2⅛ x 33
F. Back	¼ x 29¾ x 33
G. Web frame front rails (4)	¾ x 2¾ x 33
H. Web frame back rails (4)	¾ x 3 x 33
J. Web frame stile	¾ x 3 x 12¾
K. Drawer guides (4)	¼ x 1 x 17¾
L. Kickers (6)	¾ x 1 x 17¾
M. Cleats (2)	1 x 1⅛ x 17¾
N. Front feet (4)	3 x 5¼ x 8
P. Splines (2)	¼ x 2 x 5¼
Q. Front brackets (2)	¾ x 6 x 6
R. Front mounting blocks (2)	1⅜ x 5 x 5
S. Back feet (2)	3 x 5¼ x 7
T. Back blocks (2)	2 x 4½ x 6
U. Back brackets (2)	¾ x 6 x 7
V. Back mounting blocks (2)	1⅜ x 5 x 6¾
W. Top drawer face	⅜ x 4½ x 32¾
X. Top drawer front	⅝ x 3⅝ x 31⅞
Y. Top drawer sides (2)	¾ x 3⅝ x 18⅝
Z. Top drawer back	¾ x 3⅝ x 31⅛
AA. Upper middle drawer face	⅜ x 5½ x 32¾
BB. Upper middle drawer front	⅝ x 4⅝ x 31⅞
CC. Upper middle drawer sides (2)	¾ x 4⅝ x 18⅝
DD. Upper middle drawer back	¾ x 4⅝ x 31⅛
EE. Lower middle drawer face	⅜ x 7 x 32¾
FF. Lower middle drawer front	⅝ x 6⅛ x 31⅞
GG. Lower middle drawer sides (2)	¾ x 6⅛ x 18⅝
HH. Lower middle drawer back	¾ x 6⅛ x 31⅛
JJ. Bottom drawer face	⅜ x 8 x 32¾
KK. Bottom drawer front	⅝ x 7⅛ x 31⅞
LL. Bottom drawer sides (2)	¾ x 7⅛ x 18⅝
MM. Bottom drawer back	¾ x 7⅛ x 31⅛
NN. Drawer bottoms (4)	¼ x 17⅜ x 31
PP. Dust shields (8)	¼ x 12⅝ x 12⅝

Hardware

#10 x 1¾″ Roundhead wood screws (18)
#10 Flat washers (18)
#10 x 1½″ Flathead wood screws (20)
1″ Brads (1 box)
Chippendale drawer pulls (8)

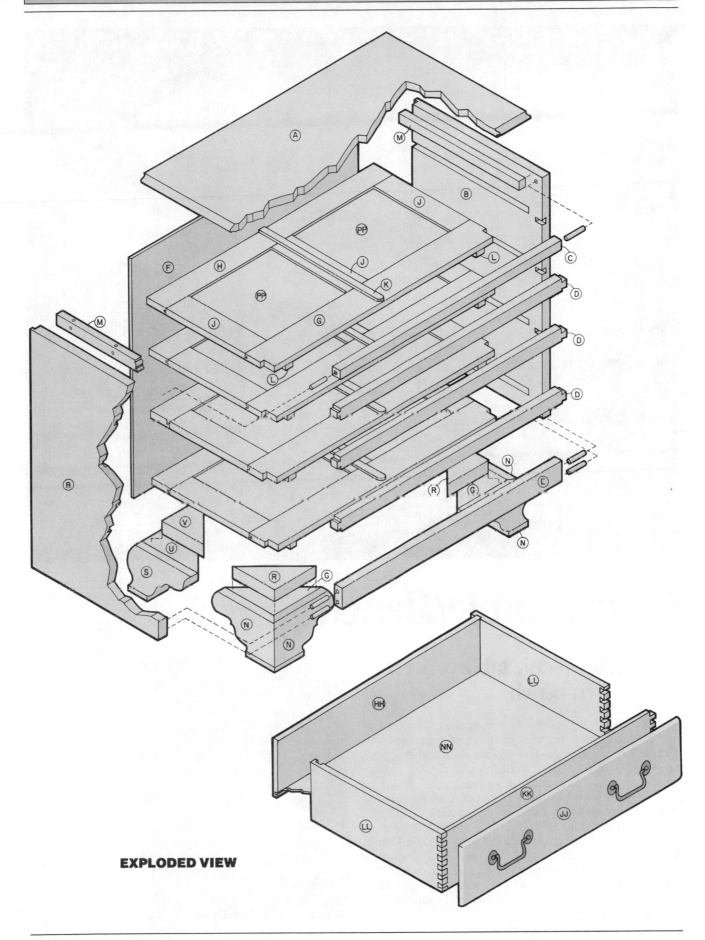

EXPLODED VIEW

Designed by Nick Engler, built by Adam Blake

Picnic Table/Bench

This clever picnic table converts to a garden bench.

Figure 1. Two table clamps, one on either side of the table tops, hold the table/benches together to make a standard-size picnic table.

Here's an ingenious variation on the classic country table/chair. You've seen the project, perhaps — a kitchen table that converts to a chair, so that you can easily store it against a wall. Well, this is an outdoor version. When you need a picnic table, it's a picnic table. When the picnic's over, it folds into a bench to create more room — and more comfortable seating on your patio or deck.

We suggest you make two of these table/benches, so that you can hook them together to make a single 3′ x 5′ table, with two parallel seats, facing each other — in other words, a standard picnic table. We've designed a simple coupler that will hold the tops together and flush with each other when you need a wide table, but that can be easily disconnected when you don't. (See Figure 1.)

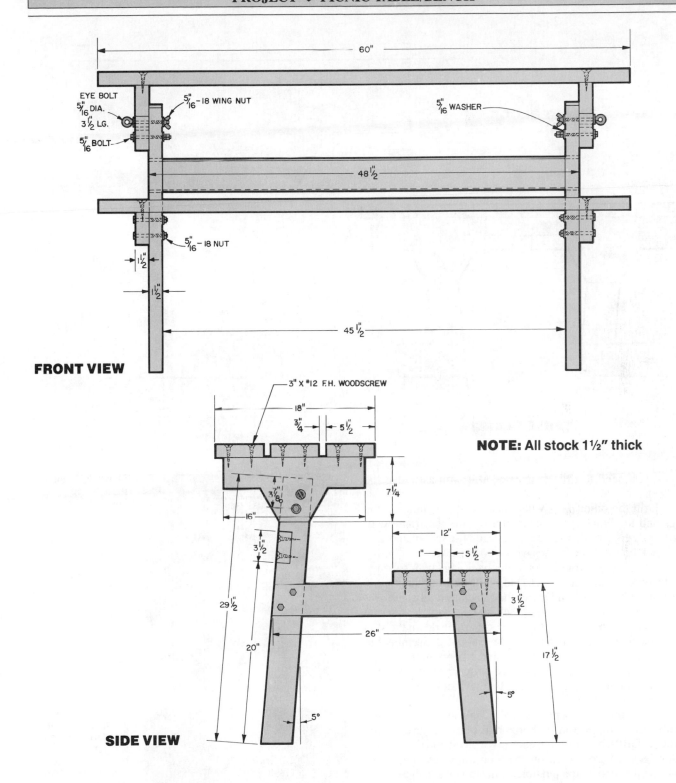

FRONT VIEW

SIDE VIEW

NOTE: All stock 1½″ thick

Making the Table/Bench

Make this project from redwood, cedar, or cypress. These woods are particularly well-suited for outdoor projects. They have natural oils which make them resistant to rot and water damage. If you use pressure-treated lumber, let this project sit outside through several rainstorms before you eat off it. Most pressure-treated woods are impregnated with cupric arsenate (an arsenic compound), and it takes a little weathering before the chemical leeches out of the surface of the wood.

This project is made from standard lumber sizes, so you shouldn't have to do any ripping or planing. Start construction by cutting all the pieces to length. Miter the legs and one end of the leg braces at 5°, as shown in the working drawings. With a dado cutter or a saber saw, cut a dado joint in the back legs for the back brace.

Cut the pivot block to the proper size and shape, using a bandsaw or saber saw. Drill the pivot holes, but do not drill the stop pin holes just yet. To accurately position the stop pin

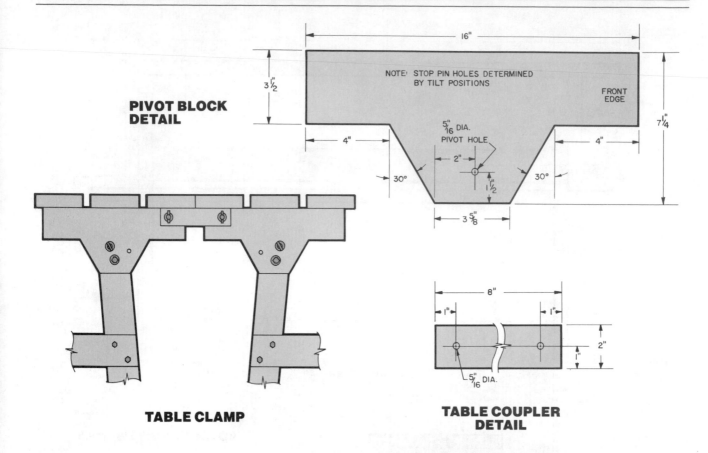

PIVOT BLOCK DETAIL

NOTE: STOP PIN HOLES DETERMINED BY TILT POSITIONS

FRONT EDGE

16"

$3\frac{1}{2}$"

$7\frac{1}{4}$"

4"

4"

$\frac{5}{16}$" DIA. PIVOT HOLE

2"

$1\frac{1}{2}$"

30°

30°

$3\frac{5}{8}$"

TABLE CLAMP

TABLE COUPLER DETAIL

8"

1"

1"

2"

1"

$\frac{5}{16}$" DIA.

holes, you need to drill them later, after you assemble the project.

Drill the other parts where needed. Make holes in the legs and leg brace for bolts, then assemble the frame with carriage bolts, washers and nuts. Attach the seat planks and the back brace to the frames with wood screws.

Attach the pivot blocks to the back legs with carriage bolts, washers and stop nuts. (Stop nuts will remain secure, even when you raise and lower the top continually.) Put two washers in between the pivot block and the back legs, so the wood won't rub when the top moves. Tighten down the stop nuts just tight enough to take any play out of the assembly, but not so tight that the pivot blocks bind when you try to turn them. Once the pivot blocks are properly attached and adjusted, attach the top planks to the blocks with wood screws.

Place the table/bench assembly on a level surface, and clamp the table top in its horizontal position, level to the ground. Drill a hole through each pivot block and through the back legs, where shown on the working drawings. These holes will become stop pin holes. Put stop pins in these holes when you want the table horizontal.

Loosen the clamps, and re-clamp the top in a nearly vertical position, tilted at just 5°. Drill another set of stop pin holes in the legs, using the stop pin holes in the pivots as guides. Use eye bolts for stop pins, securing the eye bolts in the stop pin holes with washers and wing nuts. When you want to raise the table top to its horizontal position, simply remove the eye bolts, tilt the top up, and replace the eye bolts in the first set of stop pin holes. To lower the table top, reverse the procedure. (See Figures 2 and 3.)

Figure 2. To secure the table top in the horizontal (table) position, insert the eye bolts in the first set of stop pin holes.

Figure 3. To lower the table top to the vertical (bench) position, remove the eye bolts and re-insert them in the second set of stop pin holes.

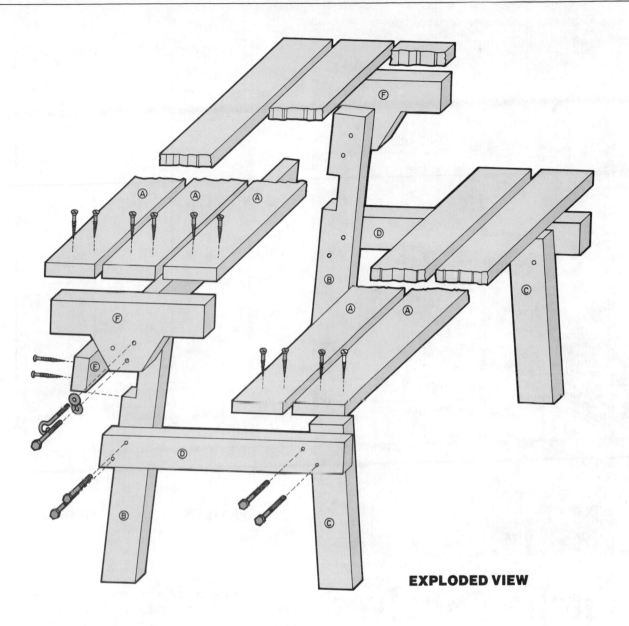

EXPLODED VIEW

To complete the project, make the couplers needed to hold two table/benches together. Cut the couplers to size, and drill holes in the ends, where shown in the working drawings. Then put the table benches together, back to back, with both table tops in the horizontal position. Clamp the couplers in place and drill holes in the pivot blocks, using the holes in the couplers as guides. Remove the clamps and insert eye bolts, washers, and nuts through the holes you just drilled to hold the table tops together.

There's no need to finish this project — the wood is naturally resistant to decay, and it will take on a warm gray-brown tone as it sits out in the weather. However, do sand the wood, especially the top and seat planks, to lessen the chance of splinters.

This project plan was first published by Shopsmith, Inc. in **Hands On!** *magazine. Our thanks to Shopsmith for allowing us to use it here.*

BILL OF MATERIALS — Picnic Table/Bench

Finished Dimensions in Inches

A.	Top/seat planks (5)	1½ x 5½ x 60
B.	Back legs (2)	1½ x 3½ x 29½
C.	Front legs (2)	1½ x 3½ x 17½
D.	Leg braces (2)	1½ x 3½ x 26
E.	Back brace	1½ x 3½ x 48½
F.	Pivot blocks (2)	1½ x 7¼ x 16

Hardware

⁵⁄₁₆″ x 3½″ Carriage bolts (10)
⁵⁄₁₆″ Hex nuts (8)
⁵⁄₁₆″ Stop nuts (2)
⁵⁄₁₆″ Flat washers (18)
⁵⁄₁₆″ x 3½″ Eye bolts
⁵⁄₁₆″ Wing nuts (2)
#12 x 3″ Flathead wood screws (24)

Designed and built by Chalmer Crowell

SIDE PATTERN

I SQUARE = ½"

5⅝" DIA
⅜" DP

SIDE VIEW

3⅝"

¾" 4½"

5⅝" DIA
⅜" DP

1½"

1¾"

5⅜"

Kitchen Shelves

You can never have too many shelves — especially in the kitchen.

If you're short of shelving space to store those little things that clutter up a kitchen, here's an idea. This storage project features several small shelves for spices and knickknacks, a small cabinet for more spices and particularly ugly knickknacks, and a rack for hand towels. If you want to make the rack removable, you can also use it to hold rolls of paper towels.

Making the Kitchen Shelves

Start by cutting all the parts to size. Enlarge the side pattern and trace it on the side stock, but don't cut the pattern until *after* you cut the joinery.

With a router and a ¾" straight bit, rout four blind dadoes where shown in the working drawings. Clamp the sides securely to your worktable and use a straightedge to guide the router. (See Figure 1.) Square off the corners of the dadoes with a hand chisel. (See Figure 2.)

Tip ◆ As you set up to cut the dadoes, remember that each side is a *mirror image* of the other.

Figure 1. Rout the blind dadoes, using a straightedge to guide the router.

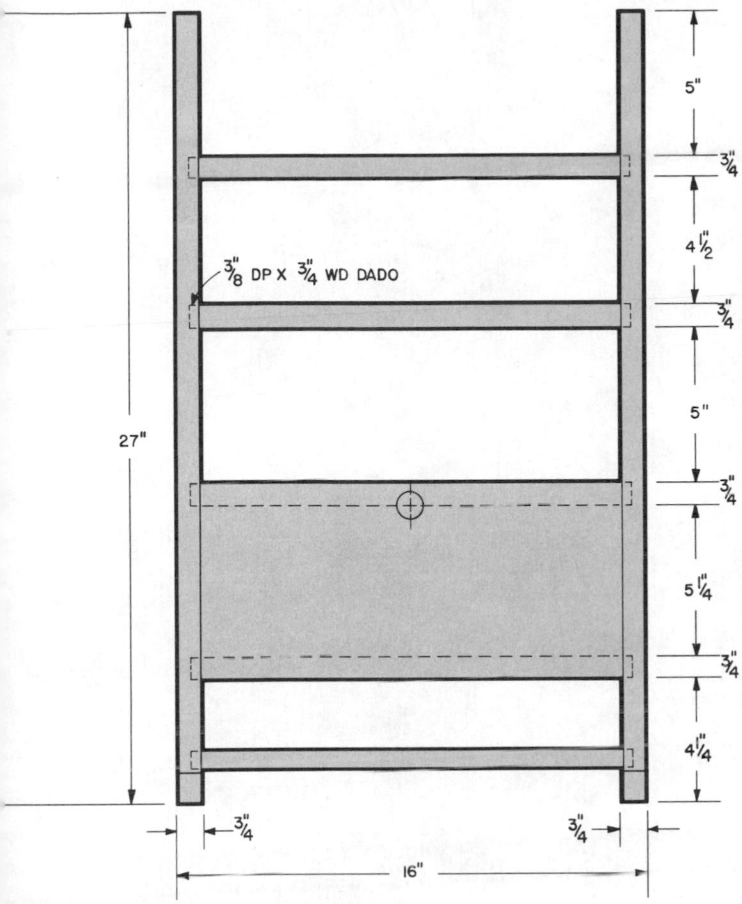

FRONT VIEW

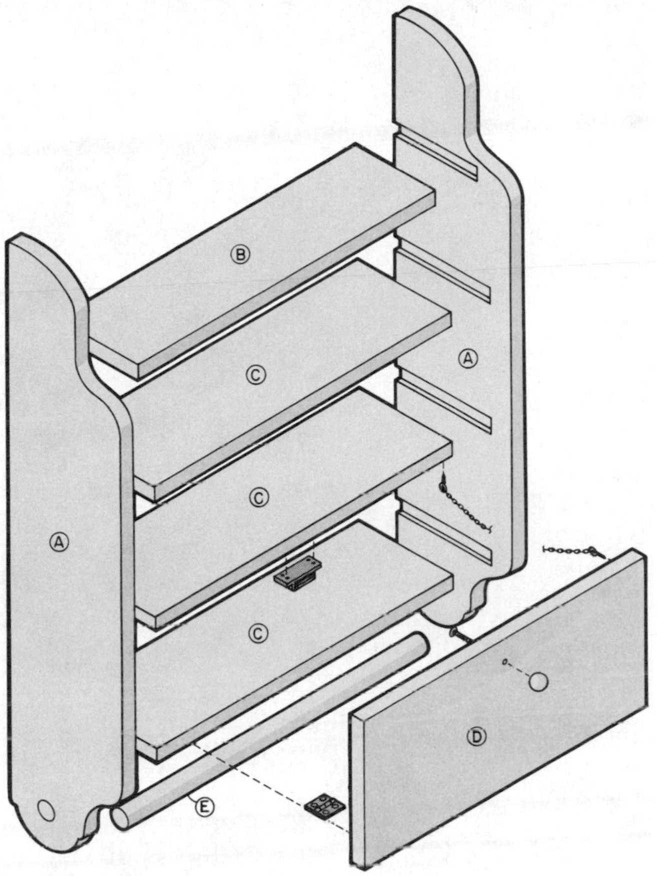

EXPLODED VIEW

Drill the holes that will hold the rack. Note that these holes are 'stopped' — they're only 3/8″ deep. Then 'dry assemble' all the parts to check their fit. If you're satisfied, take the project apart again and finish sand all parts.

Reassemble the project with glue. Reinforce the joints where the shelves join the sides with finishing nails or wood screws. Hinge the door of the cabinet to the bottom shelf. Add a magnetic catch to hold the door closed, and a chain to keep the door horizontal when you open it. Finally, apply a waterproof, easy-to-clean finish to the completed project.

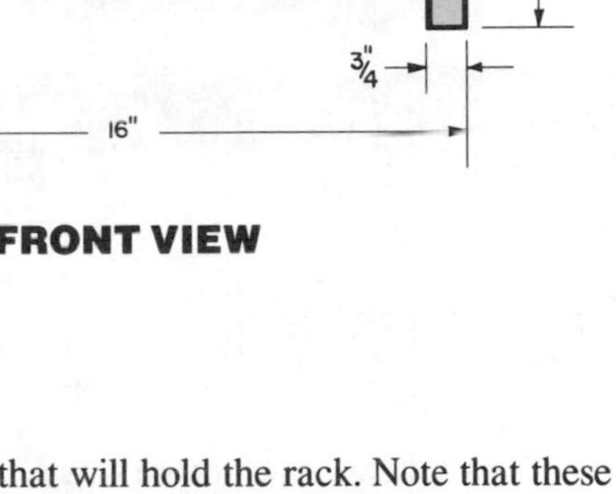

Figure 2. Square the blind ends of the dadoes with a hand chisel.

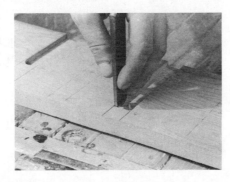

BILL OF MATERIALS — Kitchen Shelves

Finished Dimensions in Inches

A.	Sides (2)	3/4 x 5 3/8 x 27
B.	Top shelf	3/4 x 3 5/8 x 15 1/4
C.	Middle/bottom shelves (3)	3/4 x 4 1/2 x 15 1/4
D.	Cabinet door	3/4 x 6 3/4 x 14 3/8
E.	Rack	5/8 dia. x 15 1/4

Hardware

1 1/2″ x 2″ Butt hinges and mounting screws (1 pair)
Door pull
Magnetic catch
3/4″ Eye screws (2)
Small S-hooks (2)
Small chain (Approx. 8″)
3d Finishing nails or #8 x 1 1/4″ flathead wood screws (16)

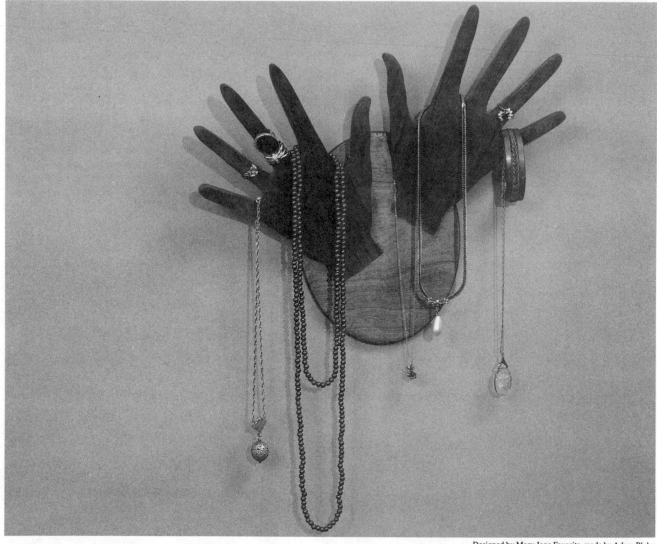

Designed by Mary Jane Favorite, made by Adam Blake

Helping Hands

Contemporary jigsaw sculpture provides a place to store and display your jewelry.

Looking for a way to keep jewelry or other small items organized and easy to find? These 'helping hands' provide a place to hang all sorts of things, out in plain sight, where you can find them in no time. You can even organize things by the finger or by the hand — rings according to the finger they fit; right hand for silver, left hand for gold, etc.

To make this project, start by cutting the pieces out of ⅜″ thick stock. You'll need an oval-shaped plaque and two hands — one right and one left. All of the parts are best cut out with the jigsaw. After cutting, sand away any saw marks from the edges.

On a belt sander, taper the wrists of the hands, as shown in the working drawings. (See Figure 1.) Drill the plaque to make mounting holes — ³⁄₁₆″ holes to mount the plaque to the wall, and ⅛″ holes to mount the hands to the plaque. Countersink the ⅛″ holes on the back of the plaque. Round over the edges of the plaque, then finish sand all parts.

Glue the hands to the plaques so that the wrists just cover the ⅛″ mounting holes. Reinforce the glue joints with #6 x ⅝″ flathead wood screws. After the glue dries, do any necessary touch-up sanding and apply an oil finish.

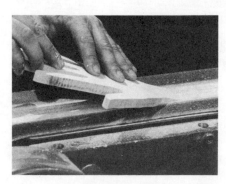

Figure 1. Taper the wrist with the aid of a belt sander.

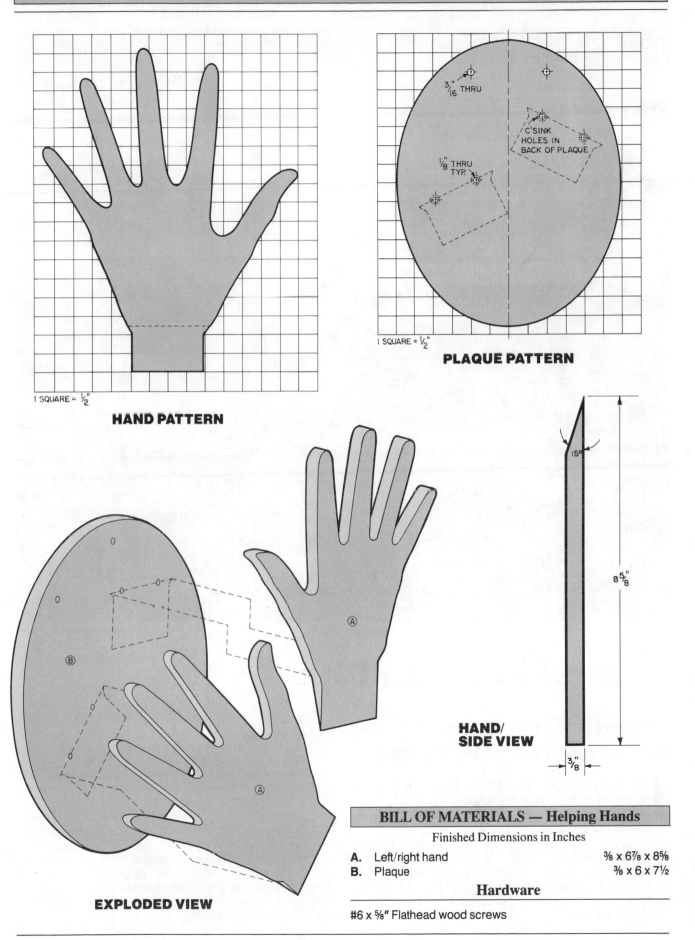

1 SQUARE = ½"

HAND PATTERN

1 SQUARE = ½"

PLAQUE PATTERN

³⁄₁₆" THRU

C'SINK
HOLES IN
BACK OF PLAQUE

⅛" THRU
TYP.

15°

8⅝"

³⁄₈"

**HAND/
SIDE VIEW**

EXPLODED VIEW

BILL OF MATERIALS — Helping Hands

Finished Dimensions in Inches

A.	Left/right hand	⅜ x 6⅞ x 8⅝
B.	Plaque	⅜ x 6 x 7½

Hardware

#6 x ⅝" Flathead wood screws

89

Designed and built by Nick Engler

Schoolhouse Lamps

Yesterday's junk makes an elegant lamp for today's home.

Browsing through second-hand stores, you'll usually find one or two ancient "schoolhouse globes". Some are plain, some are fancy, and a good many are absolutely elegant in their simplicity or their styling.

These glass shades were originally meant to be hung from ceiling fixtures. But with a little lathe work, you can also mount them upside down on a contemporary lamp base. This blend of old and new — an antique globe on a modern pedestal — makes a striking combination that works well with most any decor.

Gluing Up Stock

The first step in turning a lamp base is to glue up the stock. A base usually requires a fairly large turning blank, and it's not likely that you'll find a large enough chunk readily available.

When gluing up stock for the lathe, you must take several precautions: First of all, make sure that all the surfaces to be glued are clean and fit together without gaps. When you clamp the stock together, don't tighten the clamps so securely that you squeeze all the glue out from between the boards. This will cause a weak, 'starved' joint. And finally, let the glue set up for *at least* 24 hours before you turn the stock. If the glue joints are ill-fitting, weak, or improperly cured, the stock may come apart on the lathe.

You can glue up the stock in one of two configurations — with the grain running either parallel or perpendicular to the axis of rotation. If you opt for perpendicular grain, you can cut out rings of different diameter on your bandsaw and laminate them together in a rough approximation of the finished turning. (See Figure 1.) In some ways this simplifies the turning, since there is less waste to remove. But it also limits you to *scraping* the turning. It's all but impossible to cut or shear when the grain is perpendicular to the rotation.

Gluing up grain parallel to the turning axis takes more time, more planning, and more care. But the stock is easier to turn. You can also achieve some intriguing designs by laminating pieces of *contrasting* woods. (See Figure 2.)

Whichever method you use, remember to leave a ½" x ½" shaft down the middle of the turning and a small cavity in the bottom. (See Figure 3.) The shaft is for the hollow threaded rod that holds the light socket and provides a safe channel for the lamp cord. The cavity is to provide space for the wiring connections you'll need to make between the cord and the switch.

Turning the Base

Before you can mount the turning blank on your lathe, you'll need to put two wooden 'caps' on either end. These caps will cover the shaft and the cavity, so that you have solid wood for the lathe centers to bite into. (See Figure 4.) The caps can be either a permanent part of the turning, or temporary. If permanent, *do not* glue the bottom cap in place. Just fix it to the block with screws. You must be able to remove it in order to wire the lamp.

Start turning at a slow speed — 800 RPM or less. Until you get the blank completely rounded, the blank may be slightly out of balance. A large turning blank, revolving at a high speed, could start to vibrate dangerously.

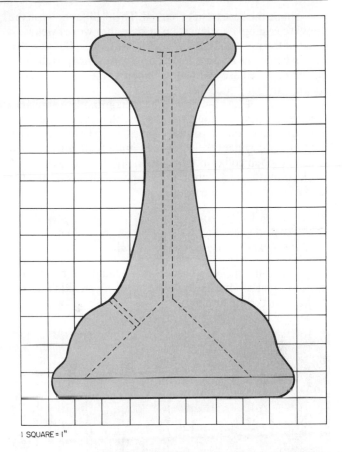

1 SQUARE = 1"

LAMP BASE PATTERN

Figure 1. If you don't mind turning with the grain running perpendicular to the axis of rotation, you can glue up the turning blank by laminating wood rings of different diameters.

Figure 3. Leave a small shaft down the center of the turning blank and a cavity in the bottom of the lamp base to accommodate the necessary lamp hardware and wiring connections.

Figure 2. By laminating contrasting colors of woods in the turning blank, you can make some striking designs in the finished lamp base.

Figure 4. 'Cap' the ends of the turning blank so that you have someplace solid to mount the lathe centers. If you wish, these caps can become part of the turning.

Shape the base to suit yourself. The profile shown in the drawing is simply a suggestion, a base that works well with some of the most common schoolhouse globes. But as we've shown you in the lead shot, there are many other possibilities. As long as the base adequately supports the globe, you can shape it any way you wish.

The top of the base must either accommodate a collar to hold the globes, or it must serve as a collar for the globes. If you buy a metal collar, you may have to turn a small recess in the top so the collar fits flush. (See Figure 5.) If you decide to turn a wooden collar in the base, make the ring at least ¼" thick so that it stands up to the weight of the globe and the heat from the light. (See Figure 6.)

> **Tip** ◆ To save time, sand *and* finish the base of the lathe. A good penetrating finish, such as tung oil or Danish oil, works well for lathe turnings.

Dismount the lamp base from the lathe and remove the bottom cap. Remove the top cap as well, if you didn't elect to make it part of the turning.

Wiring the Lamp

To complete the base, drill two holes through the side and into the cavity, as shown in the drawings. The lower hole is for the lamp cord, the other is for the switch.

The lamp switch shown here is a 'turn-on/turn-off' switch with a threaded base and wire leads. To mount it in the lamp base, just smear the threads with epoxy glue and press it into the hole. (See Figure 7.) The switch hole should be ever-so-slightly undersized for a good, snug fit.

Cut the hollow threaded rod to the length required, then mount a lamp socket (and a metal collar, if needed) on one end. Insert the other end in the shaft hole at the top of the base and push it all the way through. There should be approximately ½"-¾" of the rod showing in the cavity. Put a fender washer and a stop not on the bottom end of the thread rod to hold it in place.

Insert the lamp cord in the appropriate hole in the base. Thread the cord up through the hollow rod, and attach the cord to the leads in the socket. Pull any extra wire back down through the hollow rod into the cavity.

Figure 7. Install the switch by pressing it into a hole drilled in the turning. The hole should be slightly smaller than the threaded base of the switch. To prevent the switch from coming loose, rub some epoxy glue on the threads.

Figure 8. Secure the wiring connections with wire nuts, then staple the lamp cord to the side of the cavity so that the connections can't be pulled apart.

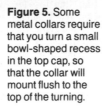

Figure 5. Some metal collars require that you turn a small bowl-shaped recess in the top cap, so that the collar will mount flush to the top of the turning.

Figure 6. If you turn a collar in the wood itself, leave at least ¼" of stock so that the wooden collar can stand up to the weight of the globe and the heat of the light.

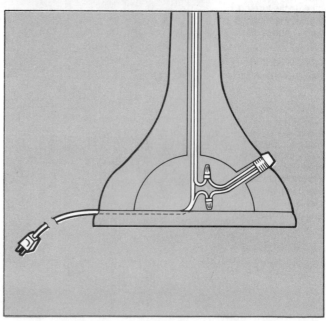

Cut one of the wires in the cord 2"-3" *before* the cord enters the hollow rod. Peel the cut wire back from the cord slightly and strip the ends. Then attach the stripped ends to the switch leads with wire nuts. To prevent these connections from being pulled apart, staple the lamp cord to the wall of the cavity where it enters from the outside. (See Figure 8.)

Install a plug at the end of the lamp cord, then test your wiring by installing a light bulb and plugging the lamp in. If everything works correctly, unplug the lamp and remove the bulb.

Finishing Up

If you've elected to make the bottom cap part of the lamp base, screw it back onto the base to cover the cavity. If not, cover the base with felt. It's essential that you somehow cover the wiring connections for safety's sake.

Put the bulb back in the socket, and sit the globe in place. If you're using a metal collar to hold the globe, tighten the three mounting screws that came with this collar. The screws should touch the globe above the lip, but do not tighten so tight that they actually press against the globe.

If you've turned a wooden collar on top of the lamp base, drill three ⅛" holes in this collar, 120° apart. Insert a #4 x ¾" roundhead wood screw in each hole. Put the globe in place, then tighten these screws as you would for a metal collar. (See Figure 9.) Once again, be sure not to tighten the screws too tight.

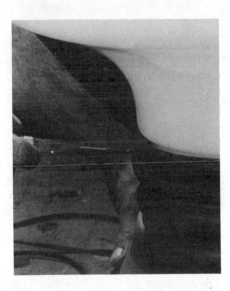

Figure 9. Use small roundhead screws to secure the globe in a wooden collar.

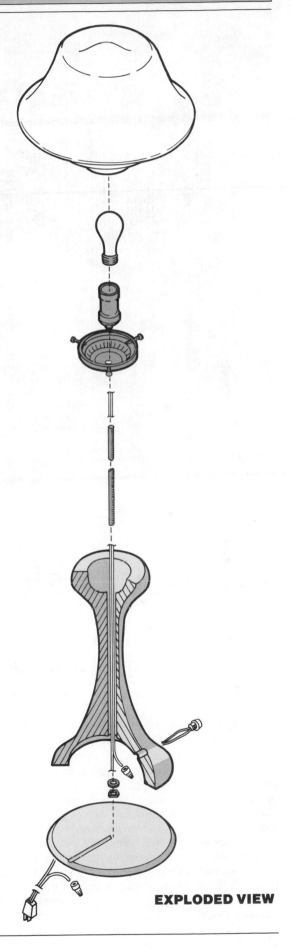

EXPLODED VIEW

Hardware List — Schoolhouse Lamp
½" Hollow threaded rod (12"-18")
Light socket with threaded base
½" Stop nut and fender washer
14-Gauge lamp cord (10'-12')
Turn-on/turn-off switch with wire leads
Plug
Wire nuts (2)
Wire staples (2-3)
Metal collar (optional)
#4 x ¾" Roundhead wood screws (3 — for use in wooden collars)

Text and photography by David Donnelly

Lowboy Desk

A classic Queen Anne design is skillfully adapted to make a modern desk.

The latter half of the 18th century is sometimes known as the Golden Age of American furniture design. It was during this short period in our history that many of the furniture styles that we now refer to as 'classic' were developed: Queen Anne, Chippendale, the Federal styles of Sheraton and Hepplewhite. Many furniture forms developed that are still popular today: the secretary desk, the drop-leaf table, the highboy — and the lowboy.

The project you see here is not a classic form, but it is adapted from a Queen Anne lowboy design. The lowboy has been stretched in several directions to make a modern-sized desk, while preserving the classic lines — the arrangement of drawers, the cabriole legs, and the prominent cyma or S-curves throughout.

Traditionally, an American Queen Anne piece is made from cherry, walnut, or mahogany, with mahogany the preferred wood. You need only purchase these expensive woods for the *visible* parts, such as the desk top, legs, drawer fronts, etc. The hidden parts, such as the drawer supports and guides, can be made from cheaper hardwoods, such as poplar or beech.

Making the Cabriole Legs

The cabriole legs, while they look hard to make, are really quite simple. In brief, all you have to do is trace the pattern on two adjacent sides of the stock; cut the cabriole shape in one side, then the other; then round and smooth the surface. Let's replay that in slow motion.

Enlarge the leg pattern to full size. Glue or tape the pattern to a piece of stiff cardboard or hardboard, and cut it out with a bandsaw. Use this as a template for tracing the pattern on all four legs.

Tip ◆ There are several easy ways to blow the pattern up to full size. You can use an opaque projector, an enlarging/reducing copier, or a local graphic arts company. I prefer the latter. Ask them for a 'stat' of the leg pattern enlarged to 29½″ in length.

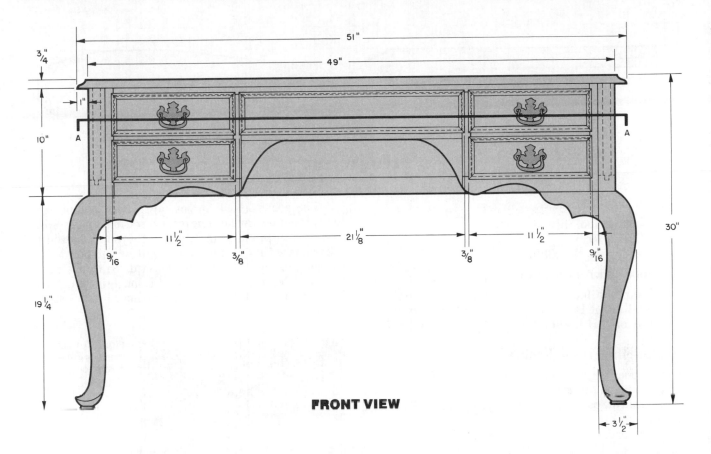

FRONT VIEW

Trace the pattern onto a leg blank — the straight side of the template (the back of the leg) should line up with the edge of the wood. Turn the blank 90°, flip the template, and trace another pattern. (See Figure 1.) Notice that the knees of the two patterns meet at a corner. *Do not* trace the patterns so the backs of the legs meet. The template won't work properly that way.

The corner posts or stiles of the desk are incorporated into the leg. It's much easier to cut the joinery in these stiles *before* you cut the shapes of the legs. Carefully lay out the joinery on the corners *opposite* to the patterns you drew. (See Figure 2.) Rout the mortise with a router and a ⅜″ straight bit. (See Figure 3.) Square the ends of the mortises with a chisel.

Now you're ready to cut the shape of the legs on a bandsaw. To make the cabriole shape, you'll have to cut each leg twice. After you cut the pattern in one side, tape the waste back to the stock. Then turn the stock and cut the pattern in the second side. (See Figure 4.) When you remove all the waste, you'll have the rough shape of a cabriole leg.

Finish shaping the pad feet with a hand chisel and a rasp. Secure the leg in a vise and carefully round the pad and the foot, as shown in the lead photograph. Be careful to avoid rasping across the grain, since this may tear the wood. Instead, cut across the grain with a *very* sharp chisel. Finish the legs by rounding over the hard corners and smoothing out the saw marks with a pneumatic drum sander. (See Figure 5.)

By the way, pneumatic drum sanders are a fairly new invention, and they aren't available everywhere. However, you can get them through several mail-order sources. Here are two addresses:

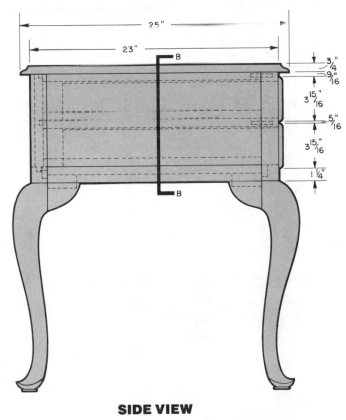

SIDE VIEW

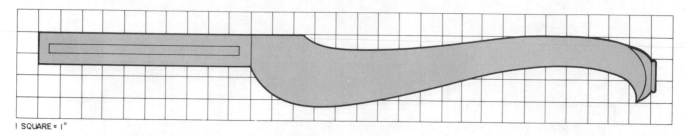

| SQUARE = | "

LEG PATTERN

For hand-held sanders, write:

The Fine Tool Shops
P.O. Box 7093
Portsmouth, NH 03801

For a stationary drum sander, write:

Shopsmith, Inc.
3931 Image Drive
Dayton, OH 45414

Cutting the Frame Joinery

Cut the board to size for the sides and the back. If necessary, glue stock edge to edge to make the wide stock required. Also cut all the parts you need for the face frame, kickers, and drawer supports.

The ends and bottom edge of the sides and the back have tenons ⅜″ wide x ½″ long. The face frame end stiles have similar tenons. You can cut these tenons with either a straight bit on a router, or a dado cutter mounted on your table saw. Notice that each tenon has a 'shoulder' — it stops ½″ from the corners of the piece. Cut this shoulder with a backsaw.

The side and back aprons have tenons *and* mortises. Rout the mortises in the same manner you made the mortises in the legs' stiles, and cut the tenons just as you cut those in the sides and the back. (Note that the apron tenons only have a shoulder on the *bottom.*) When finished, the tenons on the bottom of the sides and back should fit snugly in the mortises in the aprons, and the tenons of the mated pieces should line up.

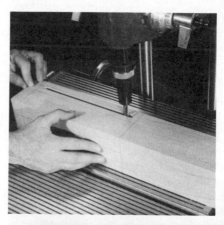

Figure 3. Rout the mortises in the legs *before* you cut the shapes.

Figure 4. Cut one leg pattern, tape the waste back on the stock, and cut the second.

Figure 1. Mark the leg patterns with a cardboard or hardboard template. Be sure that the knees meet at the corner.

Figure 2. Mark the stiles and the mortises on the corners *opposite* the leg patterns.

Figure 5. Use a pneumatic (or airfilled) drum sander to sand the cabriole legs.

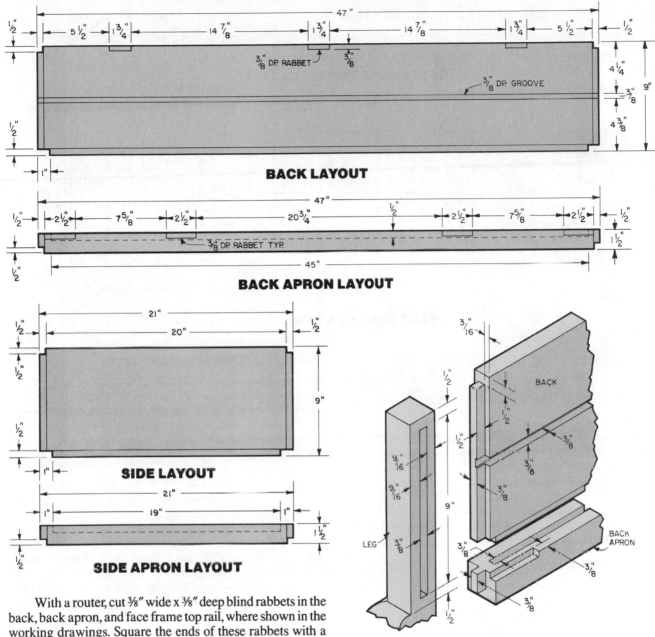

BACK LAYOUT

BACK APRON LAYOUT

SIDE LAYOUT

SIDE APRON LAYOUT

LEG AND BACK JOINERY

With a router, cut ⅜″ wide x ⅜″ deep blind rabbets in the back, back apron, and face frame top rail, where shown in the working drawings. Square the ends of these rabbets with a chisel. Then rout a ⅜″ wide, ⅜″ deep groove in the back. The rabbets and groove will hold the kickers and the drawer supports.

With a ³/₁₆″ drill and a small rasp, make three ³/₁₆″ wide, ½″ long slots in the kickers — two near the ends and one in the middle. The long dimension of the slots should be parallel to the long dimension of the kickers. With a ⅜″ straight bit in your router, 'counterbore' the slots ¼″ deep on the undersides of the kickers. Later on, you'll use these slots to attach the top to the case with wood screws. The counterbores will keep the heads of the screws from interfering with the action of the drawers.

Finally, cut a ⅜″ wide x ⅜″ deep rabbet in the *back* ends of the drawer supports, and *both* ends of the kickers. These will form tenons that fit in the blind rabbets and grooves in other parts of the project. Notice that the upper single drawer supports are notched to fit around the leg stiles. Cut these notches with a bandsaw or backsaw.

Piecing Together the Face Frame

The face frame consists of several small parts that are dowelled together. Lay out the frame pieces, except for the ears (which you will add later). Check your measurements, and be sure that all pieces fit together. Each joint is joined with two ⅜″ x 2″ dowels. Mark the position of these dowels and drill stopped holes where needed. You may find it handy to use a doweling jig to properly position these holes.

It's always good practice to clamp up your projects 'dry' before gluing them up. This way you can be sure your pieces fit, the joints line up properly, and you have enough clamps of the proper size. When you're satisfied that everything is as it should be, glue up the face frame.

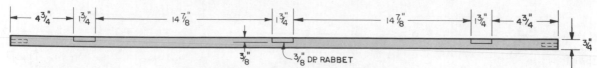

FACE FRAME TOP RAIL LAYOUT

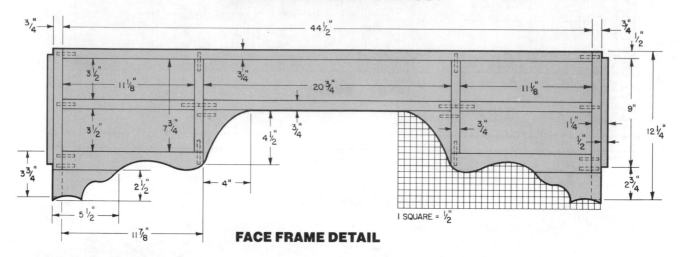

FACE FRAME DETAIL

> **Tip ◆** When you glue up the frame, clamp it to a large piece of ¾″ plywood. This will ensure that the frame is absolutely flat as the glue dries.

After the glue dries, mark the pattern for the front apron on the face frame. Cut the curves with a saber saw or bandsaw, then sand away the saw marks.

While the drawer supports rest in a groove or in rabbets at the back of the project, they are dowelled to the face frame at the front. Carefully measure the position of the drawer supports on the inside of the face frame. Then drill holes in the frame and drawer supports where needed. Dowel centers will help you to position these holes.

Assembling the Case

Finish sand all the parts. Then dry assemble the legs, sides, back, aprons, face frame, kickers, and drawer supports. When you're satisfied that everything fits together properly, disassemble the case and glue and get ready to glue the case together. This is a complex procedure and requires speed and organization. You must glue and clamp the case within 15-20 minutes, or the glue won't set properly. So I suggest you get a helper, and go through a dry run first.

When you're certain you can put the case together with the necessary speed, glue up all the parts. As you put the clamps on the case, be very careful that the case remains square and the legs plumb. Wipe off any glue squeeze-out with a wet rag. This will raise the grain slightly, but doing a little touch-up sanding is easier than scraping off a lot of glue.

After the glue dries and you remove the clamps, some parts will need additional reinforcement. Attach the corner braces to the aprons with glue and screws. Also, screw the kickers to the back and top rail.

To complete the case, cut and shape the ears; then glue them in place. After the glue dries, rasp and sand the ears so that their shape is continuous with the curves of the legs. The front ears must also conform to the curve of the apron.

Making and Installing the Drawers

There are two ways to join the drawer parts — by hand and by machine. Machine-made drawers are easier to make, and wear just as well as hand-made, if done properly. The working drawings show machine-made drawers, since most readers will probably opt for these. However, I've also included instructions for making hand-made drawers, should you want to try it.

To make the machine-made drawers, join the drawer fronts to the sides with half-blind dovetails. (These can only be seen from the sides, not the front.) Make these dovetails with a router and a dovetail template. Join the drawer back to the sides with a simple dado, set slightly in front of the back edge of the drawer sides, as shown in the working drawings. Cut a groove near the bottom edge of the front, back, and sides to hold the drawer bottom. Also cut a notch in the bottom edge of the large middle drawer, to fit over the drawer guide.

When you assemble each drawer, glue the front, back, and sides together, but leave the bottom free to 'float' in its grooves. This will allow it to expand and contract with changes in temperature and humidity. Finish the drawers by cutting ⅜″ thick drawer faces and molding the edges with an ogee bit. Then glue the drawer faces to the fronts. The edges of these faces must overlap the fronts by ⅜″, all the way around.

Making hand-made drawers is similar, though more of a challenge to make. There is no need for a drawer face; instead the front is rabbeted all the way around and the sides are joined to the front with hand-cut half-blind dovetails. (See Figure 6.) The back is joined to the sides with full dovetails. (See Figure 7.) And, like the machine-made version, the bottom floats in a groove in the front, back, and sides.

The precision of your hand-cut dovetails depends not only on skill, but your saw. In my opinion, a Japanese 'Dozuki' saw is the best tool for this task. It cuts easily, and with a very narrow kerf, so that you can actually split a pencil line.

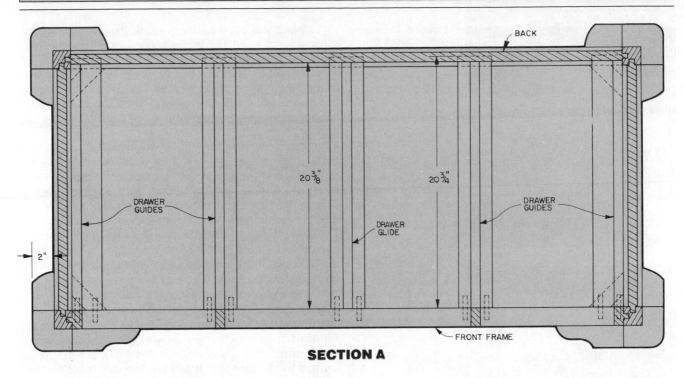

SECTION A

Labels within Section A: BACK, DRAWER GUIDES, DRAWER GUIDES, DRAWER GLIDE, 20 3/8", 20 3/4", 2", FRONT FRAME

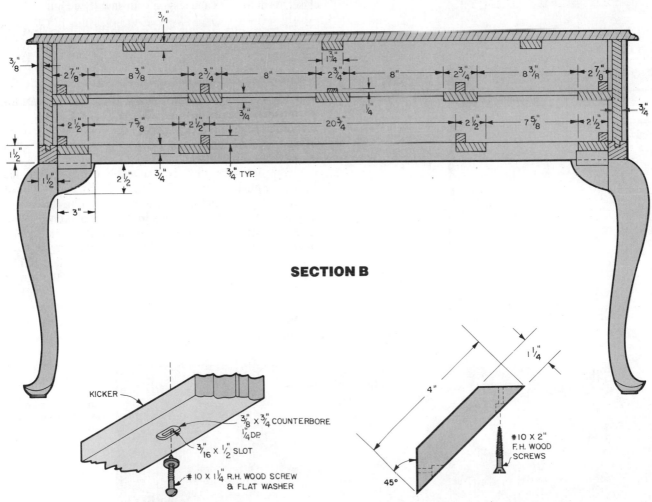

SECTION B

Labels within Section B: 3/4", 3/8", 2 7/8", 8 3/8", 2 3/4", 8", 1 1/4", 2 3/4", 8", 2 3/4", 8 3/8", 2 7/8", 3/4", 3/4", 1/4", 2 1/2", 7 5/8", 2 1/2", 20 3/4", 2 1/2", 7 5/8", 2 1/2", 1 1/2", 1 1/2", 2 1/2", 3/4", 3/4" TYP., 3"

DESK TOP JOINERY

KICKER
3/8" X 3/4" COUNTERBORE 1 1/4" DP.
3/16" X 1/2" SLOT
#10 X 1 1/4" R.H. WOOD SCREW & FLAT WASHER

CORNER BRACE DETAIL

1 1/4"
4"
45°
#10 X 2" F.H. WOOD SCREWS

Figure 6. The fronts of the drawers are attached to the sides with half-blind dovetails — you can't see the joint from the front.

Figure 7. The back is attached to the sides with full dovetails.

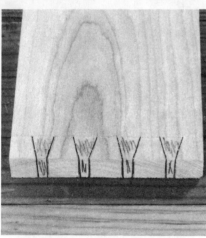

Figure 8. Mark the dovetail 'tails' first in the sides, using a sliding T-bevel.

Figure 9. Carefully cut along the marks with a saw. A Japanese 'Dozuki' saw works best.

Before you cut the joinery, plane the thickness of the sides and back to ½". Use ¾" thick wood for the front, and ¼" for the bottom. The hardwood for the front should match the type of wood you used to make the legs, sides, back, and face frame. However, you can use a less expensive hardwood for the drawer sides and drawer back. The contrasting woods will accent the dovetails, rather than detract from the appearance of the project.

Start by making the back dovetails. (That way, if you make a few mistakes at first, they won't be visible. By the time you get to the front dovetails, you'll be an expert — and less likely to make mistakes.) Using a protractor, set a sliding T-bevel to 80°. Use the bevel to mark the 'tails' of the dovetails on the sides. (See Figure 8.) Saw the lines with the Dozuki saw, then remove the waste between the tails with a hand chisel. (See Figure 9.) Use the tails as a template to mark the mating 'pins' on the back. Once again, saw the lines and chisel out the waste.

The half-blind dovetails on the front are little trickier. Mark the tails as before, only make these tails just ⅜" long. Cut the tails in the sides, and remove the waste. Then use the finished tails to mark the pins on the edge of the rabbet, where you want the sides to join the drawer front. Because of the lip formed by the rabbet, you will have to rely more on your chisel to cut the pins and less on your saw. (See Figure 10.)

> **Tip ◆** After you mark the pins on the front, remove as much waste as you can with a flat-bottom Forstner drill bit. This will greatly simplify the hand work with the chisel.

After you've cut the dovetail joinery, rout grooves for the drawer bottom in the front, sides, and back. Cut a notch in the bottom edge of the large middle drawer. Shape the overlapping 'lips' of the drawer front with an ogee bit. Then assemble the drawers with glue.

To install the completed drawers in the case, first glue the drawer guides in place. Carefully measure the position of the drawer guides and glide, and mark them on the drawer supports. Then put the drawers in the case and check your measurements. The drawers should clear the marks by ¹⁄₁₆" on both sides — all except for the middlemost drawer *glide*. The large middle drawer rides on *top* of this glide. When you're satisfied that you have properly positioned the drawer guides, glue and screw them to the drawer supports. Note that all the side guides are ¾" thick. The one middle guide is just ¼" thick. *Do not* screw this middle guide in place; just glue it to its drawer support.

Figure 10. The pins of the half-blind dovetails should only be cut halfway through the drawer fronts.

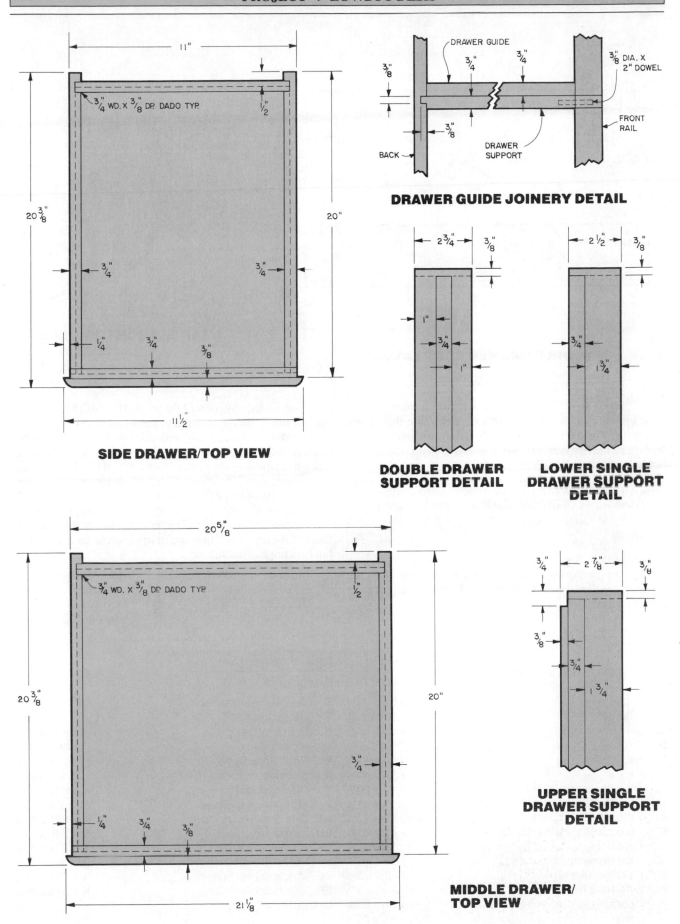

SIDE DRAWER/TOP VIEW

DRAWER GUIDE JOINERY DETAIL

DOUBLE DRAWER SUPPORT DETAIL

LOWER SINGLE DRAWER SUPPORT DETAIL

MIDDLE DRAWER/ TOP VIEW

UPPER SINGLE DRAWER SUPPORT DETAIL

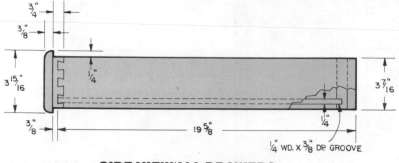

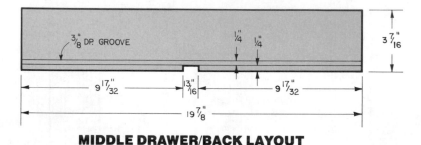

SIDE VIEW/ALL DRAWERS

MIDDLE DRAWER/BACK LAYOUT

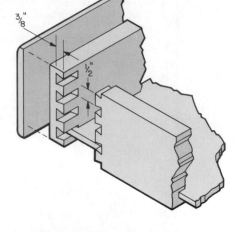

DRAWER FRONT JOINERY

Finishing Up

Glue up wide stock for the desk top. Make sure that all the end grain curves in the same direction, *towards* the top surface. That way, if the wood wants to cup, the screws holding it to the case will prevent it.

> **Tip ◆** To make sure the wood doesn't cup, use quarter-sawn or rift-sawn lumber. Because of the way the wood is cut from the tree, it has little tendency to cup.

Attach the top to the case with roundhead screws, driven up through the slots in the kickers. These slots will allow the desk top to expand and contract with changes in temperature and humidity.

Finish sand any parts of the project that still need it, then apply a finish. Be very careful to put as many coats of finish on the inside of the case and underside of the desk as you do to the outside of the desk. By evenly finishing the desk, inside and out, all the wooden parts will absorb and release moisture at the same rate. The case will have less tendency to warp, and the joints will stay solid longer.

After you've rubbed down the finish and applied a good coat of paste wax, install Chippendale drawer pulls on the faces of the drawers. There are many sources for these pulls, but here are two addresses:

Remodeler's and Renovators
1920 N. Liberty
Boise, ID 83704

Horton Brasses
Nooks Hill Road
P.O. Box 120
Cromwell, CT 06416

BILL OF MATERIALS — Lowboy Desk

Finished Dimensions in Inches

A.	Legs	3½ x 3½ x 29¼	**S.**	Double drawer supports (3)	¾ x 2¾ x 20¾
B.	Sides (2)	¾ x 9 x 21	**T.**	Drawer guides (8)	¾ x ¾ x 20⅜
C.	Side aprons (2)	1½ x 1½ x 21	**U.**	Drawer glide	¼ x ¾ x 20⅜
D.	Back	¾ x 9 x 47	**V.**	Kickers (3)	¾ x 1¾ x 21⅛
E.	Back apron	1½ x 1½ x 47	**W.**	Corner braces (4)	1¼ x 1¼ x 4
F.	Face frame top rail	¾ x 1½ x 44½	**X.**	Side drawer fronts (4)	¾ x 3⁷⁄₁₆ x 11
G.	Face frame middle rail	¾ x 1½ x 20¾	**Y.**	Drawer sides (10)	¾ x 3⁷⁄₁₆ x 19⅝
H.	Face frame side rails (2)	¾ x 1½ x 11⅛	**Z.**	Side drawer backs (4)	¾ x 3⁷⁄₁₆ x 10¼
J.	Face frame end stiles (2)	1¼ x 1½ x 12¼	**AA.**	Side drawer bottoms (4)	¼ x 10¼ x 18¾
K.	Face frame middle stiles (2)	¾ x 1½ x 7¾	**BB.**	Side drawer faces (4)	⅜ x 3¹⁵⁄₁₆ x 11½
L.	Face frame aprons (2)	1½ x 3¾ x 11⅞	**CC.**	Middle drawer front	¾ x 3⁷⁄₁₆ x 20⅝
M.	Face frame apron curves (2)	1½ x 4 x 4½	**DD.**	Middle drawer back	¾ x 3⁷⁄₁₆ x 19⅞
N.	Front leg ears (2)	2 x 2½ x 5½	**EE.**	Middle drawer bottom	¼ x 18¾ x 19⅞
P.	Side/back leg ears (6)	2 x 2½ x 3	**FF.**	Middle drawer face	⅜ x 3¹⁵⁄₁₆ x 21⅛
Q.	Upper single drawer supports (2)	¾ x 2⅞ x 20¾	**GG.**	Desk top	¾ x 25 x 51
R.	Lower single drawer supports (4)	¾ x 2½ x 20¾			

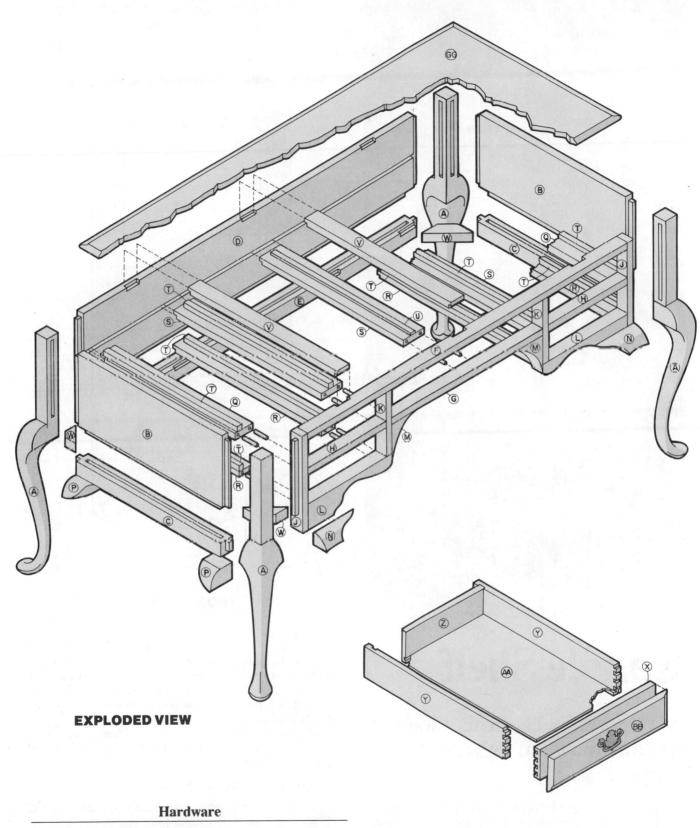

EXPLODED VIEW

Hardware

#10 x 1¼″ Roundhead wood screws (9)
#10 x 2″ Flathead wood screws (8)
#8 x 1¼″ Flathead wood screws (12)
Chippendale drawer pulls (6)

Designed and built by Harry Cooper

FRONT VIEW

Candle Shelf

A mirrored-back display shelf will throw a lot of light on the subject.

Back in the days when candles were the primary source of light at night, folks soon learned that if they put a mirror or a piece of polished metal behind the candle, it would throw more light on whatever they were trying to illuminate. By colonial times, the mirrored-back 'candle shelf' had become a common household accessory.

Today, this antique form is still interesting and useful. In its traditional role as a candleholder, it makes a pleasant wall decoration that will complement a roomful of country, colonial, or classic furniture. In a non-traditional role, it also makes a wonderful display shelf for small items that are better displayed from all sides — dolls, figurines, and so forth. The mirror lets you see both the front *and* the back of the object at the same time.

Making the Candle Shelf

Using a bandsaw or a jigsaw, cut out the shapes of the back, shelf, and brackets. Sand away any saw marks.

Carefully measure the back and mark the opening for the mirror. Cut the opening, making a piercing cut with a jigsaw or saber saw. (See Figure 1.) Mount a rabbeting bit in your router, and cut a shallow rabbet in the back side of the

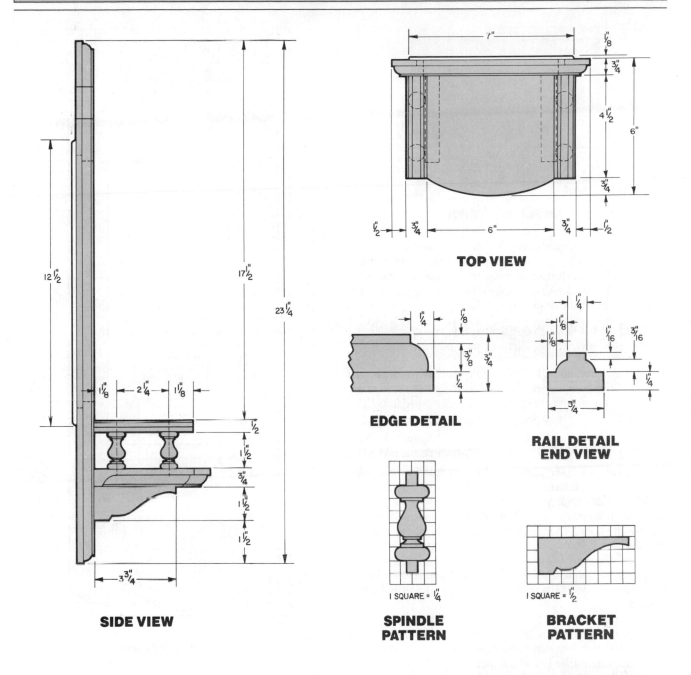

SIDE VIEW

TOP VIEW

EDGE DETAIL

**RAIL DETAIL
END VIEW**

I SQUARE = 1/4"

**SPINDLE
PATTERN**

I SQUARE = 1/2"

**BRACKET
PATTERN**

back, all the way around the opening, for the mirror to rest in. You'll have to square the corners of this rabbet with a hand chisel. (See Figure 2.)

Figure 1. Cut the mirror opening by making a 'piercing cut' with a jigsaw or saber saw.

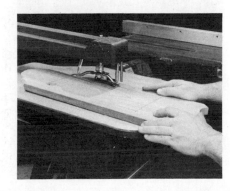

Figure 2. Use a hand chisel to square off the corners of the rabbet in the back.

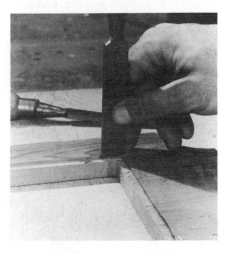

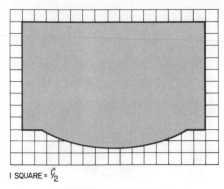

SHELF PATTERN

I SQUARE = ½"

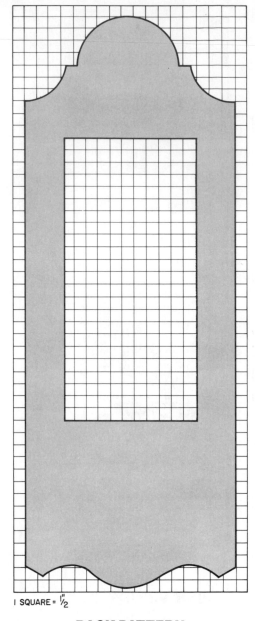

I SQUARE = ½"

BACK PATTERN

Mount an edge-shaping bit in your router, such as a quarter-round or an ogee, and shape the front side of the back — the inside of the mirror opening and all around the outside edge. (See Figure 3.) Also, shape the bottom edge of the shelf, where shown on the drawings.

> **Tip ◆** It's easier to do all the routing on this project with your router mounted to a router table.

Make the railings for the candle shelf. If you wish, you can purchase both the spindles and the rails from mail order woodworking supply companies. Here are two addresses:

The Woodworker's Store 21801 Industrial Blvd. Rogers, MN 55374

Woodworker's Supply 5604 Alameda Pl., NE Albuquerque, NM 87113

Or, you can make your own. Turn the spindles on a lathe, using miniature lathe tools to form the beads and the coves. Make the rails with your router. Cut the shapes in a wide board with a quarter-round bit, then rip the rails from the edge of the board. (See Figure 4.) Never attempt to shape or rout thin stock; it may come apart in your hands.

Drill the shelf and the rail for the spindles. Finish sand all the parts; then assemble them with glue and screws. When the glue dries, do any necessary touch-up sanding and apply a finish.

Install a mirror in the back, and hold it in place with a small piece of ⅛" thick hardboard. Tack the hardboard in place with brads, but *don't* glue it, in case you someday need to replace the mirror. Install a hanger on the back, above the mirror, to hang the completed candle shelf.

Figure 3. Shape the inside edges of the mirror opening to match the outside edges of the back and the bottom edges of the shelf. It's easiest to use a router table to do all this shaping.

Figure 4. To make the rails, first cut the shape in a wide board, then rip the thin rail free of the board.

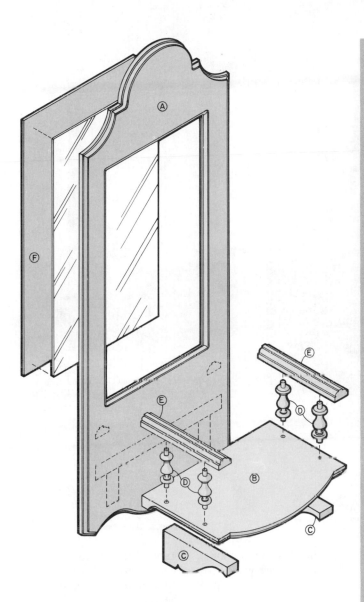

EXPLODED VIEW

BILL OF MATERIALS — Candle Shelf

Finished Dimensions in Inches

A.	Back	¾ x 8½ x 23¼
B.	Shelf	¾ x 5¼ x 7½
C.	Brackets (2)	¾ x 1½ x 3¾
D.	Spindles (4)	¾ dia. x 2
E.	Rails (2)	½ x ¾ x 4½
F.	Mirror back	⅛ x 7 x 12½

Hardware

⅛" Thick mirror, 6" x 12"
#8 x 1¼" Flathead wood screws (2-4)
⅝" Brads (6-8)
Picture hanger

CANDLE SHELF

Miniature Lathe Turning

Making your own miniature turnings — such as gallery spindles — requires a different technique than ordinary lathe turning. Miniature turnings are normally done on a drill press or horizontal boring machine, using smaller-than-usual lathe tools.

◆　Make a jig, as shown in Figure A, to help support the miniature turning. The hole in the jig should be ¹⁄₃₂"-¹⁄₁₆" larger than the round hardwood stock you're turning. A simple block of wood supports the lathe chisels. Clamp the jig to the worktable.

◆　Mount the round stock in the drill chuck, and adjust the quill feed so that several inches of the stock protrude through the jig. Adjust the drill or boring machine so that it turns at its *slowest* speed. You may want to wax the inside of the hole in the jig to prevent the stock from burning.

Figure A. You can make miniature turnings on a drill press or horizontal boring machine with this simple jig.

Gun Case designed and built by James Hasson
Ship Case designed and built by Phil Stock

Display Cases

One fine piece of craftsmanship deserves another.

Many of us first learned what a pleasure it is to work with our hands by building models when we were kids. I was probably typical. I started out with simple airplanes, then gradually advanced to the bigger things — square-rigged sailing ships were my own private passion. The satisfaction of finishing an intricate model is something I never got out of my blood; to this day I still try my hand at an occasional model.

A woodworking friend of mine, Phil Stock, is another one of the breed. But he's gone a step farther. After watching the dust collect in the rigging of his best handiwork, he decided it was time to design and build a display case. The results, as you can see, were well worth the effort. It's hard to decide which is the finer piece of craftsmanship — the ship or the case?

Jim Hasson is another woodworker who appreciates fine craftsmanship and knows the importance of displaying it properly. However, his passions are firearms; handguns, in particular. The display case that he designed and built holds a rare Colt .45. Unlike Phil's glass case, Jim's is a solid hard-wood box, inlaid with contrasting hardwoods. Whether the box is opened or closed, Jim's reverence for its contents is evident from the care he took in making the display case.

Adjusting the Design

Both cases are, of course, specifically designed for the things that they hold. It's unlikely that the treasures you want to display will be exactly the same size — or the same style.

To adjust the dimensions on Phil's or Jim's working drawings, first decide how you want to mount the object that you want to display. It goes without saying that the position a model (or anything else) is held in determines just what size space it takes up. If the object is to be displayed in an unusual position, it would be best to mount it *before* you build the case, so that you can accurately measure the space required.

When calculating the space, remember to add at least 3″ to the length and depth of the case, and 1½″ to the height to give the object enough room for proper viewing. You don't want the case to fit too snugly around the object. If it does, the object will appear cramped. If the object is to be cradled — like the handgun in Jim's case — then leave room for the foam.

Depending on the type of object to be displayed, you may also wish to adjust the style of the display case. An old-time sailing ship or an antique firearm deserves a classic case. The intricate lines of Phil's and Jim's cases are reminiscent of some of the best Chippendale cabinetry. But a contemporary piece — say, a small modern sculpture — might look better in a contemporary setting. Change the lines of the case to suit the object.

You also want to be sure that the design of the display case does not overwhelm the object. After all, the purpose of the case is to show off the object — not to show off the case. You wouldn't want to put a huge, intricate case around a model of a rowboat or a derringer; the result would be ludicrous. The same rule applies to making display cases as applies to framing pictures: First and foremost, consider where the viewer should focus his or her attention.

A Few Tricks

If you elect to build a classic display case like those shown here, you'll find it's really an exercise in creative molding and shaping. Phil and Jim used several different knives and cutters to achieve the intricate lines you see here. Some profiles required several passes with several different cutters.

Before you get started, let me share a few woodworking secrets about shaping and molding:

◆ When you need to shape (or mold) a long, narrow piece, shape the edge of a wider board first, *then* rip the narrow piece from the wide stock. (See Figures 1 and 2.) Shaping or molding a narrow board can be dangerous. The board could easily break, and your fingers pass too close to the cutters.

◆ When molding the edge of a board, attach a wide extension fence to your rip fence. (See Figure 3.) This helps keep the board square to the knives.

◆ Both shaping and molding require that you keep the wood pressed tightly against the worktable and/or the fence as you feed it past the cutters. Featherboards or 'spring sticks' do this for you. (See Figure 4.) They clamp to the power tool and hold the wood so that you don't have to get your fingers near the cutters.

◆ When cutting a shape that requires two or more passes, always cut more stock than you actually need on all but the last pass. You can use the extra stock as scraps to test the setup for the next pass.

There's more to be said about shaping and molding, of course, but we'll cover any other tricks you need to know as we go along.

Making the Molding

In order to discuss how to make the molding, it's necessary first to define what molding we're talking about. After all, there are several types of molding in these cases. Let's start with Jim's case:

Jim's firearm display case uses two simple moldings. At the top of the box is a *cove molding,* and at the bottom is a *quarter-round* or *bead molding.* Both of these moldings were made with single passes on a molding knife or shaper cutter.

Figure 1. To make your own molding, first cut the shape in the edge of a wide board. *Guard removed for clarity.*

Figure 2. Then rip the molding from the board. *Never* try to shape a narrow board; it may break or kick back.

Figure 3. A wide extension fence, bolted to your rip fence, helps keep a board at the proper angle to the molding knives.

Figure 4. Featherboards become extra 'hands', holding the wood securely against the fence and the worktable while you feed it past the cutter.

It's not surprising that the names of these knives correspond to the names of the moldings: Jim used a *cove* cutter and a *bead* cutter.

Phil's glass-sided case is more complex. There are five different moldings in the project, and some of them require more than one pass with more than one cutter. At the very top of the case is the *top molding,* as you might expect. Just below that is something we're going to call the *soffet molding,* for want of a better term. It forms a tiny soffet around the top of the display case. At the bottom of the case, the glass is held in place by the *glass molding.* The *base molding* skirts the bottom of the case, and the feet are made from *foot molding.*

Let's talk about how to make these various moldings. For a quick reference as to which molding is which, refer to Figure 5. You already know how to make the cove, bead, and outside glass moldings: Pass the edge of the board across a single cutter, then cut the molding free of the board. But for the other moldings, you must combine cutters in the proper order.

Top molding — The top molding is a long ogee formed by three passes. On the first pass, cut a cove. Use a blank knife for the second pass to make a long chamfer. Finally, put a small bead on the end of the chamfer. (See Figure 6.)

Soffet molding — The soffet molding is formed in a single pass with a three-bead cutter, but only a portion of the cutter shape is used. (See Figure 7.)

Base molding — Make the molding for the bottom of the case in two passes. First, cut an ogee. Then, round off the outside edge of the ogee with a bead. (See Figure 8.)

Foot molding — The molding for the feet is cut in two passes. Round over the top edge with a quarter round or large bead cutter, then put a small bead in the bottom edge with a small bead cutter. (See Figure 9.)

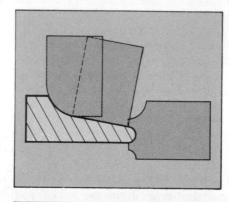

Figure 6. Make the top molding in three separate passes, using a cove cutter, blank or straight cutter, and bead cutter.

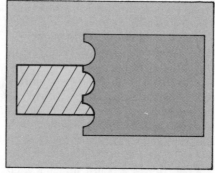

Figure 7. Make the soffet molding in a single pass using a three-bead cutter, using the shape of only one and a half beads.

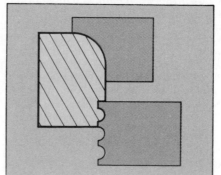

Figure 8. Make the base molding in two passes, using an ogee cutter and a bead cutter.

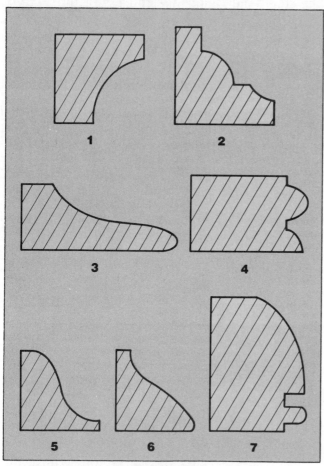

Figure 9. Make the foot molding with a quarter-round cutter and a bead cutter.

Figure 5. There are seven types of molding in the two projects shown here. For our purposes, we'll call them the **cove molding** (1), **bead molding** (2), **top molding** (3), **soffet molding** (4), **glass molding** (5), **base molding** (6), and **foot molding** (7).

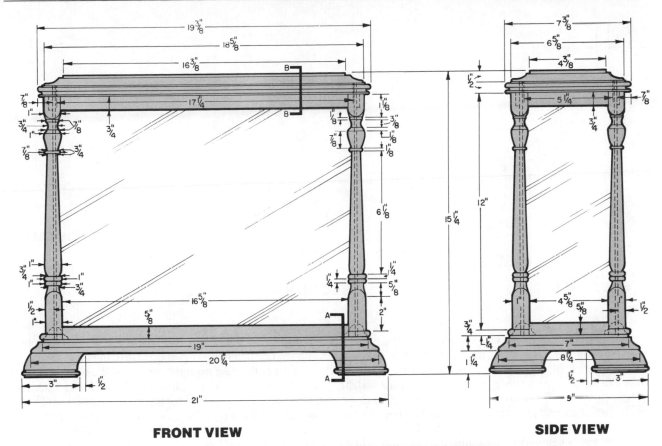

FRONT VIEW

SIDE VIEW

GLASS-SIDED DISPLAY CASE

Making the Glass-Sided Display Case

Aside from the moldings, the most striking thing about Phil's glass-sided case are the support posts. These special posts are turned three-quarters round to accommodate the glass. This looks pretty tricky, but it's not all that difficult to do.

Begin by cutting a ½" x ½" rabbet along one corner of the turning stock. Then cut a ½" x ½" strip to fill that rabbet while you're turning the post. But don't glue it in place. Instead cut the turning stock about 2"-3" longer than necessary, and anchor the strip in place with two wood screws — one near each end. (See Figure 10.)

Mount the stock on the lathe as if it were an ordinary spindle turning, and turn the shape desired. However, take extra care to feed the chisels *very* slowly and only remove a small amount of stock at one time. Otherwise a chisel may catch the strip and tear it out.

> **Tip ◆** Turn the middle of the post first, then put a piece of tape around the middle to help secure the strip in the post. (See Figure 11.)

When you've completed the post, remove the screws and the strip. You'll be left with a perfect three-quarters round spindle.

Phil's case is assembled in two parts — the base and the case. These come apart so that you can get the objects you wish to display in and out. Let's start with the case:

Miter the top molding, then glue the pieces to the top. While the glue is drying, glue the post blocks to the bottom of

Figure 10. After you've cut a rabbet in the turning stock, fill it temporarily with a strip of wood. Attach the wood to the stock with wood screws near either end.

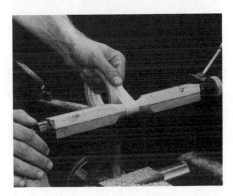

Figure 11. Turn the middle of the post first and wrap a piece of tape around it to help hold the strip in place.

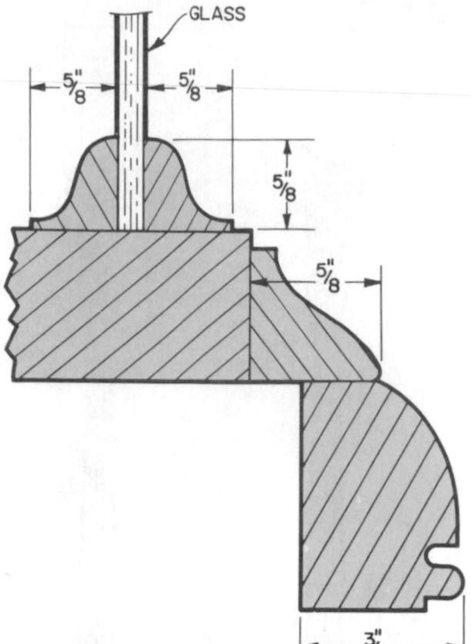

SECTION A

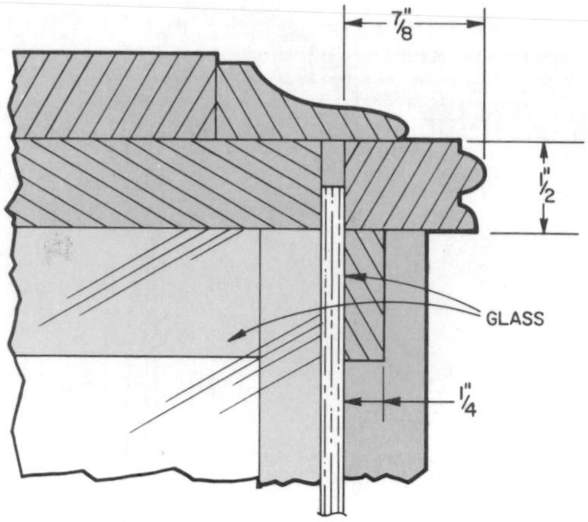

SECTION B

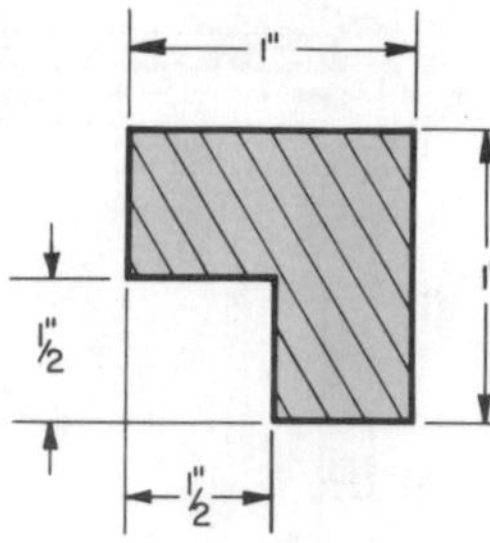

POST DETAIL

the posts. Glue the cap to the top, being careful to position it correctly. Then miter the soffet molding and glue it around the perimeter of the top assembly. You may wish to use 1/8″ spacers, to make sure that the gap between the soffet and the cap is wide enough to accommodate the glass. Dowel the posts to the soffet, and glue the top rails in place between the posts. Set this assembly aside while the glue dries.

Miter the base molding and glue it to the base, just as you attached the top molding to the top. While the glue is drying on the base, glue up an 8″ x 8″ frame out of the foot molding. With a bandsaw, cut the corners from this 'frame' to make the feet. (See Figure 12.) Remember to cut curves on the 'side' edges of these feet, then carve beads with rasps and files to continue the shape of the bead all around the visible edges of the feet. (You don't need to carve the beads on the inside or back edges of the feet, where you'll never see them.) Glue the finished feet to the underside of the base.

Center the case assembly on top of the base, and mark the position of the posts. Drill pilot holes for screws, then screw the case and base together, passing the screws up through the base into the posts. (See Figure 13.) With the posts secured in place, carefully glue the glass molding in place on the base. Once again, use 1/8″ spacers to keep the moldings properly spaced.

Disassemble the base and case assemblies, and do any necessary finish sanding. Apply a finish, then mount your model — or whatever you want to display — to the base. Reassemble the base and case with glass in place.

Tip ◆ You may also want to drill several small holes in the base. This helps equalize the humidity and the temperature inside the case with the outside air.

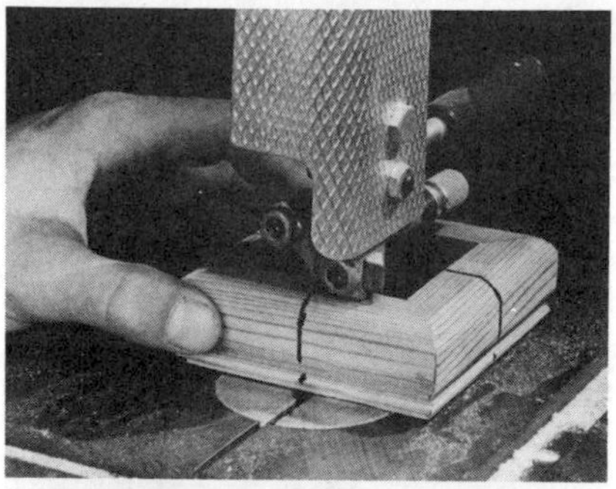

Figure 12. Using a bandsaw, cut the feet from a frame made with the foot molding.

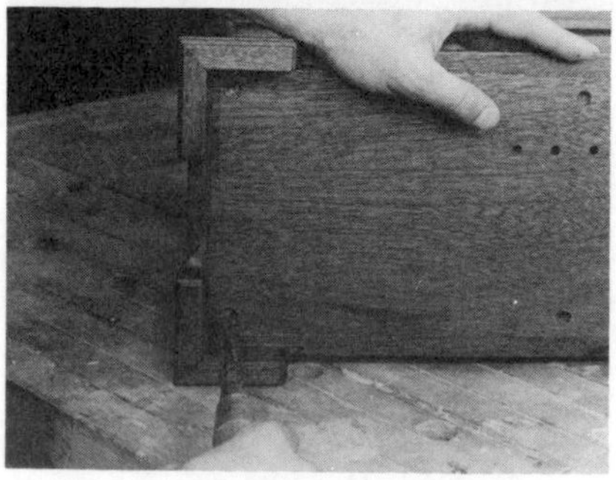

Figure 13. Screw the case to the base by passing screws up through the base into the posts.

BILL OF MATERIALS — Glass-Sided Display Case

Finished Dimensions in Inches

A.	Top	1/2 x 4 3/8 x 16 3/8
B.	Top molding (total)	7/16 x 1 1/8 x 50 1/2
C.	Cap	1/2 x 5 1/4 x 17 1/4
D.	Soffet molding (total)	1/2 x 7/8 x 53 1/2
E.	Top rails (total)	1/4 x 3/4 x 42 1/2
F.	Posts (4)	1 x 1 x 12
G.	Post blocks (4)	1/4 x 1 3/16 x 1 3/16
H.	Glass molding (total)	5/8 x 5/8 x 87 1/2
J.	Base	3/4 x 7 x 19
K.	Base molding (total)	5/8 x 3/4 x 57
L.	Foot molding (total)	3/4 x 1 1/4 x 28
M.	Dowels	1/4 dia. x 3/4

Hardware

1/8″ x 12 3/4″ x 17 3/8″ Glass (2 pieces)
1/8″ x 5 3/8″ x 12 3/4″ Glass (2 pieces)
#8 x 1 3/4″ Flathead wood screws (4)

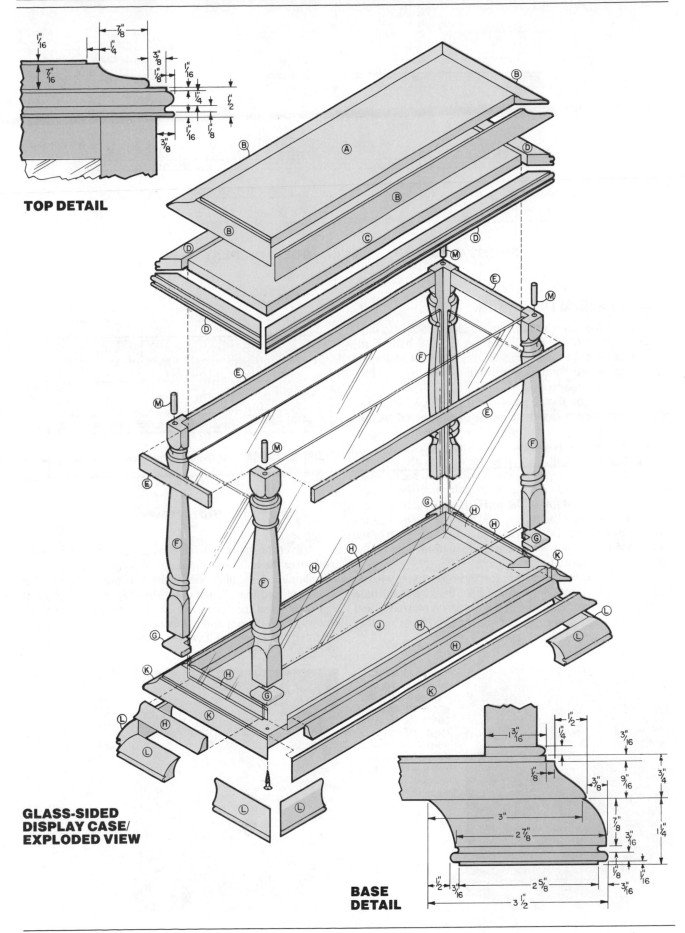

TOP DETAIL

GLASS-SIDED DISPLAY CASE/ EXPLODED VIEW

BASE DETAIL

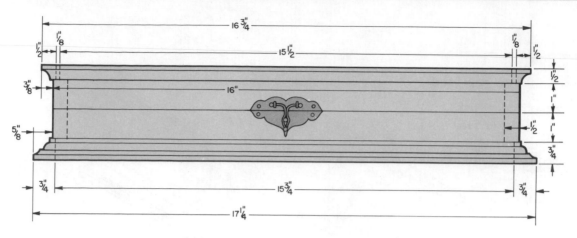

FRONT VIEW

SOLID DISPLAY CASE

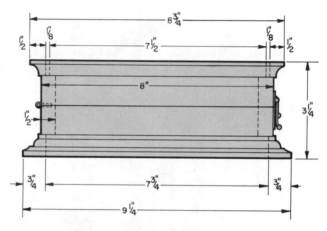

SIDE VIEW

Making the Solid Display Case

Jim's case is simpler to make than the glass-sided case, but it requires just as much care. Like the top and base of the glass-sided case, the top and base of this solid case are framed with moldings. Apply the cove molding to the top, and the bead molding to the base.

However, the top is framed with a ⅛″ wide strip of contrasting wood *before* the cove molding is glued on. (See Figure 14.) This gives the impression of an inlaid strip of wood all around the perimeter of the top.

To make the front, back, and sides of the case, miter the parts and glue them together. If you wish, reinforce the miter joints with splines. On a table saw, rip the assembly in half. Glue the completed top to the top half, and the base to the bottom half. Finish sand the top and the base, then hinge the two halves together. Be careful to match up the grain of the wood so that it's continuous from top to bottom. Remove the hardware and apply a finish.

To make a foam 'cradle' for the object you wish to display, cut two pieces of foam, each ½″ thick, to fit the base of the case. Trace the outline of the object on one piece; and cut it out, discarding the inside. Glue the two pieces together with contact cement. (See Figure 15.)

Cover the foam with felt, velvet, or satin, wrapping the cloth over the hollowed-out piece of foam, down the sides, and gluing it to the underside of the solid piece. Then set the cloth-wrapped foam in the case. You may glue it in place, if you wish. After the object has set in the case for a time, the cloth will stretch out and conform to the contours, making the foam cradle look as if you had molded it to the object.

Figure 14. Glue a ⅛″ wide strip of *contrasting* wood to the edges of the top *before* you apply the molding. This will make the top look as if it has been inlaid with a second piece of wood.

Figure 15. To make a foam cradle, trace the outline of the object you wish to display on a piece of foam. Cut out the outline, discarding the inside. Then glue the foam to a second, solid piece of foam.

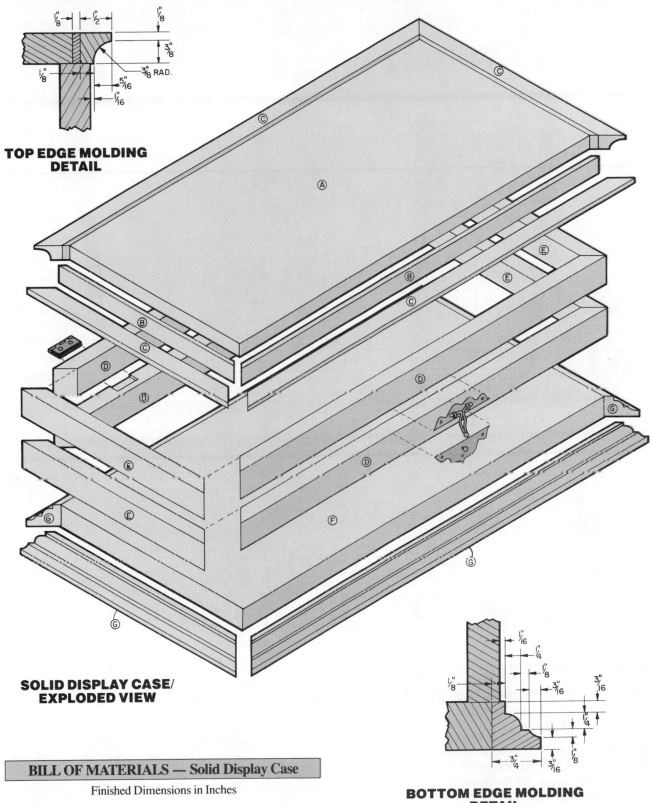

TOP EDGE MOLDING DETAIL

SOLID DISPLAY CASE/ EXPLODED VIEW

BOTTOM EDGE MOLDING DETAIL

BILL OF MATERIALS — Solid Display Case

Finished Dimensions in Inches

A.	Top	½ x 7½ x 15½
B.	Inlay (total)	⅛ x ½ x 47
C.	Cove molding (total)	½ x ½ x 51
D.	Front/back (2)	½ x 2 x 16
E.	Sides (2)	½ x 2 x 8
F.	Base	¾ x 7¾ x 15¾
G.	Base molding (total)	¾ x ¾ x 53

Hardware

1″ x 1½″ Hinges and mounting screws (1 pair)

Clasp

Designed by Nick Engler, built by Adam Blake

Space Age Doodle Maker

It takes the serious doodler where no doodler has ever gone before.

Every now and then you run across a toy that appeals to both children and adults. This is one of those toys: A doodle maker. An *automatic* doodle maker, to boot. Just set the drawing surface in motion with a little push, and presto! It starts to doodle.

The gizmo works on the simple principle of pendular motion — the same principle that keeps a grandfather clock running. The pendulum, in this case, is the drawing board. It swings back and forth under a pen. However, because of the way the drawing board is suspended, the board also swings around, describing a circular or oval motion. It also twists

clockwise and counterclockwise. The result of all these various motions is that you can get the machine to draw some pretty amazing doodles — and no two doodles will ever be the same. (See Figure 1.)

The doodle maker takes up a good deal of space —more than most doodlers have room for. So we designed this machine to come apart and fold up inside its base. (See Figure 2.) The base makes a handy storage and carrying case, so you can take your doodler wherever you need to doodle — school lectures, business meetings, IRS audits, etc.

Making the Base

Start by making the base. Cut the parts to size, mitering the ends of the front, back, and sides. Glue these parts together, along with the mounting blocks. You can also glue the bottom in place — this will help to hold the assembly square

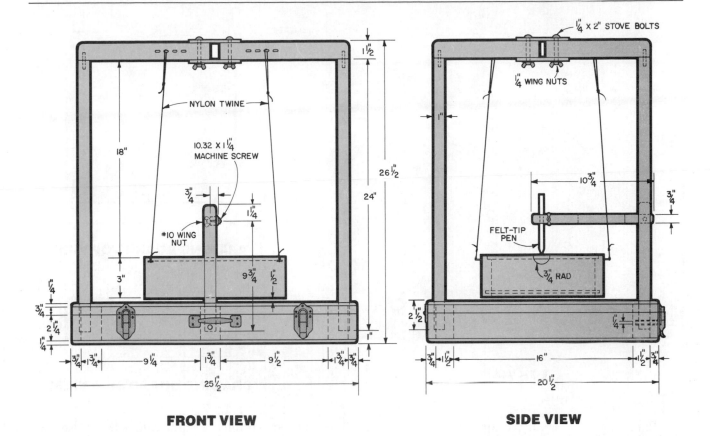

FRONT VIEW   **SIDE VIEW**

— but set the top aside until later. You'll find it impossible to clamp the mounting blocks in place with *both* the top and the bottom attached.

Note that the working drawings show an alternate position for the drawing arm. The drawing arm works well in both positions, though one position restricts the movement of the drawing board to and fro, while the other restricts it back and forth. You may want to attach the drawing arm mounting block in the alternate position, or in both positions, so you can see which position you like best.

After the glue sets up, remove the clamps and mark where the drawing arm mounting block(s) are on the *outside* of the base assembly. Then attach the top. Reinforce the miter joints with finishing nails, if you wish. (See Figure 3.)

Carefully measure and mark the holes for the drawing arm and the support dowels. Drill these holes on a drill press; don't attempt them by hand unless you've a very steady grip. They *must* be straight up and down.

Figure 2. The doodle maker comes apart and fits in its base, for carrying and storage.

Figure 3. Reinforce the miter joints with finishing nails. Drive these nails from two directions, perpendicular to each other.

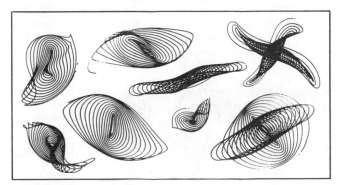

Figure 1. The doodle maker will draw any number of doodles, and no two will be alike.

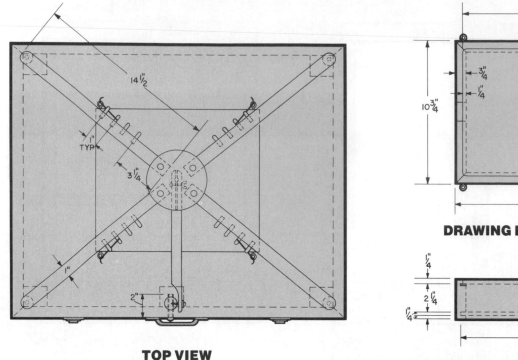

TOP VIEW

DRAWING BOARD/TOP VIEW

DRAWING BOARD/SIDE VIEW

Rip the top from the completed base assembly, using a table saw. (See Figure 4.) Cut both sides and the back. Then put ⅛″ spacers in the kerfs and clamp them in place while you cut the back. This will prevent the top and bottom part of the case from squeezing together as you finish the rip cut, pinching the blade and putting a 'step' in the top or bottom cut.

> **Tip ◆** Note that the bill of materials specifies that the back, front and sides of the base should be 3⅛″ wide, while the working drawings show it as 3″ wide. You'll lose that ⅛″ when you rip the base in two.

Reattach the top and the bottom portions of the base assembly with hinges and clasps. To make sure that the holes line up exactly, put 1″ dowels in all the holes until you finish attaching the hardware. If you wish, you can also add a handle at this time.

Making the Drawing Board

Cut all the parts to size and, once again, miter the ends of the front, back, and sides. With a dado cutter or a router, cut a ¼″ wide, ¼″ deep groove near the bottom edges of the back,

front, and sides. This groove will hold the bottom. Also, cut a ¼″ wide, ¼″ deep rabbet in the top edge of these parts. This rabbet will hold the top.

In one of the sides, cut a small, semi-circular notch in the top edge. This notch will enable you to easily remove the top, when you need to. (See Figure 5.)

Glue the front, back, and sides together with the bottom in place. However, don't glue the bottom in the grooves — just let it 'float'. After the glue sets up, reinforce the miter joints with finishing nails. Attach eye screws to the sides, near the top edge, as shown in the working drawings. Finally, lay the top in place. *Don't* glue the top in the rabbet; as mentioned before, you'll need to remove the top from time to time.

Making the Supporting Frame

Cut the supporting dowels to length and drill holes in the top ends. Cut the supporting arm to length, and drill matching holes in the bottom edge, near the 'outside' end. Glue ¼″ dowels in the holes in the supporting arms. After the glue dries, insert these dowels in the holes in the ends of the supporting dowels. However, *don't* glue the supporting

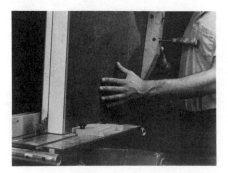

Figure 4. Rip the top from the base on a table saw. On the last cut, insert ⅛″ spacers in the kerfs and clamp them in place. This will keep the top from pinching the blade on the last cut.

Figure 5. Notch one end of the drawing board so that you can easily remove the top.

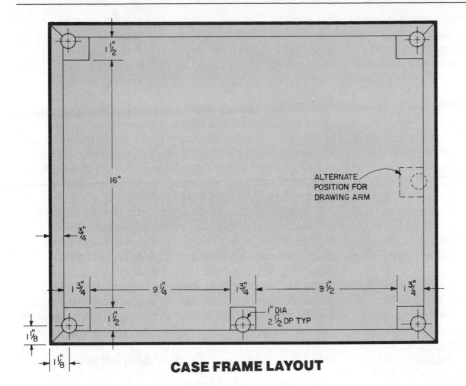

CASE FRAME LAYOUT

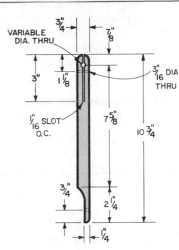

DRAWING ARM LAYOUT

dowels and the supporting arms together — you want to be able to take them apart to store the finished Doodle Maker.

Cut the round gussets out on a bandsaw, and 'pad' drill ¼" holes in them. (See Figure 6.) Then put together the base, supporting dowels, and supporting arms. Lightly clamp the gussets in place, and carefully line up the arms diagonally. When you're satisfied that the arms are aligned, mark the 'inside' ends of the arms where you want to drill them. Carefully mark which arm goes in what position, then remove the gussets and the arms. Drill the inside ends of the arms all the way through.

> **Tip ◆** Positioning the gussets and lining up the arms is a task that will try the patience of a saint. We strongly suggest you have a helper for this operation, to share your misery.

While you're at it, also drill the faces of the arms for pegs, as shown in the working drawings. The pegs should angle upwards at 10°. Glue the pegs in place. Later on, you'll use these pegs to hang the drawing board.

Figure 6. Pad drill the gusset, so that the holes are exactly the same on both.

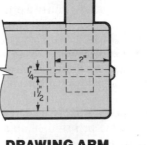

DRAWING ARM PEG DETAIL

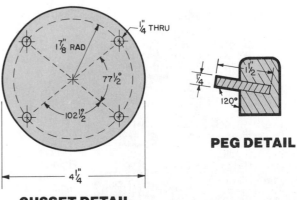

DRAWING ARM MOUNTING DETAIL

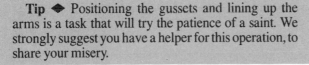

GUSSET DETAIL

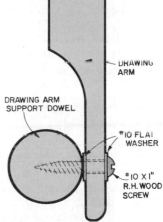

PEG DETAIL

Reassemble the supporting arms and gussets, using ¼" stove bolts, washers, and wing nuts. The supporting arms should spread out from the gussets in a rigid 'X', with their outside ends doweled to the supporting dowels. The pegs must all face either the back or the front of the assembly.

Hang the drawing board from the pegs with nylon twine, as shown in the working drawings. It's important to use nylon, or some other non-stretchable material, to suspend the board. All four lengths of twine must be exactly the same length, and the drawing board should hang ¼"-½" above the base.

Making the Drawing Arm

Cut the drawing arm support dowel to size and put it in place in the mounting block. It's very important that this dowel does not turn in the mounting block, so it should be pegged in place. With a hand drill, drill a ¼" hole through the outside of the base, through the bottom portion of the drawing arm support dowel, and into the mounting block. Insert an 'axle peg' in the hole to hold the dowel in place. (See Figure 7.) These pegs can be purchased from most woodworking supply houses, or you can turn your own with miniature lathe tools.

Cut the drawing arm from 1 x 1 stock, 'thinning out' the outside end on a bandsaw. Drill a hole in the inside end to hold felt-tipped pens. The size of this hole will depend on the make of the felt tipped pens you decide to use — the hole should be ¹⁄₆₄"-¹⁄₃₂" smaller than the diameter of the pen. On the bandsaw, cut a ¹⁄₁₆" kerf in the inside end, through the pen hole and down the middle of the drawing arm for about 3". Near the pen hole, drill another hole, ³⁄₁₆" in diameter, through the drawing arm and perpendicular to the pen hole. Drill another ³⁄₁₆" hole, through the thinned out portion of the arm.

Mount the pen in the drawing arm by sliding it into the pen hole. To secure the pen, put a 10-32 machine screw through the ³⁄₁₆" hole, and fasten it in place with a wing nut. Adjust the pen so that when you attach the drawing arm to its support, the pen will be straight up and down with the point resting on the drawing board.

Hold the drawing arm-and-pen assembly against the drawing-arm support dowel, with the pen straight up and down and the pen point resting on the exact middle of the drawing board. Carefully mark where to drill the pilot hole to mount the drawing arm on the dowel, then drill it. Fasten the drawing arm in place with a #10 roundhead wood screw and

Figure 7. Use a toy 'axle peg' to pin the drawing arm support dowel in place.

Figure 8. To enhance the pendulum action of the drawing board, place weights on the inside.

flat washers. Note the positions of the flat washers on the working drawings — put them on either side of the drawing arm. Tighten down the screw so the arm does not wobble back and forth, but not so tight that it won't pivot up and down.

Finishing Up

Disassemble the Doodle Maker and remove all the hardware — hinges, clasps, handle, screws, nuts, and bolts. Finish sand all parts, rounding any sharp corners and edges. Be careful not to sand the ends of the support dowels that fit in the mounting holes. If you do, there may be too much slop when you put the project back together.

You'll probably want to paint your Doodle Maker with bright, cheerful colors. We suggest you also use these colors to 'code' the different parts that go together. For example, you always want to attach a certain support arm to a certain support dowel, and place that particular support dowel in a particular mounting hole. Paint the support arm and support dowel the same color, and put the same colored ring around the mounting hole. You'll need four different colors to do this coding.

Do *not* paint the end of the dowels that fit into the holes, or the drawing arm peg. These should be left unfinished.

Using the Doodle Maker

Now that you've built it, how do you use it? Simple. First reassemble the finished project, and hang the drawing board from the pegs. Take off the top of the drawing board and fill the box with something heavy. *This is very important!* If the drawing board doesn't have enough weight, it won't swing for very long.

Gravel and sand work well, but you may not want these in the house. Nuts and bolts also work well, but you may not want a kid to have these. The two best alternatives we found were to use two or three 2½ pound weights from a barbell set, or a whole bunch of marbles. (See Figure 8.) If you use marbles, make sure that they cover the bottom of the box to a depth of 1" or more. If there are too few marbles and they slosh around inside the box, the doodler won't work properly. Replace the top of the drawing board.

Insert a felt-tip pen (you choose the color) in the drawing arm, and adjust the position of the pen so that it's straight up and down when the tip is resting on the board. Then raise the pen up and tape a clean sheet of paper to the drawing board. Give the drawing board a little push in any direction, let it swing for a few seconds to make sure it's not going to bump into any of the support dowels, then lower the pen onto the paper. As the drawing board continues to swing, the pen will draw an incredible doodle.

Let the drawing board come to a rest, raise the pen off the paper, and give the box a push in some other direction. You might even give it a twist *and* a push. Lower the pen, and the doodler will begin to embellish the first doodle with another one.

There are other things you can try: Move the twine that suspends the drawing board to different pegs. Switch pen colors. Change the position of the paper. Knock the drawing board in the middle of a swing to change directions. All of these things will alter the design and help you in your quest for the perfect doodle.

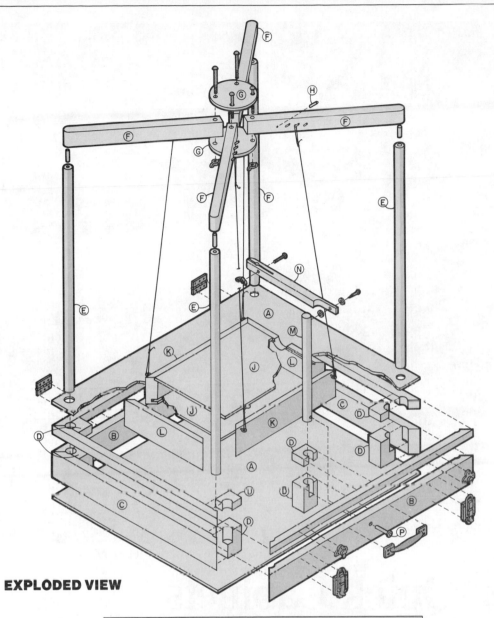

EXPLODED VIEW

BILL OF MATERIALS — Space Age Doodle Maker

Finished Dimensions in Inches

Hardware

A.	Base top/bottom (2)	¼ x 20½ x 25½
B.	Base front/back (2)	¾ x 3⅛ x 25½
C.	Base sides (2)	¾ x 3⅛ x 20½
D.	Mounting blocks (5-6)	1½ x 1¾ x 3⅛
E.	Support dowels (4)	1 dia. x 24
F.	Support arms (4)	1 x 1½ x 14½
G.	Gussets (2)	4¼ dia. x ¼
H.	Pegs (20)	¼ dia. x 1½
J.	Drawing board top/bottom (2)	¼ x 9¾ x 11¾
K.	Drawing board front/back (2)	¾ x 3 x 12¾
L.	Drawing board sides (2)	¾ x 3 x 10¾
M.	Drawing arm support dowel	1 dia. x 11
N.	Drawing arm	¾ x ¾ x 10¾
P.	Drawing arm peg	¼ dia. x 2

1½" x 3" Butt hinges and mounting screws (1 pair)
Catches and mounting screws (1 pair)
Handle and mounting screws
4d Finishing nails (24-36)
¼" x 2" Stove bolts (4)
¼" Flat washers (8)
¼" Wing nuts (4)
10-32 x 1¼" Machine screw
10-32 Wing nut
#10 x 1" Roundhead wood screw
#10 Flat washers (4)
#10 Eye screws (4)
Nylon twine (Approx. 4')
Felt-tipped pens (several colors)
Weights or marbles (5-7 pounds)

Designed by Nick Engler, built by Adam Blake and Nick Engler

Super-Quick Cabinets

Build a lot of cabinet space in a hurry — no muss, no fuss, no fancy joinery.

When you need work space *and* storage space in the same place, there's nothing that beats a built-in cabinet. This simple structure provides a counter to work on, and drawer and shelves to store things in, all in the same floor space. Because there's nothing better, you hardly ever see a kitchen without kitchen cabinets.

Built-in cabinets would work just as well in a variety of other applications — laundry room, workshop, garage — anywhere you keep a lot of stuff to do a lot of work. However, cabinets are rarer in these places because they are expensive and time-consuming to build. Who wants to put all that time and money into a project that's going to sit in the garage and collect oil stains and old lawnmower parts?

Well, here's a design for built-in cabinets that could change all that. It may not look as nice as kitchen cabinets — it dispenses with niceties such as doors and laminated countertops. But it serves the same purpose. Best yet, it's cheap and super-quick to build. You can make the entire project out of plywood or chipboard, and nail or screw it together. There's not a single junction more complex than a butt joint in the entire structure. With a single exception, all the parts are simple rectangles, so you can cut them out in no time.

Making the Cabinet Frame

Before you start on this project, determine how long you want to make this cabinet. As you can see from the photographs, the cabinet is made up of two similar modules — an 'end unit' and a 'middle unit'. (The only practical difference between the two units is that the end unit has a solid side.) Measure the space you have available, then plan to fill it with up to two end units and as many middle units as you can

122

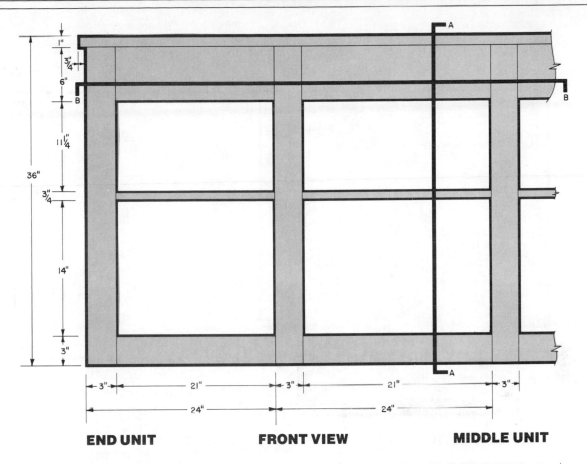

END UNIT   **FRONT VIEW**   **MIDDLE UNIT**

squeeze in. As shown, each unit is 24″long. However, you can adjust this, if you need to. Simply make the opening between the front stiles narrower or wider, as desired.

Once you've planned out your cabinet, figure out how many of what parts you'll need. Then rip them to width and cut them to length. You can use a table saw, radial arm saw, or contractor's saw for all the ripping and cutting. The only piece that needs to be 'shaped' at all is the top brace. Make the notch in the brace with a saber saw or hand saw. (See Figure 1.)

Figure 1. The only part in this project that isn't a simple rectangle is the top brace. Cut a notch in one end of the braces to fit around the top back rail.

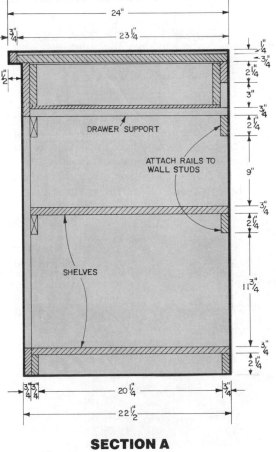

DRAWER SUPPORT

ATTACH RAILS TO WALL STUDS

SHELVES

SECTION A

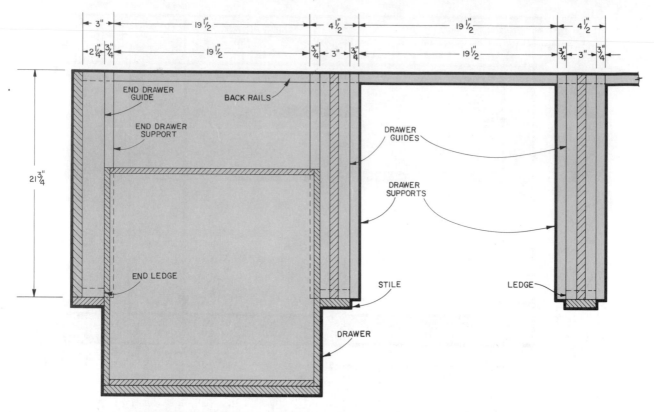

SECTION B (One drawer part way open, the other removed)

Labels in figure: 3"; 19 1/2"; 4 1/2"; 19 1/2"; 4 1/2"; 2 1/4"; 3/4"; 19 1/2"; 3/4" 3" 3/4"; 19 1/2"; 3/4" 3" 3/4"; 21 3/4"

END DRAWER GUIDE; BACK RAILS; END DRAWER SUPPORT; DRAWER GUIDES; DRAWER SUPPORTS; END LEDGE; STILE; LEDGE; DRAWER

Tip ◆ If you can, rip the front rail so that it runs the entire length of the cabinet. If you have to make this piece in two or more sections, plan the break so that it happens behind a toeboard, *not* behind a stile. (See Figure 2.)

Part of the reason that this project is so quick and inexpensive to build is that it uses the wall to support the cabinet. There is no back to the cabinet; instead, attach the back rails to the wall at the intervals shown in the working drawings. Use 1/4" lag screws, and make sure that the screws bite into the frame studs. If you're working with a masonry wall, install expansive lead anchors where you want to attach the rails. (See Figure 3.)

Glue and nail the cleats to the front stiles. Then nail and glue the stiles and toeboards to the front rail. Work with a framing square, being very careful to get the stiles perpendicular to the rails and toeboards. You may want to lay out these parts on a large, flat surface — such as your driveway — and clamp them up before nailing them together.

Nail or screw the cabinet sides to the ends of the back rails, as shown in the drawings. Then nail and glue the front rail-and-stile assembly to the front edge of the cabinet sides.

Figure 2. If you have to make the front rail in two or more sections, plan the break between the sections so that it happens behind a toeboard, *not* behind a stile.

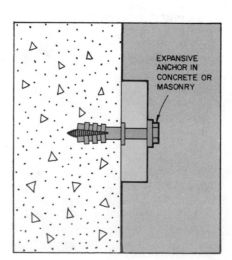

Figure 3. To attach the back rails to a masonry wall, drill the masonry with a cement drill and insert expansive lead anchors.

EXPANSIVE ANCHOR IN CONCRETE OR MASONRY

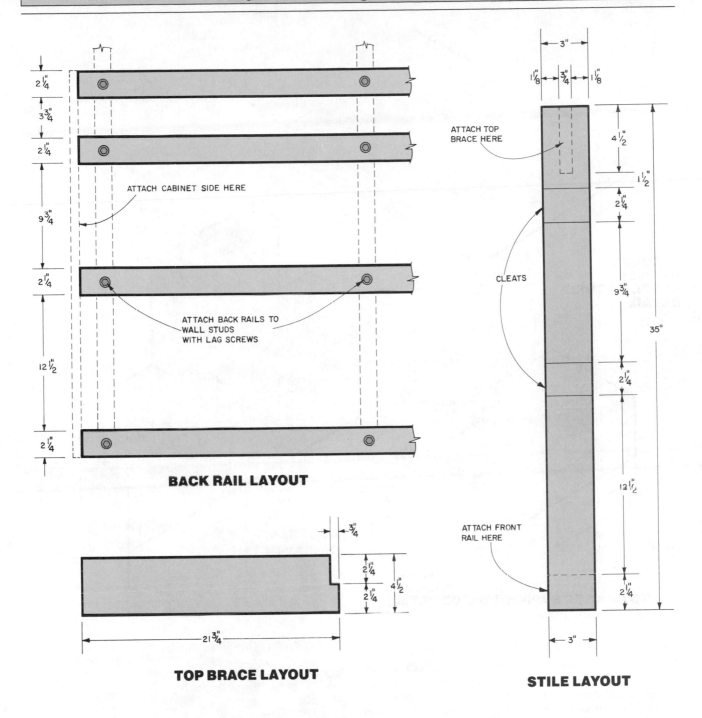

BACK RAIL LAYOUT

TOP BRACE LAYOUT

STILE LAYOUT

Installing the Shelves

With a helper, drop the bottom shelf in place so that it rests on the front rail and bottom back rail. You may have to shift the cabinet sides and front rail slightly to get it to drop in place, if these parts aren't perfectly square to each other. Once you have the part positioned properly, nail it to the rails.

Repeat this procedure for the top shelf, resting this part on the second back rail and the bottom cleat. Check the spacing between the stiles, and make sure the stiles are square to the toeboards before nailing the top shelf in place.

Nail and glue the drawer guides to the drawer supports. Mark the drawer guides for the middle units so you know where to attach the top braces, when the time comes. Place the drawer support assemblies so that they rest on the third back rail and the top cleat. Check the spacing between the supports, and be sure that the middle drawer supports stick out ¾" on either side of the stiles. When you're satisfied that these parts are properly positioned, nail them in place.

Next, nail and glue the top braces in place. The notched end of each brace fits around the top back rail, while the other end rests against the inside face of the stiles. The top edge of the braces must be flush with the top end of the stiles and the top edge of the top rail.

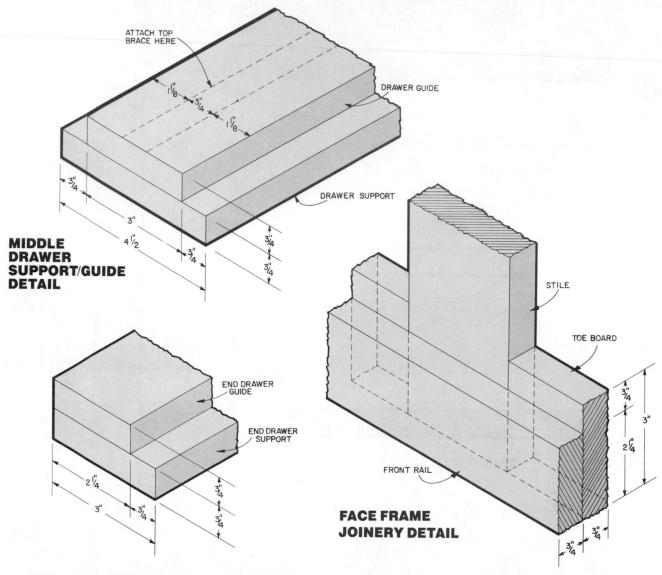

ATTACH TOP BRACE HERE

DRAWER GUIDE

$1\frac{1}{8}''$

$3\frac{1}{4}''$

$1\frac{1}{8}''$

DRAWER SUPPORT

$3\frac{1}{4}''$

$3''$

$4\frac{1}{2}''$

$3\frac{1}{4}''$

$3\frac{1}{4}''$

$3\frac{1}{4}''$

MIDDLE DRAWER SUPPORT/GUIDE DETAIL

END DRAWER GUIDE

END DRAWER SUPPORT

$2\frac{1}{4}''$

$3''$

$3\frac{1}{4}''$

$3\frac{1}{4}''$

$3\frac{1}{4}''$

END DRAWER SUPPORT/GUIDE DETAIL

STILE

TOE BOARD

$3\frac{1}{4}''$

$3''$

$2\frac{1}{4}''$

FRONT RAIL

$3\frac{1}{4}''$

$3\frac{1}{4}''$

FACE FRAME JOINERY DETAIL

Finishing Up: Countertop and Drawers

Put the countertop in place, resting it on the top back rail, the top braces, the sides, and the stiles. Check that all parts are square to each other, then nail the countertop in place. Cover it with a sheet of ¼″ hardboard. Don't glue the hardboard in place; just tack it down with brads. This will create a 'disposable' counter surface that you can replace from time to time, as the hardboard becomes discolored, stained, or beat-up.

If you wish, trim the edges of the covered countertop with ¾″ thick, 1″ wide stock. (See Figure 4.) This isn't necessary, but it hides the edges over the countertop and makes the project look more 'finished'.

Nail and glue together the drawer fronts, backs, and sides. Slide these assemblies in place on the drawer supports and check that they do not rub against the guides. If they do, you will have to shave down the sides somewhat. When you're satisfied that the drawers slide in and out properly, attach the drawer bottoms and the drawer faces with nails and glue.

Figure 4. Trim the edges of the covered countertop with ¾″ thick, 1″ wide stock. This will hide the edges of the countertop and hardboard surface, giving the project a more 'finished' look.

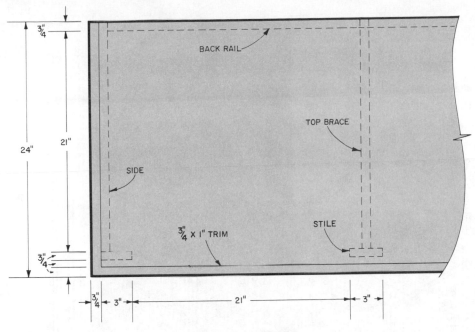

TOP LAYOUT

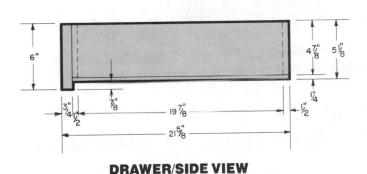

DRAWER/SIDE VIEW

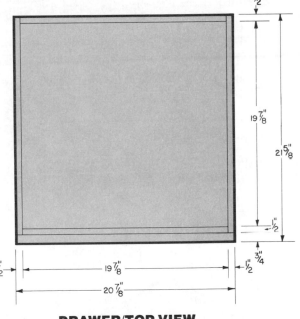

DRAWER/TOP VIEW

Tip ◆ Rub some paraffin wax on the drawer supports and drawer guides to help the drawers slide a little easier.

Install the completed drawer in the cabinet and check the sliding action. It isn't necessary to install pulls; the 'lip', where the drawer face overlaps the drawer front, makes a good pull.

To complete the cabinet, paint or stain the exterior. *Don't* paint the hardboard counter surface; instead, rub in several applications of furniture wax. This will help protect the surface from spills. If you're going to use the cabinet in your workshop, it will also keep glue from sticking to the surface. Just let the glue dry, and peel it up.

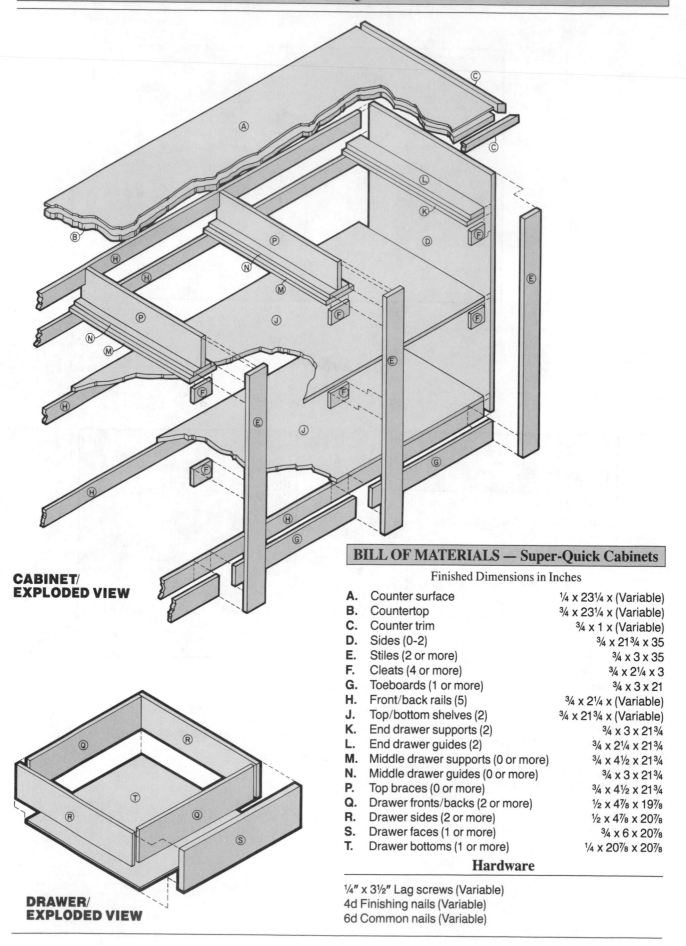

**CABINET/
EXPLODED VIEW**

**DRAWER/
EXPLODED VIEW**

BILL OF MATERIALS — Super-Quick Cabinets

Finished Dimensions in Inches

A.	Counter surface	¼ x 23¼ x (Variable)
B.	Countertop	¾ x 23¼ x (Variable)
C.	Counter trim	¾ x 1 x (Variable)
D.	Sides (0-2)	¾ x 21¾ x 35
E.	Stiles (2 or more)	¾ x 3 x 35
F.	Cleats (4 or more)	¾ x 2¼ x 3
G.	Toeboards (1 or more)	¾ x 3 x 21
H.	Front/back rails (5)	¾ x 2¼ x (Variable)
J.	Top/bottom shelves (2)	¾ x 21¾ x (Variable)
K.	End drawer supports (2)	¾ x 3 x 21¾
L.	End drawer guides (2)	¾ x 2¼ x 21¾
M.	Middle drawer supports (0 or more)	¾ x 4½ x 21¾
N.	Middle drawer guides (0 or more)	¾ x 3 x 21¾
P.	Top braces (0 or more)	¾ x 4½ x 21¾
Q.	Drawer fronts/backs (2 or more)	½ x 4⅞ x 19⅞
R.	Drawer sides (2 or more)	½ x 4⅞ x 20⅞
S.	Drawer faces (1 or more)	¾ x 6 x 20⅞
T.	Drawer bottoms (1 or more)	¼ x 20⅞ x 20⅞

Hardware

¼" x 3½" Lag screws (Variable)
4d Finishing nails (Variable)
6d Common nails (Variable)

Designed by Nick Engler, built by Adam Blake

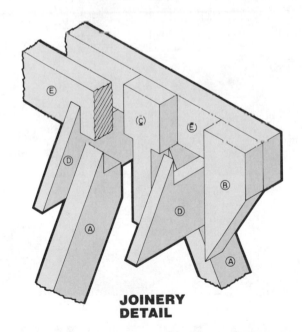

TOP VIEW

END VIEW   SIDE VIEW

JOINERY DETAIL

New Improved Sawhorse

It holds both ends of a board up — even after you cut the wood.

There's always a way to build a better mousetrap — or in this case, a better sawhorse. And if you've ever had to run and get a helper just to hold the end of a board while you cut it off, you'll understand what makes this a better sawhorse. The slot down the middle enables you to crosscut or rip boards of all sizes *alone*, with no need to bother anyone.

This sawhorse is made from 2 x 4's and scraps of plywood. The legs are braced in all directions by the gussets and the end braces. These legs support not one, but two 2 x 4's, held apart by end braces and spacers.

To use the sawhorses, simply align your cutting mark with the space between the 2 x 4's, and cut down the center. Instead of the short end of the board dropping to the ground, it will remain where it is. We suggest you make three of these sawhorses, to properly support your work.

Caution: *Do not* stand on these sawhorses, or use them to support scaffolding.

BILL OF MATERIALS — New Improved Sawhorse

Finished Dimensions in Inches

A.	Legs (4)	1½ x 3½ x 25¾
B.	End braces (2)	1½ x 3½ x 9¾
C.	End spacers (2)	1½ x 3 x 9¾
D.	Gussets (2)	¾ x 8 x 10
E.	Horizontal members (2)	1½ x 3½ x 48

Designed by Nick Engler, built by Adam Blake and Nick Engler

Modular Wall System

Use these oversize 'blocks' to build any type of storage system you need.

The concept behind children's building blocks is as ingenious as it is simple: Given enough wooden cubes, of the proper size and shape, you can build almost *anything*. The possibilities are only limited by your childhood imagination.

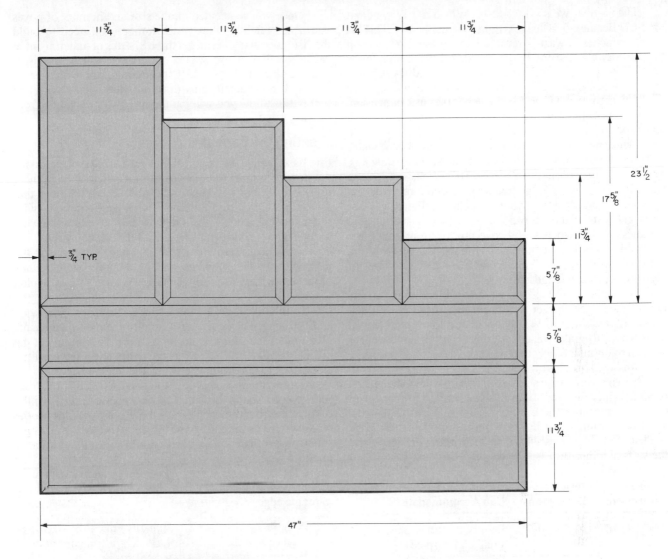

POSSIBLE BOX SIZES

That same concept can be applied to furniture — in particular, wall systems. In this case, the 'blocks' become open ended boxes. Some of the boxes are left empty; others house drawers, shelves, and doors. The dimensions of these boxes are carefully calculated so that they can be stacked together in an infinite number of combinations. From one simple set of these 'modules', you can build a desk, display shelves, a bookcase, an audio/video center, a pantry, and so on. The possibilities are only limited by your adult imagination — and the amount of lumber you can afford.

Planning the Boxes You Need

The boxes are made from plywood. The top, bottom and sides are cut from ¾″ plywood, mitered at the edges, and joined with splines. The back is made from ¼″ plywood, and it sits in a rabbet in back edge of the box assembly. The front edge of the box is faced with ¼″ thick strips of solid wood, to hide the plies.

The dimensions of these boxes are of utmost importance. First of all, you must be able to stack them together in a variety of configurations. To do this, the outside dimensions

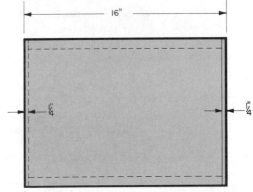

BASIC BOX/SIDE VIEW

must all be divisible by the same number. (If the boxes were random sizes, it would be difficult to stack them in any sort of sensible order.) Second of all, that number must be large enough that even the smallest box will be useful. And, finally, the number must divide into the dimensions of a sheet of plywood (48″ x 96″) so that there is a minimum of waste.

The number we used was 5⅞″. Why 5⅞″? Why not an even 6″? Because 5⅞″ leaves room for the *saw kerf*. There is only two inches of waste over a full 96″. A box 5⅞″ wide on the outside, made from ¾″ plywood, will have an interior dimension of 4⅜″. That's wide enough for a drawer, a few books, about two dozen records, and a lot of other things you might want to store. Using 5⅞″ inches as the basic dimension, the other possible dimensions are 11¾″, 17⅝″, 23½″, 47″, and so on.

Please note that these dimensions are just for the width and length of the boxes, as shown on the working drawings. The depth is a constant 16″. Why 16″? Well, 16″ is deep enough to store some large items like a stereo receiver or a tape deck. And it's small enough that books and magazines don't get lost on the shelves. And when you subtract the thickness of the wood strips covering the front edges, the plywood is only 15¾″ deep. Even with the saw kerf, you can get three strips of 15¾″ material out of a 4′ x 8′ sheet of plywood, cutting it lengthwise.

Using these dimensions, we were able to make all fifteen of the boxes you see here from four sheets of ¾″ thick plywood, one sheet of ¼″ plywood, and four board feet of solid wood (to make the edge strips). Furthermore, we had enough material left over that we could have made one more medium-sized box, had we needed it.

When you plan the sizes of boxes you want to build, first of all consider the types of things you want to store in them. Carefully measure these objects, and make sure that the *inside* dimensions of the boxes will accommodate them. Here is a list of the box sizes shown in the working drawings, and the sorts of things they will hold:

Outside Dimensions	Inside Dimensions	Can Accommodate:
5⅞″ x 11¾″	4⅜″ x 10¼″	Letters, cassettes, papers, small plates, spices
11¾″ x 11¾″	10¼″ x 10¼″	Small books, file folders, plates, glasses
11¾″ x 17⅝″	10¼″ x 16⅛″	Records, large books, magazines, small stereo components, pots and pans
11¾″ x 23½″	10¼″ x 22″	Large stereo components, adjustable display shelves
5⅞″ x 47″	4⅜″ x 45½″	Drawers for tape cassettes, papers, or silverware
11¾″ x 47″	10¼″ x 47″	Stereo components, display shelves, file drawers

By no means are these the only things these boxes can hold. Nor are they the only size boxes you can build. You can also make boxes 5⅞″ x 17⅝″, 23½″ x 35¼″, or whatever you need. We suggest you don't make anything larger than 23½″ x 47″ (approximately 2′ x 4′). Beyond this size, the boxes become too heavy to be easily rearranged, and they lose some of their sturdiness.

Once you've decided on the size and number of boxes you need, calculate how much lumber you need to build them. Figure that you can get three 8′ strips of material out of each sheet of plywood. A 11¾″ x 11¾″ box will use precisely half of a strip. An 11¾″ x 23½″ box requires three quarters of a strip. And so on. If it helps, draw the sheets of plywood and plot out just how you will cut the pieces for each box from them.

Building the Basic Box

Purchase ¾″ and ¼″ thick cabinet grade (A-B) plywood for the boxes. (We built our boxes from standard birch-veneer plywood.) When you cut up the plywood, remember that there is an 'A' side, and a 'B' side. The 'A' side is covered with heartwood veneer — the grain is prettier and somewhat darker. The 'B' side may be covered with sapwood, or a combination of heartwood and sapwood. Always saw the plywood with the 'A' side up, and use this side for the *outside* of the boxes, as well as any doors and drawer faces you plan to make.

Carefully cut the ¾″ thick sheets into strips 15¾″ wide and 96″ long. Then cut each strip into the pieces you need. Don't miter the edges at this time. You may want to cut the pieces slightly (¹⁄₁₆″-⅛″) oversize, so that you have a little extra stock to play with when you do miter the edges.

Tilt your table saw at 45°, and make a practice box from scrap wood. Clamp this box together and make sure that the corners are mitered properly. If there are any gaps on the *insides* of any corners, then the table saw is tilted at an angle slightly *more* than 45°, and you should adjust it to a smaller angle. If there are gaps on the *outsides* of the corners, then the saw is set to an angle *less* than 45°, and you need to increase the angle. Only after you get the saw set perfectly, should you miter the edges. (See Figure 1.)

> **Tip ◆** As you work, continually check the size of the piece and the angle of the miter, just in case your table saw creeps out of adjustment.

Without changing the angle of the table saw, reposition the rip fence close to the blade. Using the rip fence as a guide, cut ⅛″ wide, ⅜″ deep grooves in all the mitered edges. (See Figure 2.) When the mitered edges are fitted together, the spline grooves should line up precisely. (See Figure 3.)

Return the table saw back to the usual (90°) angle, but leave the dado cutter attached. Cut ⅝″ wide, ¼″ deep rabbets in the back edges of all the pieces. (See Figure 4.)

Cut ⅛″ thick, ¾″ wide splines from the ⅛″ hardboard. Also, cut all the back pieces you need. Then 'dry assemble' all the boxes and check the fit of the joints. If you're satisfied, finish sand all parts (except the splines), and reassemble the box tops, bottoms, and sides with glue. Insert the back to keep the boxes square while the glue dries, but *do not* glue the back in place at this time.

You'll need both band clamps and bar clamps to assemble the boxes. You'll probably only be able to glue up one or two boxes at a time, unless you want to invest a small fortune in clamps. As you glue up the boxes, carefully wipe away any glue squeeze-out with a wet rag. The water will raise the grain slightly, but it won't harm the wood. You'll find it's a lot easier and a lot safer to remove the glue from the thin veneer now, rather than wait until it's dry. When you have glued up

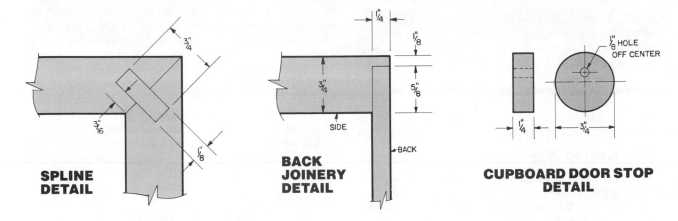

SPLINE DETAIL

BACK JOINERY DETAIL

CUPBOARD DOOR STOP DETAIL

all of the boxes, do any necessary touchup sanding — especially those areas that you wiped with the rag.

Cut ¼″ thick edge strips from solid wood. Carefully miter and attach these to the front edges of the boxes with glue. Hold them in place with strips of masking tape until the glue dries. You may wish to use brads to tack them in place, but this really isn't necessary, and it does detract slightly from the appearance of the finished boxes. If you spread the glue evenly and hold the strips firmly in place with the tape while the glue is drying, then you should get a good, solid glue bond. (See Figure 5.)

We finished our boxes by installing 'campaign' hardware — brass L-brackets and T-brackets — at the corners. These are optional, but they add visual interest to the boxes. To install them, you must first rout out a ¹⁄₁₆″ recess for them, then attach them with brass brads.

Figure 1. Miter the edges of the box tops, sides, and bottoms. Keep the good side of the plywood up when you cut.

Figure 2. Before you change the angle of the table saw, make the spline grooves.

Figure 3. The spline grooves should line up precisely when you put the miter joint together. The splines strengthen the joint and keep it properly aligned while the glue is drying.

Figure 4. With the dado cutter, make a rabbet in the back edges of the tops, sides, and bottoms. These rabbets will hold the backs in place.

Figure 5. To hide the plies on the front edges of the box, glue solid wood strips to the plywood. Hold the strips in place with masking tape while the glue dries.

Tip ◆ Make two small U-shaped jigs of scrap wood, and clamp these to the boxes while you rout the recesses for the brackets. These will serves as guides and 'stops' for the router. (See Figure 6.)

At this point, the boxes are completed. If you want, you can attach the backs with glue and brads, and apply a finish. However, if you wish to install drawers, doors, or shelves, leave the backs unattached and don't finish the boxes just yet.

Making and Installing Drawers

There are two types of drawers you can install in these boxes: plain old drawer-type drawers and full-extension drawers. (See Figures 7 and 8.) The plain drawers require no hardware (other than drawer pulls), while the full extension drawers require special full extension slides.

Plain old drawers — Plan your drawers so they are ⅛" smaller than the opening you want them to fit. For example, if the opening is 4⅜" high and 10¼" wide, make the drawers 4¼ high and 10⅛" wide. This will give you ¹⁄₁₆" of 'slop' all the way around — the drawers will fit well, but not too tight.

Make the front of the drawer from veneered plywood, with the 'A' side out. The back, sides, and bottom can all be made from scraps. Join the front, back, and sides with half-blind dovetails, using a router and a dovetail template. With a dado cutter, cut a groove on the inside of the drawer pieces to hold the bottom. Notch the bottom edge of the back of the drawer to fit over the drawer guides.

Make the drawer guides from hardwood, and glue them to the bottom inside surface of the box. Doing this, you'll come to understand why we told you to leave the drawer back unattached. This operation would be almost impossible with the backs in place. Be very careful when you position the

drawer guides. They must match the position of the notches in the drawer backs, and they must be perfectly parallel.

Glue the drawer front, sides, and backs together, with the bottom in place. Don't glue the bottom to the other parts of the drawer; just let it 'float' in the grooves. After the glue cures, finish sand the drawer, and slip it into the box. The notches in the back should fit over the drawer guides, holding the drawer ¹⁄₁₆" above the bottom of the box. (See Figure 9.) When the drawer closes, the drawer guide should stop the drawer when the face is flush with the front edges of the box.

Full-extension drawer — This is made in a similar manner to the plain old drawer. The front, back, and sides are dovetailed together, and the bottom rides in a groove. However, there the similarity ends.

Make the drawer a full inch (1") narrower than the width of the opening. This gives you room to install the *extension slides* on either sides of the drawer. (Some slides may require more room. Check the directions that come with the slides.) Use 14" slides, even though you can make the drawer a little longer.

The front of the drawer is faced with a piece of plywood ('A' side out). The drawer face hides the hardware. You can make this drawer face from ¼" plywood, if you wish, so that the drawer can be a little longer. However, we opted to make ours from ¾" plywood so that it would take more abuse.

This type of drawer is particularly handy for files. You'll find the 11¾" dimension provides just enough height to accommodate standard file folders.

Making and Installing Doors

There are three types of doors you can mount to these boxes: cabinet doors (made from plywood), glass doors, and drop-leaf doors. Each door requires a special type of hardware.

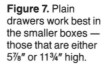

Figure 6. If you wish to install the optional brass brackets, cut recesses for them with your router. Use two U-shaped jigs, as shown, as stops for the router.

Figure 7. Plain drawers work best in the smaller boxes — those that are either 5⅞" or 11¾" high.

Figure 8. Full-extension drawers are mounted on extension slides. Notice that the front of the drawer is 'faced' with a piece of plywood.

Figure 9. The back of the plain drawer is notched so that it will fit over the drawer guides.

Cabinet doors — The cabinet doors, like the drawers, are made ⅛″ smaller than the openings. And, like the drawers, they are *flush mounted.* Flush mounted doors require special hinges that allow you to open and close the doors without rounding off a corner somewhere. (See Figure 10.)

The types of hinges we used are European 'Blum' hinges. These particular hinges not only let you flush mount a door without rounding a corner, they also allow you to adjust the position of that door in the opening in *all three* dimensions — front-to-back, up-and-down, and back-and-forth. This, in turn, lets you center the door precisely.

The only trick to mounting these particular hinges is that they must be inset in the door. You need to drill a 1⅜″ hole, ½″ deep, with a flat bottom. Most of the hardware companies that sell Blum hinges also sell the special multi-spur bit you need to make this hole. However, we used a holesaw, then cleaned out the bottom of the hole with a smaller, flat-bottom drill bit. You could also use a router to clean out the waste.

The hinges are self-closing, but you do need to put door stops on the other sides of the doors. We used an old cabinet-maker's trick; our stops are ¾″ diameter wheels with off-center holes. (See Figure 11.) Mount these stops with a roundhead screw through the holes, then turn the wheel until it stops the door right where you want it. Tighten the screw to keep the stop from turning.

Glass doors — Glass doors also require special hardware. We used a type of 'no-drill' hardware, so that we wouldn't have to drill holes in the glass. (See Figure 12.)

The glass doors pivot on two metal bracket/hinges. They are held in these hinges by screws and a pressure plate. For these particular hinges, we had the glass cut ¼″ narrower and ⅜″ shorter than the opening. The hinges you choose may require different dimensions — check the directions that come with the hardware.

The glass door closes and opens with the aid of a magnetic 'Tutch' latch. This latch sticks to a metal striker plate that is friction-fit to the glass door. When you push on the striker plate from the outside, the latch releases, and the door swings open. Push the door closed, and the magnet engages the striker plate again.

Drop-leaf door — You may want to make a box or two whose door drops down and forms a shelf or desk top. For this, you need special drop-leaf hinges and a drop-leaf support. (See Figure 13.)

Like the Blum hinges, the drop-leaf hinges allow you to flush mount the door without rounding the corners. However, they also ensure that the door drops down flush with the bottom of the box, and that it *only* opens to 90°. These hinges aren't enough to support the full weight of the door, especially if you want to use it as a desk, so you also need to install a support or two. Install one on small doors that will function as shelves, and two on larger doors that will double as desks.

Keep the drop leaf closed with a simple magnetic catch. Since the door has a wire pull on the outside, you don't need to go to the expense of a 'Tutch' latch.

Making and Installing Shelves

There are two types of shelves you may want to install in the boxes: adjustable shelves and pull-out shelves. Once again. each of these requires a special type of hardware.

Adjustable shelves — Adjustable shelves can be made from either wood or ¼″ thick glass. (If you use wood, cover the front edge with solid wood strips to hide the plies.) These shelves rest on metal pins, or 'shelf supports'. These supports fit in ¼″ diameter, ⅜″ deep holes, drilled in the inside of the

Figure 10. The cabinet doors are hung on special hinges that let you mount them flush with the front edge of the box.

Figure 11. To make an adjustable door stop, cut a small wheel from ¼″ plywood and drill an off-center pilot hole for the mounting screw. To adjust the stop, just turn the wheel.

Figure 12. Glass doors are hung on 'no-drill' pivot hinges, and opened or closed with a magnetic 'Tutch' latch.

Figure 13. Drop-leaf doors are mounted on special drop-leaf hinges. Drop-leaf supports help to keep the doors horizontal, even when used as a shelf or desk.

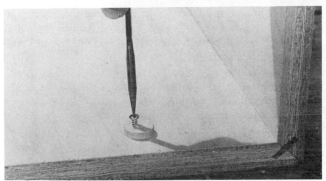

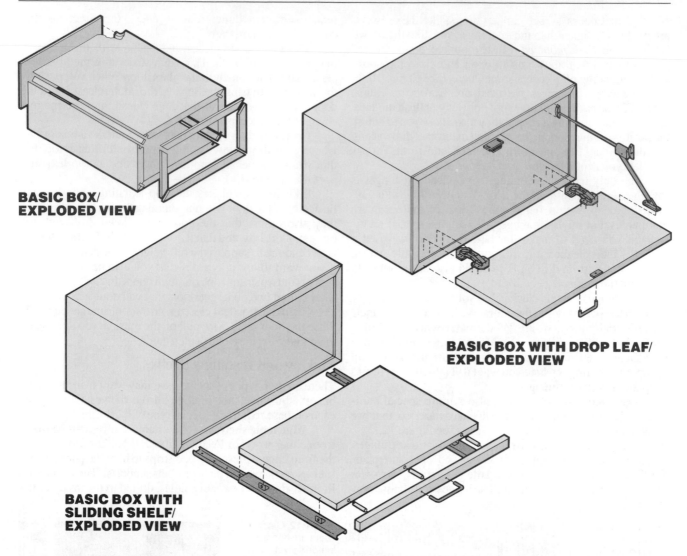

**BASIC BOX/
EXPLODED VIEW**

**BASIC BOX WITH DROP LEAF/
EXPLODED VIEW**

**BASIC BOX WITH
SLIDING SHELF/
EXPLODED VIEW**

boxes. The holes are usually spaced every 2″, as shown in the working drawing. To raise or lower a shelf, simply move the supports to a new set of holes.

Pull-out shelves — There may be some things you want to store on a shelf that you'll also need to pull out from time to time, such as a turntable, video and audio cassettes, a top-loading VCR, etc. To do this, you need to mount the shelf on 14″ shelf slides. (See Figure 14.)

Figure 14. Mount pull-out shelves on shelf slides. These pieces of hardware are similar to extension slides for drawers.

These slides are a good deal like the extension slides, except that they're made for shelves. You can mount them to either the side or the bottom of the box, then mount the shelf on top of them. The slides we used required that we make the shelf ¾″ narrower than the opening, to allow room for the hardware. However, this dimension may vary from manufacturer to manufacturer. Consult the directions that come with the slides.

Since the pull-out shelf must be made from wood, you'll probably want to make it from plywood so that it matches the rest of the box. Attach strips of solid wood to the front edge to hide the plies.

Once you've installed the drawers, doors, or shelves in the boxes, remove the hardware. Finish sand any parts that still need it, and apply a finish to the wood. Reassemble the boxes and their components with the hardware, *then* (finally!) attach the backs.

By the way, all of the hardware mentioned in this chapter — including the 'campaign' hardware and brass pulls — can be bought from mail order hardware suppliers. Here are two sources:

The Woodworker's Store   The Wise Company
21801 Industrial Blvd.   6503 St. Claude Avenue
Rogers, MN 55374   Arabi, LA 70032

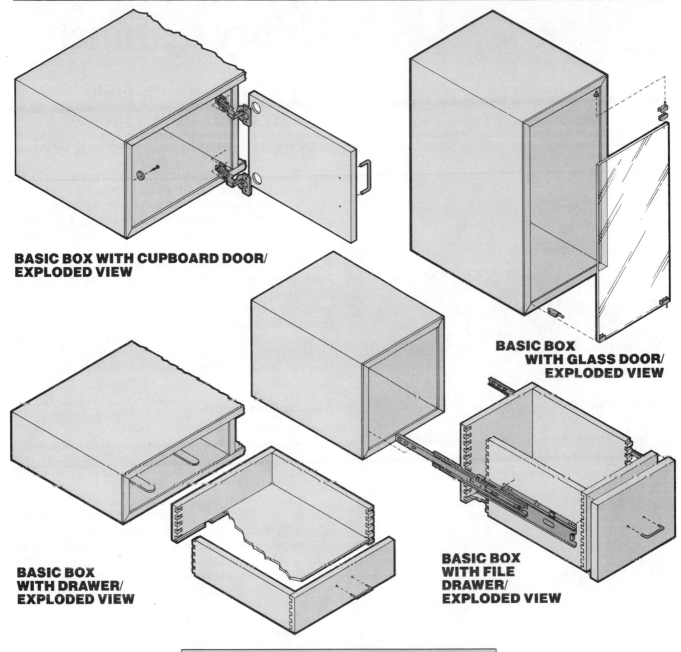

**BASIC BOX WITH CUPBOARD DOOR/
EXPLODED VIEW**

**BASIC BOX
WITH GLASS DOOR/
EXPLODED VIEW**

**BASIC BOX
WITH DRAWER/
EXPLODED VIEW**

**BASIC BOX
WITH FILE
DRAWER/
EXPLODED VIEW**

BILL OF MATERIALS — Modular Wall System

Shopping List

The following list of materials and hardware will build the fifteen boxes shown in the lead photograph. Your own shopping list may differ somewhat, depending on the number and size of boxes you wish to build, and what sorts of drawers, doors, or shelves you wish to install in them.

¾″ x 4′ x 8′ Sheets of A-B cabinet grade plywood (4)
¼″ x 4′ x 8′ Sheet of A-B cabinet grade plywood
¾″ Hardwood to match plywood veneer (4 board feet)
⅛″ x 4′ x 4′ Tempered hardboard

Hardware

3″ Brass wire pulls (9)
14″ Full-extension drawer slides and mounting screws (1 pair)
Self-closing flush door hinges and mounting screws (3 pair)

#6 x ¾″ Roundhead wood screws and washers (3)
'No-drill' glass door pivot hinges (2 pair)
Magnetic 'Tutch' latches (2)
'No drill' glass door striker plates (2)
¼″ x 10″ x 21⅝″ Glass doors (2)
Drop-leaf hinges and mounting screws (1 pair)
Drop-leaf support and mounting screws
Magnetic catch and striker plate
Pin-style shelf supports (16)
¼″ x 10⅛″ x 13½″ Glass shelves (4)
14″ Shelf slides and mounting screws (1 pair)
#8 x 1¼″ Flathead wood screws (16)
¾″ Brads (1 box of 100)
Campaign-style brass L-brackets and brads (60)
Campaign-style brass T-brackets and brads (8)

Designed by Nick Engler, built by Adam Blake

Utility Cabinet

This unique, easy-to-build cabinet offers three types of storage in one space-saving unit.

N eed more shelving space? More drawer space? How about a bin to keep dog food, rock salt, dirty clothes, or other loose items? This cabinet will give you all three, in less than three square feet of floor space. Depending on your storage needs, you may wish to build several units and place them side by side.

As designed, the cabinet is perfectly suited for a laundry room, garage, or shop. The shelves are tall and deep to store large objects; smaller things can be stored in the drawer. If you wish, you can put doors on the shelves to hide the mess inside, or leave them open for easy access. (We elected to put doors on the upper compartment, and leave the lower one open.) The bin swings out, pivoting on a large dowel. It is balanced so that you can fill it full of heavy materials and still open it easily.

Making the Cabinet

Start by making the basic case. Cut the case parts — sides, top, back, shelves, and baseboard. Since this is a utility cabinet, you needn't make it from expensive materials. Use ¾" particleboard for most of the parts, and ¼" plywood for the back.

Cut the rabbets and dadoes in the sides and the top with a router or dado cutter. If you use a router, clamp a straightedge to the stock to help guide the router. Mount a ¾" straight bit in the router, and make each joint in several passes, cutting just ⅛"-¼" deeper with each pass. (See Figure 1.) To use a dado cutter, you'll either need a table extension for your table saw, or you'll need to clamp a straightedge to the underside of the stock to serve as an auxiliary fence. Keep this fence pressed firmly against the edge of your table saw to guide the work. (See Figure 2.)

Tip ◆ The glue that holds particleboard together is particularly hard on router bits. Sharpen the straight bit from time to time with a small stone, as you're cutting the joints. Keep the bit clean with paint thinner or oven cleaner.

After you've cut the joinery, drill the 1" holes in the sides for the bin pivot. If you wish, you can also drill holes in the sides of the shelving compartments for adjustable shelves.

Assemble the sides and the shelves first, using glue and flathead wood screws. (You'll probably need a helper to hold the bigger parts while you screw them together. Then attach the top (with glue and screws), and the back (with glue and brads). Check that the case is square before you nail the back in place.

Wait for the glue to dry; then sand down any rough edges on the case. If you wish, cover the screw heads with putty or plugs.

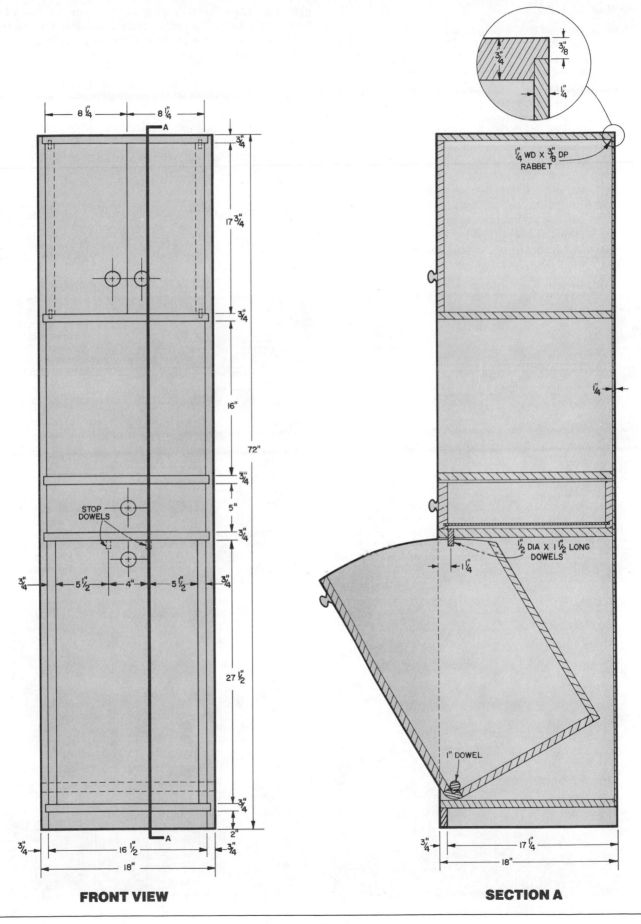

FRONT VIEW

SECTION A

Assembling the Bin

Cut out the parts for the bin. Like the case, most of these parts are made from ¾″ particleboard. The front bottom corner, however, is made from a scrap of 2 x 2, and the splines that hold it to the bin are made from ¼″ plywood.

Cut the shape of the bin sides with a saber saw, and drill the 1″ pivot holes near the front bottom corners. With a slotting cutter mounted in your router, cut ¼″ wide, ½″ deep slots in the bottom edge of the bin front, the front edge of the bin bottom, and two adjacent sides of the stock for the front corner. (See Figure 3.)

After you cut the joinery for the bin, cut a rabbet in the bottom corner stock. Clamp the stock down on your workbench, and round the outside bottom-most corner with a plane. Use a cardboard template to help gauge the curvature as you're working. (See Figure 4.)

Assemble the bin front, bin bottom, and bottom corner with glue and splines. Then attach the bin back and sides with glue and screws. When the glue dries, sand the bin down and install a pull to the front of the bin. Be sure to attach this pull *before* you put the bin in place. Otherwise, you may find it hard to get the bin out of the cabinet.

Put the bin inside the cabinet, and slide a pivot dowel through the 1″ holes. Check the action of the bin. If the top edges rub, you may have to sand them down. If the bottom corner rubs, you may have to plane it down some more. When you're satisfied with the action of the bin, cut the dowel to the proper length and tack it in place with two finishing nails, through the front edge of the sides, as shown in the working drawings.

> **Tip ◆** To keep the bin from tipping forward, out of the case, you may wish to install 'stops' in the underside of the shelf, just above the bin. These stops are just ⅜″ dowels.

Figure 1. If you cut the dadoes with a router, use a straightedge to guide your work. Make each joint in several passes, cutting just ⅛″-¼″ deeper with each pass.

Figure 2. If you cut the dadoes with a table saw, use a straightedge (clamped to the underside of the stock) as an 'auxiliary fence' to guide the work. Keep the straightedge pressed up against the edge of the table saw.

Figure 3. A slotting cutter, mounted in your router, makes quick work of the grooves for the splines that join the bottom bin corner to the bin front and bin bottom.

Figure 4. Round over the bottom corner with a hand plane. Use a cardboard cut-out to gauge the curve as you make it.

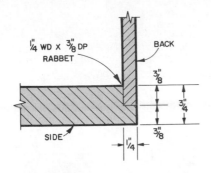

1/4" WD X 3/8" DP RABBET

BACK

3/8"

3/4"

3/8"

1/4"

SIDE

SIDE-TO-BACK JOINERY DETAIL

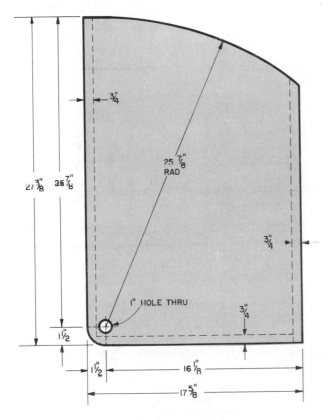

3/4"

25 7/8" RAD

27 3/8" 26 7/8"

3/4"

1" HOLE THRU

3/4"

1 1/2"

1 1/2" 16 1/8"

17 5/8"

BIN/SIDE LAYOUT

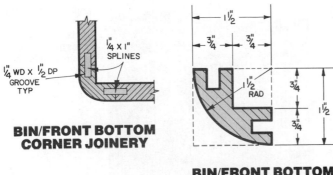

1/4 X 1" SPLINES

1/4" WD X 1/2" DP GROOVE TYP

BIN/FRONT BOTTOM CORNER JOINERY

1 1/2"

3/4" 3/4"

1 1/2" RAD

3/4"

1 1/2"

3/4"

BIN/FRONT BOTTOM CORNER DETAIL

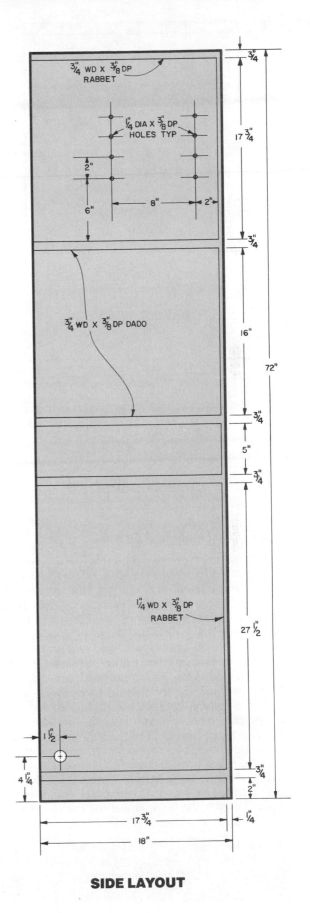

3/4" WD X 3/8" DP RABBET

3/4"

1/4" DIA X 3/8" DP HOLES TYP

17 3/4"

2"

6"

8"

2"

3/4"

3/4" WD X 3/8" DP DADO

16"

72"

3/4"

5"

3/4"

1/4" WD X 3/8" DP RABBET

27 1/2"

1 1/2"

4 1/4"

3/4"

2"

17 3/4"

1/4"

18"

SIDE LAYOUT

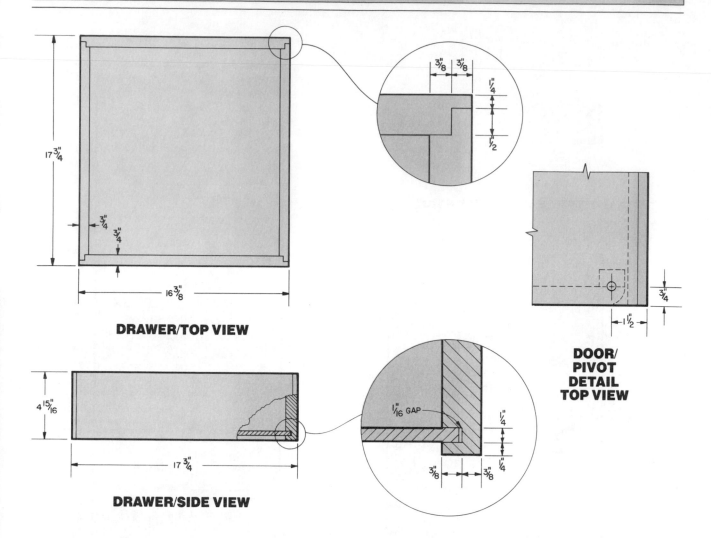

DRAWER/TOP VIEW

DRAWER/SIDE VIEW

DOOR/PIVOT DETAIL TOP VIEW

Making the Doors and Drawer

Cut the door and drawer parts from ¾" particleboard, except the drawer bottom. Make this from ¼" plywood. Round the front outside corners of the doors and glue a 1½" wide reinforcing strip to the back of each door. With a router or a dado cutter, make the grooves and rabbets in the drawer parts.

Assemble the drawer with glue and screws. However, *don't* glue the bottom of the drawer in place. Let it 'float' in the grooves. Sand the drawer smooth, mount a pull to the drawer front, and put the finished drawer in place in the case.

Install pulls on the doors, and clamp the doors in place in the cabinet. You can do this by squeezing the shelves together with some bar clamps. Drill ⅜" holes through the shelves into the outside corners of the doors. Install dowels in these holes, so the doors will pivot. Check the action of the doors. If the corners rub, you may need to sand them down slightly. Once you're satisfied with the door action, tack the dowels in place, as you did with the pivot dowel for the bin. Also, install magnetic catches to keep the doors closed.

Tip ◆ When you drill the pivot holes in the underside of the shelf, you may find it necessary to use a right angle adapter for your drill. (See Figure 5.) This accessory allows you to drill in tight quarters.

Finishing Up

If you elected to put adjustable shelves in the cabinet, cut the shelves you need. Hold them in place with dowels or movable shelving supports.

Do any touchup sanding that's necessary. Then paint the utility cabinet to match or complement the room where you'll use it. If you're going to store dog food, cat food, or bird seed in the bin, be sure to use a *latex* paint. This paint is less toxic than oil paint, and you won't risk harming the animals.

Figure 5. A right-angle adapter helps you drill holes in tight spots, like the pivot holes for the doors in the underside of the shelf.

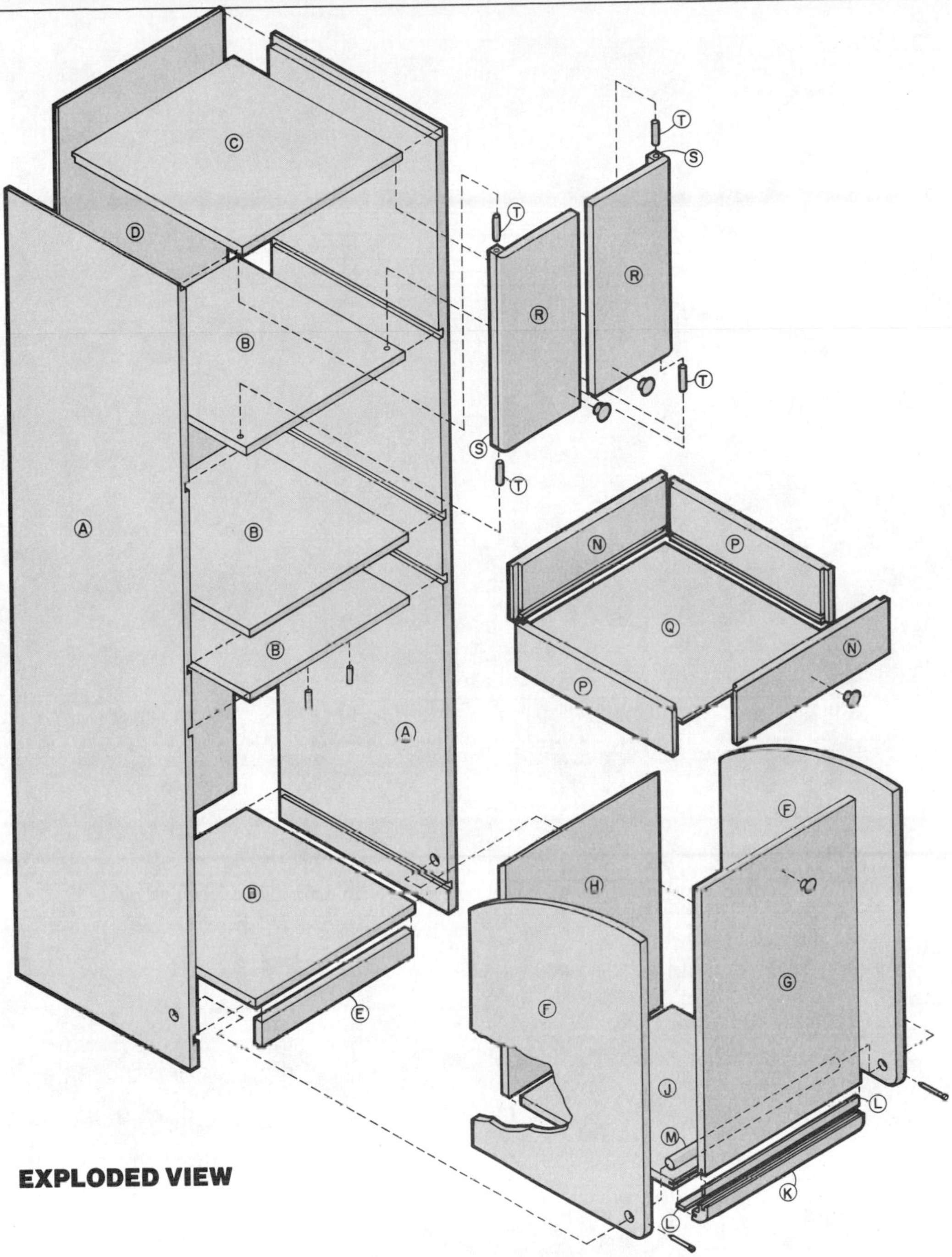

EXPLODED VIEW

BILL OF MATERIALS — Utility Cabinet

Finished Dimensions in Inches

A.	Sides (2)	¾ x 18 x 72
B.	Shelves (4)	¾ x 17¼ x 17¾
C.	Top	¾ x 17¼ x 18
D.	Back	¼ x 17¼ x 69⅝
E.	Baseboard	¾ x 2 x 16½
F.	Bin sides (2)	¾ x 17⅝ x 27⅜
G.	Bin front	¾ x 14⅞ x 25⅞
H.	Bin back	¾ x 14⅞ x 21¾
J.	Bin bottom	¾ x 14⅞ x 15⅜
K.	Bin bottom corner	1½ x 1½ x 14⅞
L.	Splines (2)	¼ x 1 x 14⅞
M.	Bin pivot dowel	1 dia. x 18
N.	Drawer front/back (2)	¾ x 4^15/16 x 16⅜
P.	Drawer sides (2)	¾ x 4^15/16 x 17¼
Q.	Drawer bottom	¼ x 15½ x 16⅞
R.	Doors (2)	¾ x 8⅛ x 17⅝
S.	Reinforcing strips (2)	¾ x 1½ x 17⅝
T.	Door pivot dowels (4)	⅜ dia. x 1¼

Hardware

1½″ Door/drawer pulls (4)
4d Finishing nails (6)
1″ Brads (1 box)
#8 x 1¼″ Flathead wood screws (36-42)

Designed by Nick Engler, built by Adam Blake and Nick Engler

Sunshade Gazebo

Simplified construction and a pole foundation make this gazebo inexpensive and easy to build.

Few outdoor structures are so appealing or inviting as the gazebo. This Victorian creation adds a touch of elegance to any backyard. The trouble is, this elegance often costs a good deal of money. Even a small gazebo, with a simple pad foundation, can cost several thousand dollars just for the materials.

The structure shown here is something of a breakthrough, as gazebos go. It has all the elegance of a gazebo built in the Victorian tradition, but it cost hundreds of dollars less to build. In most locations, it can be built for under $800 (1987 prices). I built this particular gazebo for just a hair over $500, because I waited till mid-summer when most of the building materials I needed went on sale.

Why so inexpensive? Because this gazebo uses materials and techniques that have been developed over recent years to build *decks*. (Actually, it is an eight-sided deck with a sunshade deck cover.) Because of their popularity, decks have gotten quite inexpensive lately. On the other hand, traditional gazebos are built like houses, and houses have gotten quite expensive.

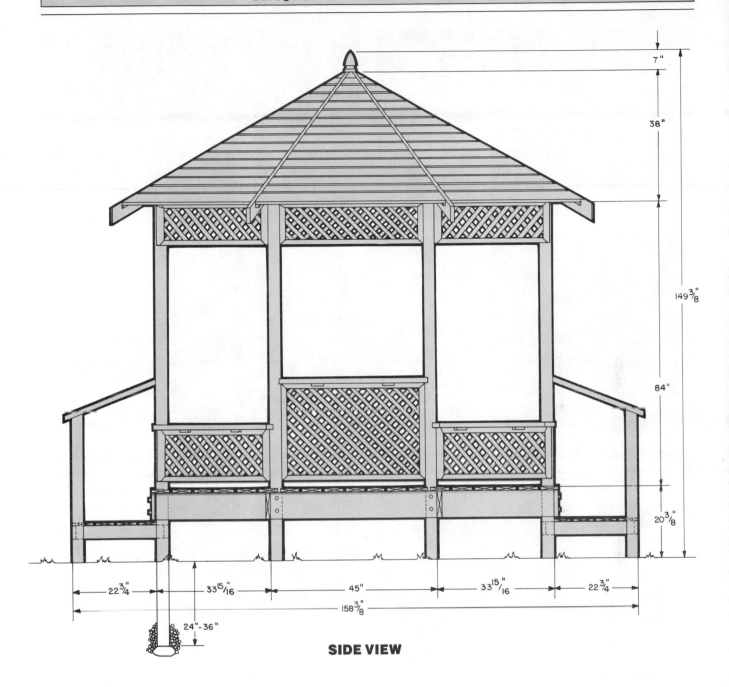

7"

38"

149³/₈"

84"

20³/₈"

22³/₄" 33¹⁵/₁₆ 45" 33¹⁵/₁₆ 22³/₄"

158³/₈"

24"-36"

SIDE VIEW

Building the Frame

One of the things that makes this gazebo so inexpensive is that there is no concrete foundation to pour. Like many decks, the gazebo uses a 'pole' foundation. These poles are part of the frame, and these two structural components — the frame and the foundation — are constructed at the same time.

Begin by building the floor frame. Because this is an eight-sided structure, the floor frame is unusual. The 2 x 8 joists are lapped to form a large 'tic-tac-toe' pattern. Notch the joists as shown in the working drawings, then fit the notches together so that two joists run north-south, while the other two run east-west. (See Figure 1.)

Cut the outside floor frame parts to fit between the joists. Make eight frame parts — cut four of them square at the ends, and miter the other four, as shown in the drawings. Nail the four square-end frame pieces in place first, then add the mitered pieces. (See Figure 2.)

With a helper, arrange the completed floor frame on the building site where you want to erect the gazebo. Mark the locations of the eight poles with wooden stakes, then lift the floor frame over the stakes and set it aside for a time. (See Figure 3.)

With a post-hole digger, dig holes for the posts where you've driven the stakes. (See Figure 4.) These holes should be at least 8″ in diameter — about twice as wide as the posts. They should also be at least 24″ deep and below the frost line

Figure 1. Assemble the 2 x 8 joists with lap joints. The joists will form a grid, like a tic-tac-toe game.

Figure 2. Nail the floor frame members to the outer ends of the joists to make an octagon. Attach the members with square-cut ends first, then the members with mitered ends.

Figure 5. Put large rocks in the bottom of the holes. Then put the floor frame back in position, and place the posts in the holes.

Figure 6. Support the floor frame approximately 12″ off the ground with concrete blocks and scraps of wood. Level the frame by adding or subtracting wood scraps at one or more of the support points.

Figure 7. Attach the posts to the floor frame with lag screws.

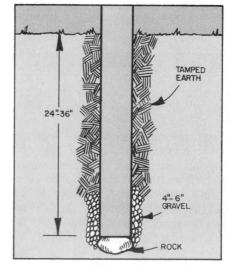

Figure 3. Put the floor frame in place on the building site, and mark where the posts will go with stakes.

Figure 4. Move the frame out of the way and dig the post holes. These holes must be at least 24″ deep, and below the frost line for your area.

Figure 8. Set the posts in the ground, at least 24″ deep and below the frost line. Put a large rock in the bottom of the hole to keep the posts from settling. At ground level, paint the sides of the posts with roofing tar to keep the posts from rotting prematurely. Throw in a bit of gravel around the base of each post to provide drainage, then fill up the holes with dirt and tamp it down firmly.

TAMPED EARTH

24″-36″

4″-6″ GRAVEL

ROCK

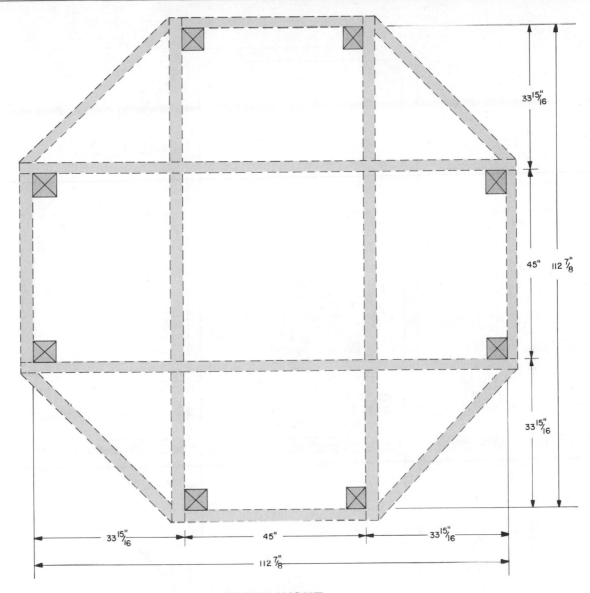

POST LAYOUT

for your area. If they aren't below the frost line, the posts may heave out of alignment during the winter. To find out where the frost line is for your area, call the local Building Inspections office.

When you've finished digging the holes, put a large, flat rock in the bottom of each hole to keep the posts from settling. Like the holes, these rocks should be twice the diameter of the posts. Then put the floor frame back in position over the holes, and put the posts in the holes. (See Figure 5.)

With concrete blocks or scrap wood, prop up the floor frame, approximately 12″ above the ground. Check that the frame is level. If it isn't, add or subtract wood scraps from one or more of the places where you have supported the frame. (Scc Figure 6.) When you're satisfied the frame is level, make sure the posts are plumb. Brace them temporarily with scrap wood to hold them perfectly upright. When the frame is level and the posts are plumb, attach the frame to the posts with ½″ x 4″ lag screws. (See Figure 7.)

To set the posts permanently in the ground, throw a few shovelfuls of gravel in each post hole. This will help drain ground water away from the posts. Then fill the holes with dirt and tamp the dirt down firmly. (See Figure 8.)

Tip ◆ To help keep the posts from rotting off at ground level, paint the sides of the posts with roofing tar 3″ above and below the surface. This should be done *before* you fill the holes with dirt.

Measure up from the top edge of the floor frame, along the posts, as shown in the working drawings. With a handsaw, cut all the posts off at the same height.

Tip ◆ To make sure that your posts are long enough, buy them at least 12″ longer than you think you'll need. This way you won't have to be quite so careful about how deep you dig the post holes.

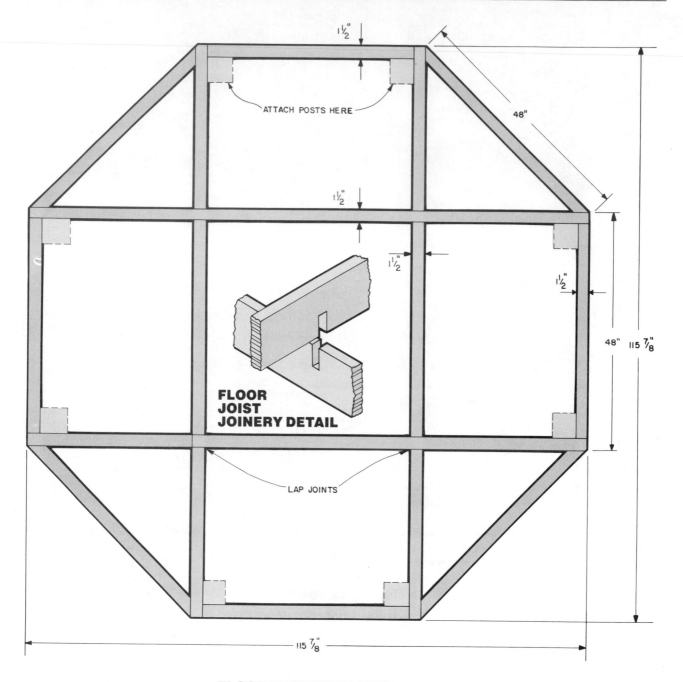

1½"

1½"

ATTACH POSTS HERE

48"

1½"

1½"

48" 115 ⅞"

**FLOOR
JOIST
JOINERY DETAIL**

LAP JOINTS

115 ⅞"

FLOOR FRAME/TOP VIEW

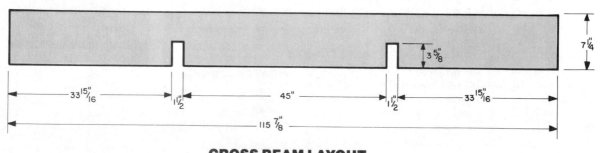

33 ¹⁵/₁₆"

1½"

45"

1½"

33 ¹⁵/₁₆"

3 ⅝"

7 ¼"

115 ⅞"

CROSS BEAM LAYOUT

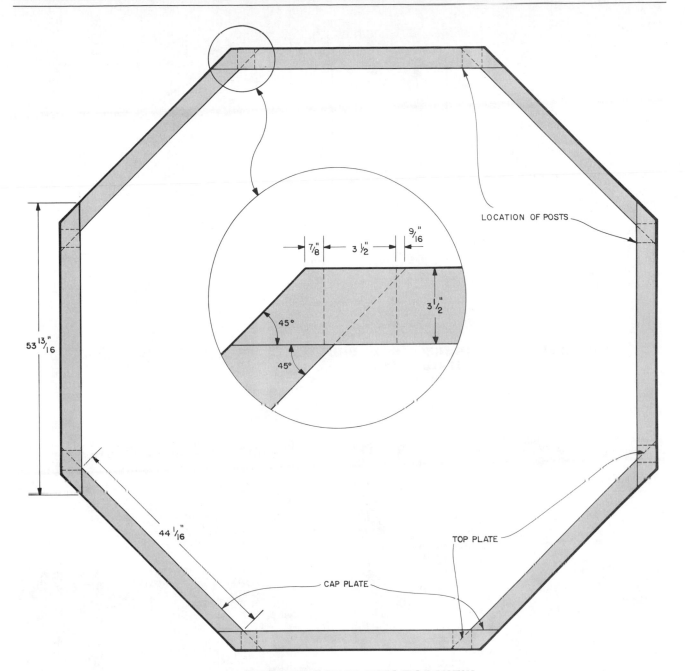

7/8" 3 1/2" 9/16"

LOCATION OF POSTS

45°

45°

3 1/2"

53 13/16"

44 1/16"

TOP PLATE

CAP PLATE

TOP AND CAP PLATES/TOP VIEW

Cut the parts needed for the top and cap plates, as shown in the working drawings. You'll need 16 pieces, all of them mitered at the ends. Nail the top plate in place first, attaching it to the tops of the posts with 16d nails. Then nail the cap plate to the top plate with 10d nails. (See Figure 9.) The ends of the cap plate members should lap the joints between the top plate members, as shown in the working drawing details.

When the top and the cap plates are in place, brace the posts and the floor joists to keep the gazebo frame square. Cut the braces from 2 x 4 stock, as shown in the drawings. To fit properly, these braces must be notched on both sides. Attach the braces to the posts, beneath the floor frame, with ¼″ x 3½″ lag screws, and to the joists with ¼″ x 2″ lag screws.

Figure 9. Attach the top plate and cap plate to the tops of the posts. The cap plate must lap the joints between the top plate members.

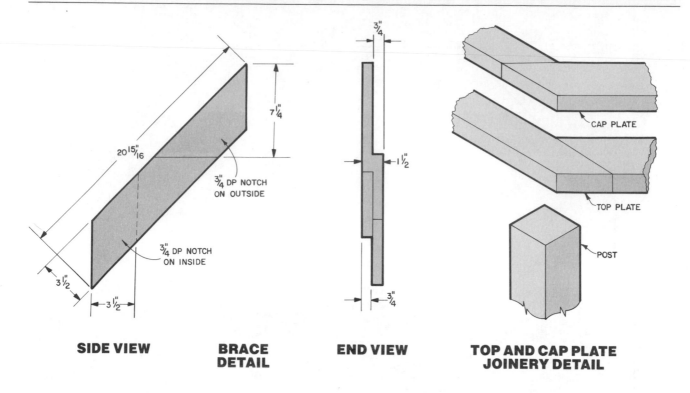

SIDE VIEW

BRACE DETAIL

END VIEW

TOP AND CAP PLATE JOINERY DETAIL

Figure 10. Install additional 2 x 4 joists in the floor frame, using metal joist hangers wherever practical.

Figure 11. Surround the posts with cleats to help support the decking all around the posts.

Tip ◆ Whenever you cut a diagonal brace, don't miter the upper end so that it's horizontal. This presents the end grain to the rain, and the brace will quickly rot. Instead, miter both ends so the end grain will be vertical. If a board must be cut so that the end grain is horizontal (like the posts), then cover the end grain with another board (like the top and cap plates).

Figure 12. Install the decking with spiral nails, spacing the planks ¼"-½" apart. If you wish, use a thin board to get the spacing even.

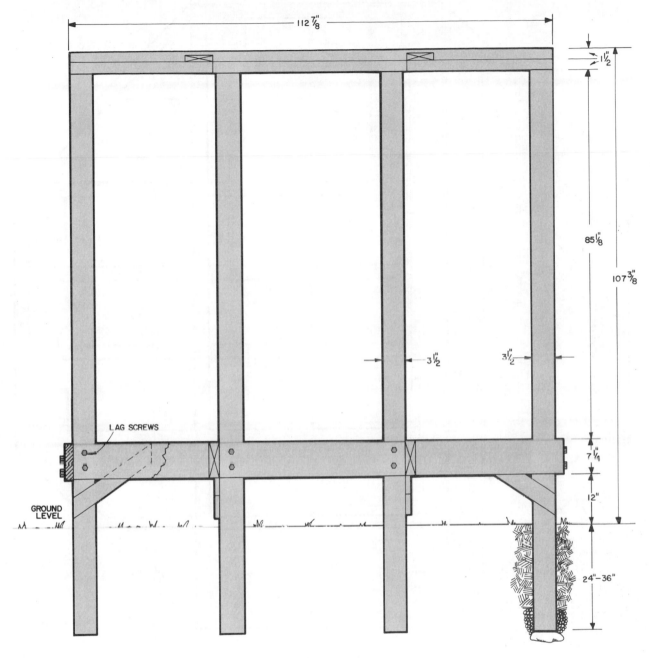

FRAME/SIDE VIEW

Covering the Floor

Before you can cover the floor frame with decking, you need to add some additional joists. These don't have to be quite as beefy as the crossed joists; they can be made from 2 x 4's. Attach these extra joists to the floor frame members, using joist hangers and 8d nails at those junctions where the 2 x 4 joists are perpendicular to the 2 x 8's. (See Figure 10.) Where they meet at an angle, miter the 2 x 4 joists and join the parts with 16d nails.

You also need to attach cleats to the posts, to create a nailing surface for the decking around the posts. Make these cleats from scraps of 2 x 4, and attach them to the posts with 16d nails. (See Figure 11.)

Once you have attached the extra joists and cleats, lay the decking across the floor frame, perpendicular to the 2 x 4 joists. Notch the planks to fit around the posts. Attach the decking planks to the frame with 12d square-shanked spiral nails. Space the planks ¼"-½" apart, to give the wood room to expand in humid weather. If you wish, use a thin board to help space the planks evenly. (See Figure 12.) When all the planks are nailed in place, cut the planks flush with the outside frame members.

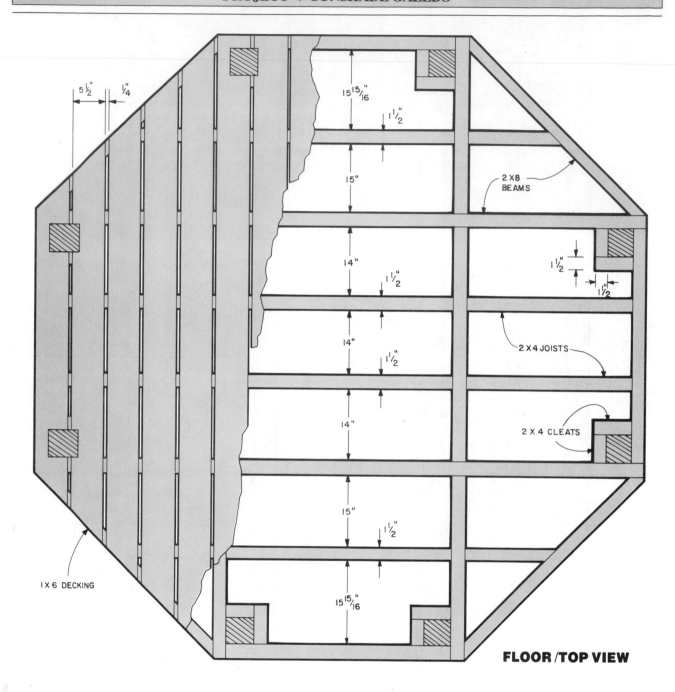

FLOOR/TOP VIEW

Covering the Roof

Once the floor is down, add a roof. Cut eight rafters from 2 x 4 stock. Miter the ends of the rafters, and cut bird's mouths in the bottom edge, where shown in the working drawings. From a scrap of 4 x 4, make a key block. Rip the block on a table saw to an octagonal shape, then turn it on a lathe to point the top. If you don't have a lathe, you can also use a bandsaw to shape the key block.

> **Tip ◆** If you plan to cover the roof with shingles, make the rafters from 2 x 6's. This will help support the extra weight.

Toenail two rafters to opposite sides of the key block and run a temporary brace from rafter to rafter to make a 'truss'. With the help of a friend, raise this truss in place and fit the bird's mouths to the cap plate, over opposite corners. Nail the rafters to the cap plate with 16d nails. Have your friend continue to hold the truss upright while you attach the third and fourth rafters at 90° to the other two. (When you have four rafters installed, your helper can stop holding the truss and you can remove the temporary brace.) Attach the last four rafters to the assembly to complete the roof frame. (See Figure 13.)

Note: As shown in the working drawings, four sides of the key block will be just 1 7/16″ wide — not quite wide enough to accommodate the rafters. You would think you would have to chamfer the ends of the last four rafters to get them all to fit, but in actual practice, this is not the case. There is

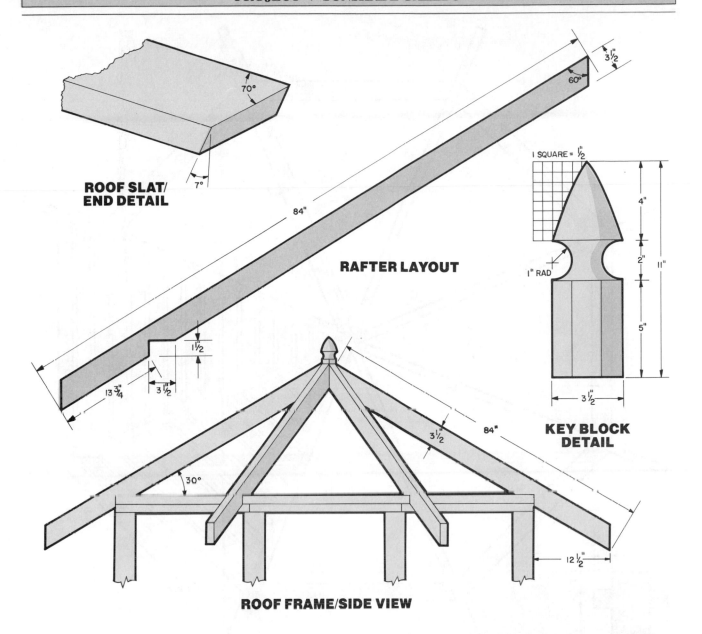

ROOF SLAT/ END DETAIL

RAFTER LAYOUT

KEY BLOCK DETAIL

ROOF FRAME/SIDE VIEW

enough 'give' in the softwood to allow you to attach all eight rafters flush to the key, with no need for fancy fitting.

Rip 1 x 1 stock to make the roof cleats. Attach these cleats to the faces of the rafters with 6d nails, starting a few inches from the lower ends of the rafters, and running almost all the way up to the key block. The cleats should be positioned ¾″ from the upper edge of the rafters.

Cut the roof slats from 1 x 4 stock. No matter how careful you are as a carpenter, there will probably be enough 'slop' in the construction of the frame that you will find it necessary to hand fit each slat. This is a slow process, but it yields the best results. Carefully mark the position of all the slats on the rafters before you start cutting and nailing. Begin at the top of each section and work your way down, spacing the slats 1″-2″ apart. (See Figure 14.) Compound-miter the ends of each slat at 7° (through the edge) and 70° (through the face), as shown in the drawings. Nail the slats in place with 8d nails. Angle these nails so that they bite into the cleats *and* the rafters.

Figure 13. Secure the lower end of the rafters to the cap plate, fitting the bird's mouths over the corners. Then nail the upper end to the key block.

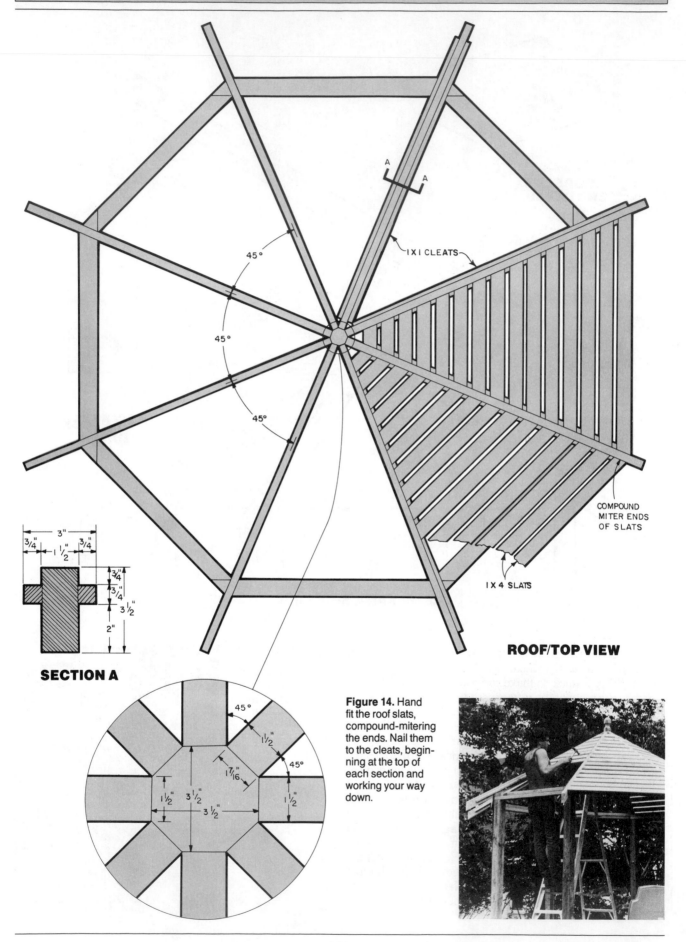

45°

45°

45°

45°

A A

1 X 1 CLEATS

COMPOUND
MITER ENDS
OF SLATS

1 X 4 SLATS

ROOF/TOP VIEW

SECTION A

3"
3/4" 1 1/2" 3/4"
3/4"
3/4"
3 1/2"
2"

45°
1 1/2"
45°
1 7/16"
1 1/2" 3 1/2" 1 1/2"
3 1/2"

Figure 14. Hand
fit the roof slats,
compound-mitering
the ends. Nail them
to the cleats, begin-
ning at the top of
each section and
working your way
down.

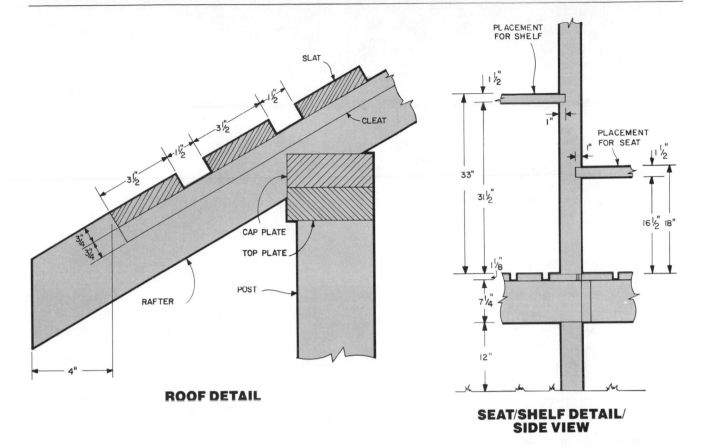

ROOF DETAIL

SEAT/SHELF DETAIL/ SIDE VIEW

Adding Seats and Shelves

As designed, this gazebo has four seats, two shelves, and two entranceways. However, you can arrange any number of seats, shelves, and entranceways that you want — provided the total equals eight. The seats and shelves are dadoed into the posts. Because of the placement and orientation of the posts, some seats or shelves can be cut square, while others require fancy miter cuts. Cut the seats and shelves that you need from 2 x 12 stock, and attach 1 x 4 battens to the undersides to keep the wide boards from cupping or splitting.

> **Tip ◆** It's best to arrange the entranceways on the same sides as the short outside floor frame members — those frame parts that were cut square. Later on, this will make it much easier to build and attach the stairs.

Cut dadoes in the posts where you will attach the seats and shelves. To do this, mark where you want the dadoes on the posts. With a handsaw, cut 1″ deep kerfs where you made the marks. Then remove the waste with a chisel. (See Figure 15.) Slide the seats and shelves in place, then toenail them in place with 16d nails. Set these nails below the surface of the wood with a punch. (See Figure 16.)

Cut braces for the seats and shelves from 1 x 4 stock. Attach these braces to the undersides of the seats and shelves, and to the sides of the posts, with 12d nails. To keep the relatively thin wooden braces from splitting, drill pilot holes before you drive the nails.

Figure 15. Cut dadoes in the posts to hold the seats and shelves. To make these joints, first cut saw kerfs on either side of the dado. Then remove the waste between the kerfs with a chisel.

Figure 16. Set the seats and shelves in place in the dadoes, then toenail them to the posts. Set the nails below the surface of the wood with a punch.

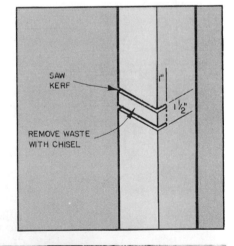

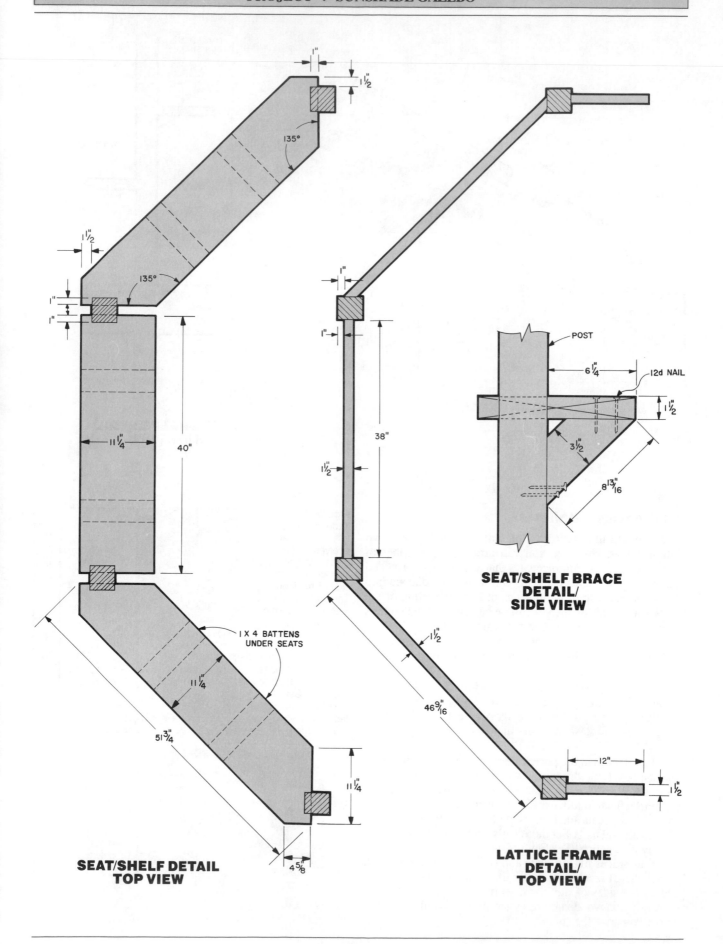

1"

1½"

135°

1½"

135°

1"

1"

11¼"

40"

1 X 4 BATTENS
UNDER SEATS

11¼"

51¾"

11¼"

4⅝"

**SEAT/SHELF DETAIL
TOP VIEW**

1"

1"

38"

1½"

1½"

46⁹⁄₁₆"

12"

1½"

**LATTICE FRAME
DETAIL/
TOP VIEW**

POST

6¼"

12d NAIL

1½"

3½"

8¹³⁄₁₆"

**SEAT/SHELF BRACE
DETAIL/
SIDE VIEW**

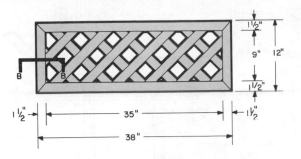

SHORT UPPER LATTICE FRAME

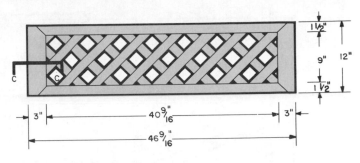

LONG UPPER LATTICE FRAME

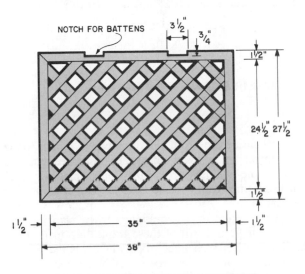

SHORT LOWER LATTICE FRAME

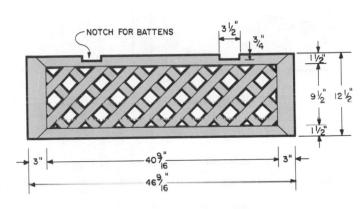

LONG LOWER LATTICE FRAME

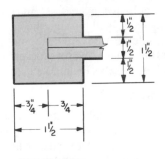

SECTION B

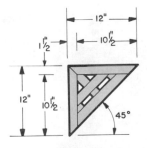

**ENTRANCE WAY
LATTICE FRAME**

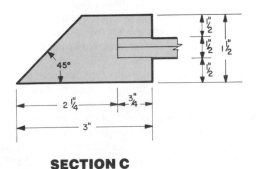

SECTION C

Installing Lattice Frames

Figure out how many lattice frames you need — and what type you need. There are several different factors that determine the type of frames needed. First of all, how many seats, shelves, and entranceways do you have? All of these require a different arrangement of frames. The lower frames for those sections with shelves are taller than for those sections with seats. The entranceways have no lower frames, and just two little triangular upper frames, to make an arch in the upper corners.

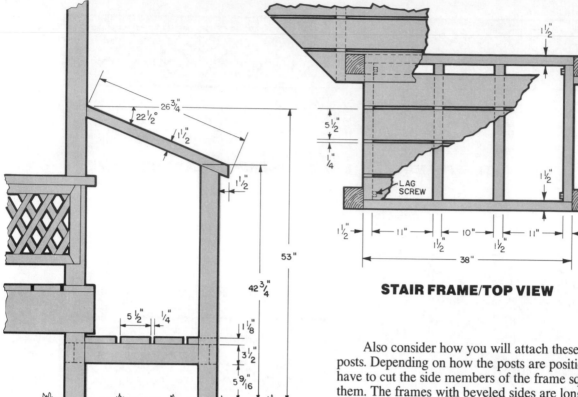

STAIRS/SIDE VIEW

STAIR FRAME/TOP VIEW

Figure 17. Notch the lower frames so they fit around the battens on the undersides of the seats and shelves.

Figure 18. Nail the frames to the posts, seats, shelves, and top plate with finishing nails. Where the sides of the frames are mitered, nail through the face of the frame member. Where the sides are square, toenail the frames in the gazebo.

Also consider how you will attach these frames to the posts. Depending on how the posts are positioned, you will have to cut the side members of the frame square, or bevel them. The frames with beveled sides are longer than those with square sides.

Refer to the working drawings when planning and building your frames. All of these frames are made from either 2 x 2 or 2 x 4 'channel' stock, mitered at the corners. The lattice rests inside the grooves in the channel, and the frames are assembled with 8d finishing nails in the corners. Notch the lower frames to fit around the battens under the seats and the shelves. (See Figure 17.)

Set the frames between the posts, and nail them in place with 8d finishing nails. Nail through the face of those frame members with mitered sides. (See Figure 18.) Where the frame members are square, and set squarely against the posts or other parts of the gazebo, toenail them in place.

Making the Stairs

For each entranceway, make a stair frame from 2 x 4's. Assemble the frame with 16d nails, then temporarily set the frames on the ground between the posts. Mark where you will put the stair posts with stakes, and remove the frames. Dig holes for the posts — once again, these holes should go down below the frost line. Place large rocks in the bottoms of the holes, and set the posts on the rocks. Brace the posts upright.

Put the stair frames back in place and attach them to the posts with 3/8" x 4" lag screws. Throw some gravel in the post holes, then fill the holes with dirt. However, don't tamp the earth down just yet.

Carefully measure the posts and cut them off, mitering the tops at 22½°. Cut the railings from 2 x 4 stock, and miter the ends of the railings the same as the posts. Attach the railings to the stair posts and the gazebo posts with 16d nails. Make sure the stair posts are plumb, then tamp the dirt down around them. Finally, cover the stair frames with decking, leaving a space between the planks, as you did when you covered the floor frame.

BILL OF MATERIALS — Sunshade Gazebo

Shopping List for Lumber and Building Materials

Treated Lumber
(Nominal Dimensions)

4 x 4 x 12'-14'	16 pieces	Main posts, stair posts, key block
2 x 12 x 12'	2 pieces	Seats, shelves
2 x 8 x 10'	4 pieces	Large floor joists
2 x 8 x 8'	4 pieces	Outside floor frame members
2 x 4 x 14'	4 pieces	Rafters
2 x 4 x 10'	8 pieces	Top plate, cap plate, mitered floor joists, floor cleats
2 x 4 x 8'	11 pieces	Floor braces, small floor joists, stair frame, stair rail
1 x 6 x 10'	19 pieces	Decking to cover floor, stairs
1 x 4 x 10'	30 pieces	Roof slats
1 x 4 x 8'	7 pieces	Rafter cleats, shelf/seat braces, battens

Special Wood Products
(Nominal Dimensions)

2 x 2 x 8' Channel	8 pieces	Lattice frames
2 x 4 x 8' Channel	3 pieces	Lattice frames
4' x 8' Lattice	2 sheets	

Hardware

6d Common nails (1#)
8d Common nails (3#)
10d Common nails (1#)
16d Common nails (3#)
12d Square-shanked spiral nails (5#)
Joist hangers (16)
½" x 4" Lag screws (24)
¼" x 3½" Lag screws (8)
¼" x 2" Lag screws (8)

Note: All hardware must be galvanized or rustproof.

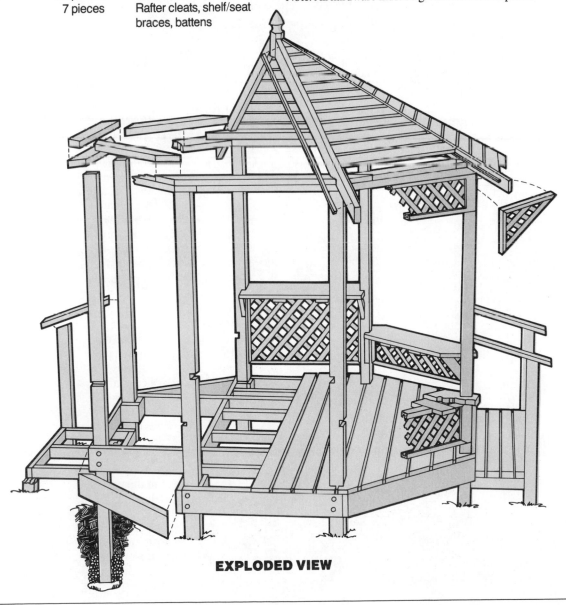

EXPLODED VIEW

TECHNIQUES

Case Construction

It's strong; it's light; and it lets the wood breathe.

Have you ever had the chance to inspect a piece of medieval furniture close up? The few of us who have are surprised by how clumsy and heavy it is. And if you go looking for a medieval piece to inspect, you'll also be surprised by just how few pieces of it there are left to inspect. For all the wood that medieval cabinetmakers used, their furniture didn't last very long.

There's a good reason for all of this. First of all, there weren't any medieval cabinetmakers. Nor were there any

carpenters. Back then, if you worked with wood, you were called a joiner. Joiners built houses during warm weather, and furniture when it was too cold or wet to work out of doors. They used the same lumber — and the same joinery — for both endeavors. Their furniture was clumsy and heavy because even the scraps left over from a medieval house-building job were pretty good-sized slabs of wood. It was short-lived because the wood was often poorly cured or the joinery was inappropriate.

As the science of woodworking advanced, and joiners began to specialize as either carpenters or cabinetmakers, furniture became better made. By the late Renaissance (an era that cabinetmakers refer to as the Jacobean Period), furniture making had advanced far beyond the crude joiner's tools and timber-frame joints of the Middle Ages. Cabinetmakers were turning out case pieces — chests and desks made from wooden frames. Instead of pegging together large slabs, as a joiner might have done, the cabinetmakers began to build lighter frames and peg those together. In these frames, they mounted thin panels. The pieces were still made of wood, but this type of construction — called case construction — required much less wood, by volume.

Consequently, Jacobean furniture was lighter and more delicate than its medieval predecessors. The frame-and-panel joinery also provided a way for the wood to 'breathe' — expand and contract with changes in temperature and humidity — so the pieces were less likely to warp, split, or pop their joints.

It is impossible to underestimate the importance of this development on cabinetmaking science. Case construction made possible many of the furniture forms we take for granted today — chests of drawers, desks with drawers, wardrobes, china cabinets, sideboards, hutches, kitchen cabinets, and wall systems, just to name a few.

Why It Works

To understand this importance, you first need to know why case construction is a better way to put together large pieces of wooden furniture than any other way cabinetmakers have developed so far. The reason is ridiculously simple: First of all, wood breathes, as we mentioned before. And case construction lets it.

Wood is made up of long, thin cells bound together with a cellulose glue. Except in 'figured' wood (burls, knots, bird's-eyes, etc.), these cells are all oriented in the same direction. This is what determines the grain. These cells were once filled with water, but by the time you buy the wood at a lumberyard, they are pretty well dried out. However, they will still collect and hold water, if given the chance.

These cells continue to breathe, as long as the wood is exposed to air. The surrounding air — and with it, any humidity in the air, passes in and out of the cells. The higher the humidity, the more water the cells collect, and they begin to swell. However, they don't swell evenly. These are long, skinny cells, remember? They grow fatter much easier than they grow longer. Therefore, when wood breathes, it expands and contracts across the grain a good deal more than with the grain — at least ten times more, for most species of wood.

How much will an average board expand and contract across the grain? This depends not only on the species, but also on the climate and the way you finish the wood. However, most experienced woodworkers expect that wood will move up to ¼″ across the grain for every 12″ of width. (See Figure 1.) Therefore, an 18″ wide board could expand to 18⅜″ on a hot, humid day. A 36″ wide board could expand to 36¾″.

You can see how this expansion and contraction could present quite a problem if you were building a large piece of furniture. Even a slight movement of the wood could be enough to warp the piece so that the doors or drawers would stick. Repeated movement — such as the wood expanding and contracting with the changes in seasons — will eventually pop the glue joints.

Consider this problem: You're building a large wooden box — sides, ends, and a bottom. You can figure out easily enough how to join the sides and the ends so that the grain all runs in the same direction, and all four boards will breathe in unison. (See Figure 2.) But how do you attach the bottom? If you attach it one way, the grain of the bottom will be perpendicular to the ends. If you attach it the other way, the grain will be perpendicular to the sides. (See Figure 3.) Either way,

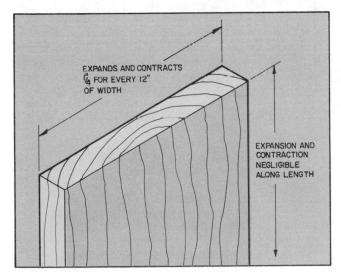

Figure 1. Wood expands and contracts *across* the grain ten times more than it does *with* the grain. On the average a board will swell or shrink up to ¼″ for every 12″ of width.

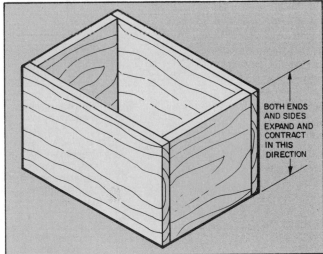

Figure 2. You can easily join the four sides of a box so that both sides and both ends breathe in the same direction.

the bottom will strain against two of the other boards, and the box will be unstable.

Since you know something about joinery, you probably already know the answer: Cut a groove near the bottom edge of the sides and ends. Let the bottom 'float' in this groove. Don't glue it in the grooves, or otherwise restrict its movement. Cut it a little smaller than need be, to give it room to expand and contract.

This is the essence of frame-and-panel joinery, and the foundation of case construction. The sides and ends of your box become a 'frame', and the bottom becomes a 'panel'. The frame parts are glued together or somehow permanently joined; the panel is left free in the grooves. All the parts can breathe without straining against any other part.

Letting the Wood Breathe

The fundamental rule in case construction, then, is not to restrict the movement of the wood; join it together in such a way that all the parts can breathe freely. The frame-and-panel joint is but one way of accomplishing this; there are many other methods. Here are a few that you've probably used at one time or another:

The French Dovetail — The french dovetail is actually a dovetail tenon that rides in a dovetail groove. (See Figure 4.) The tenon is not glued in place, so that both parts — the part with the tenon and the part with the groove — can breathe independently.

The Mortise — A mortise is no more than a dado or a groove, blind at both ends. If the grain of the board with the mortise runs contrary to the board that fits in the mortise, you can let the second board 'float' in the mortise. (See Figure 5.) To make the joint more rigid, you may want to cut a tenon in the end of the board that fits in the mortise, or peg the board in the mortise. If you peg the board, don't peg it in more than one location. Two or more pegs will restrict its movement.

The Clip — A clip is a small piece of wood or metal that joins two boards. One end of the clip is screwed to the first board, and the other rides in a groove in the second. (See Figure 6.) In this way, both boards can expand and contract without stressing the other. Clips are often used to join tops to case assemblies.

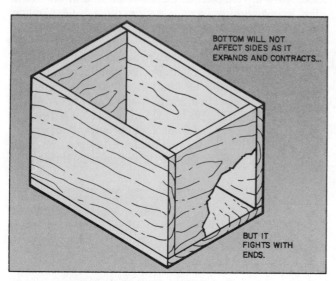

BOTTOM WILL NOT AFFECT SIDES AS IT EXPANDS AND CONTRACTS...

BUT IT FIGHTS WITH ENDS.

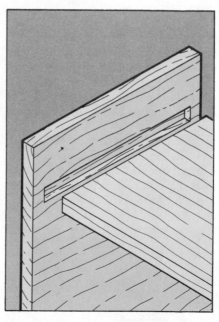

Figure 5. A *mortise* is a double-blind groove or dado. Let a second board float in this joint, so that it can expand and contract.

Figure 6. One end of a *clip* is screwed to a board, and the other end rides in a groove cut in a second board. This lets both boards breathe independently.

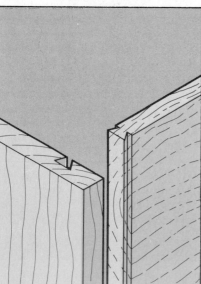

Figure 3. However, when you try to attach the bottom, the grain will either fight with the ends or the sides. Unless you let the bottom 'float' in a groove, there's no way that you can attach the bottom so that its movement won't eventually pop the joints of the box.

Figure 4. A *french dovetail* consists of a dovetail tenon that slides in a dovetail slot.

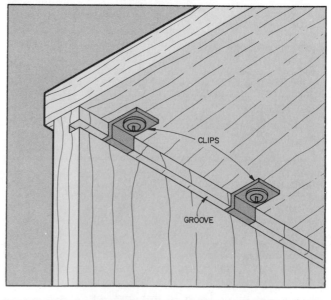

CLIPS

GROOVE

The Elongated Screw Hole — If you need to screw together two boards with the grains opposed, drill the pilot holes in the first board slightly larger than needed, then elongate the holes with a rasp. (The holes should be elongated in the direction that you expect the second board to expand and contract.) Join the boards together with round-head screws and washers. (See Figure 7.) The elongated holes make it possible for both boards to move slightly.

Figure 7. An *elongated screw hole* will also let two boards move independently. The hole should be elongated in the same direction as the movement.

When and where you use these joints and devices depends entirely on the circumstances and the location of the joint. You probably don't want to use cleats or screws on parts of a project that will be visible; these things are better suited for the inside of a case. You won't want to use mortises if the mortised board could possibly pull away from the other; use french dovetails instead. Each joint will require some thought before you decide what joinery to use. Whatever you decide on, make sure that all the boards in your project can breathe properly.

A Typical Case Construction

While the rule is simply, "Let the wood breathe", the application may be quite complex. A typical case construction has dozens of parts and twice as many joints. All of these joints must work together to let each part breathe properly *without* the parts falling apart. It's not always an easy task, but it can be done. Consider Tom Stender's "Chest of Drawers" in the **Projects** section of this book. (See Figure 8.)

The "Chest of Drawers" is a classic case construction. The sides, top, and back are solid panels, while the drawers are supported on web frames. The sides and the top are the only major parts whose grain is oriented so as to breathe in unison. All the other parts would fight with each other, were it not for Tom's careful case joinery.

Figure 8. This "Chest of Drawers" is a classic example of case construction.

Let's start with the web frames. Like most frames, they consist of rails (running the width of the chest) and stiles (running the depth). These rails and stiles are joined by tongue-and-groove joints. (See Figure 9.) At first glance, you might think that this joinery is in direct opposition to the rule — the grain of the stiles runs perpendicular to the grain of the rails. However, both the rails and stiles are no more than 3″ wide. The movement of these boards across the grain will be 1/16″ or less. (Tom has further reduced the possibility of movement by applying a finish to the inside parts of the cabinets.) Common glues — aliphatic resin (yellow) glue, polyvinyl (white) glue, and hide glue — all have a certain amount of 'give', even after they've dried. They will stand up to small movements for many, many years.

In general, you don't need to employ special joinery to let the wood breathe, if the parts are less than 3″ across the grain. You will see many examples in woodworking of frames that are joined with dowels, splines, screws, all sorts of joints and devices that don't allow for the movement of the wood. Woodworkers can get away with this if the parts are not very wide. And in Tom's design, there is a 'backup', of sorts. Even if the tongue-and-groove joints do eventually pop, they still won't fall apart because of the way the web frames are joined to the sides.

The dust shields inside the web frames are another story. These panels are wide enough that they need room to move. They rest in grooves, running around the inside edges of the web frame rails and stiles. They are not glued in place; they are allowed to 'float' free.

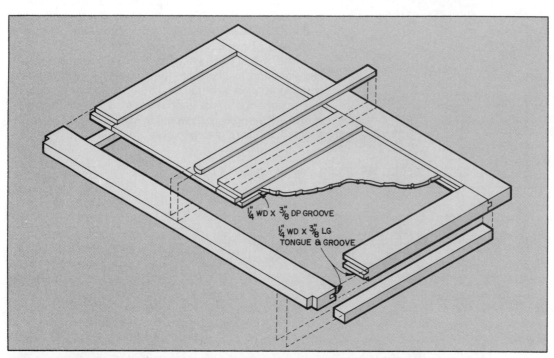

Figure 9. The web frames are joined with tongue-and-groove joints. The rails and stiles are glued together, even though their grain directions are opposed. A woodworker can get away with this, because the movement of a narrow board is small.

¼″ WD X ⅜″ DP GROOVE

¼″ WD X ⅜″ LG TONGUE & GROOVE

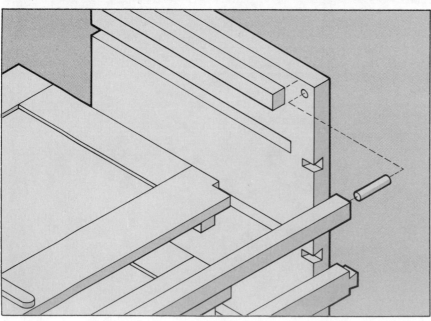

Figure 10. The front corners of the web frames are attached to the front edge of the sides with french dovetails. This is the only spot where the frames are glued in place. The frames lay in the dadoes along the sides, but they are not glued, so the sides are free to expand and contract.

Where the web frames join the sides, the grain of the stiles runs perpendicular to that of the sides. The sides, like the dust shields, are wide enough that they will move considerably with changes in temperature and humidity. If they were glued or screwed to the web frames, they would probably warp or cup, distorting the case. Within a short time, the drawers would begin to stick. To prevent this, Tom has attached the web frames to the sides only at the *front* of the case, using french dovetails. (See Figure 10.) The portions of the web frames behind the dovetails simply lay in dadoes; they are not glued or screwed to the sides.

So what keeps the sides from spreading apart at the back of the case? Just that: The back of the case. Most novice woodworkers think that the back of a case is not essential to the overall structure. They think of it as an afterthought; something to finish off the piece and help prevent dust and dirt from falling in the drawers. This is not true; the back helps to hold the sides together. (See Figure 11.) Most modern case pieces, such as this chest of drawers, have plywood backs. Plywood breathes very little, so the back can be one solid sheet, oriented in any direction. Before the days of plywood, cabinetmakers nailed thin slats of solid wood across the back, leaving tiny gaps between the slats so that each slat could expand and contract.

To complete the case, Tom attached the top across the two sides. He could have simply glued and screwed the top to the sides, since the grain of all three parts is oriented in the same direction. But he didn't want any screws — or even screw plugs — to mar the surface of the wood on the outside of the chest. So he assembled the parts with cleats and screws, on the inside of the case. (See Figure 12.) The 'cleat' frame is put together much like the web frame, with tongue-and-groove joints. And it presents the same problems — the stiles run perpendicular to the grain direction of the top. Tom's solution was to make elongated screw holes in the cleats, then assemble the top to the case with roundhead screws and washers.

Parting Thoughts

The sort of thinking that Tom Stender put into his "Chest of Drawers" is essential to good, solid case construction. Every time you join two pieces of wood, there are several questions you need to ask yourself:

Which way is the wood grain oriented?

What are the dimensions of the parts across the grain?

How much is the wood likely to move?

How will one part move in relation to the other?

Is the movement small enough that the parts can be solidly attached, or do there need to be accommodations for movement?

What sort of joint or device will best accommodate the movement?

How will this joinery affect the overall structure and strength of the completed project?

That's quite a bit to think about, perhaps. But wood is a living, breathing material; and as such it demands special considerations. As the first joiners-turned-cabinetmakers found long ago, only by treating this material with the respect and consideration it demands can you create something of lasting utility and beauty.

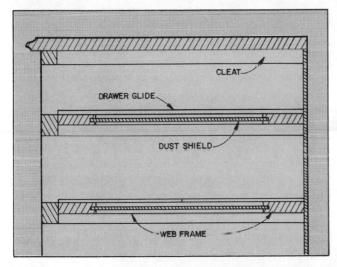

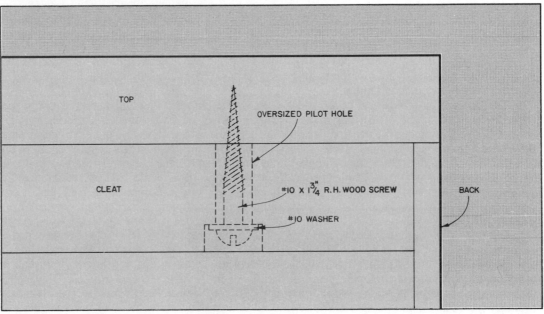

Figure 11. The back keeps the sides from spreading apart at the back of the case. Note that the web frames don't quite touch the back. This leaves room for the sides to breathe.

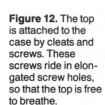

Figure 12. The top is attached to the case by cleats and screws. These screws ride in elongated screw holes, so that the top is free to breathe.

Text by John Mitchell

Working with Outdoor Lumber

Before you start to work with pressure-treated lumber, there are some important things you should know.

In any outdoor building project, such as the "Sunshade Gazebo" in the **Projects** section, the wood suffers from constant exposure to the elements. To prolong the life of the project, you will want to use types of wood that weather well — redwood, cedar, cypress, or 'pressure-treated' lumber, often referred to as 'outdoor' lumber.

The first three — redwood, cedar, and cypress — are unprocessed woods whose own oils make them naturally resistant to water, insects, fungus, and decay. The ability of these woods to survive the outdoors is legendary. On the east coast, in the early nineteenth century, shingle-makers used to 'mine' the bogs and swamps for fallen cedars. Even though some of these trees had been submerged for hundreds of years, they were still sound enough to be sawn and split into shingles.

Unfortunately, naturally decay-resistant woods have become quite expensive. A sunshade gazebo made from redwood will cost you two to four times what it would cost to build the same project from ordinary spruce and fir. However, there is an inexpensive alternative — outdoor lumber. This is ordinary spruce and fir lumber that has been 'cooked' at high

pressures in chemical preservatives so that the chemicals penetrate deep into the wood. This treatment makes the lumber every bit as decay-resistant as the natural alternatives.

It also makes the lumber potentially harmful, if not handled correctly. The chemicals used to treat outdoor lumber can be poisonous to plants, pets, and people. If you're going to work with outdoor lumber, it behooves you to know something about it — and its dangers — so that you can avoid any problems.

How Pressure-Treatments Work

Wood deteriorates in the outdoors for two reasons — fungal decay or insect attack. In either case, this deterioration requires that certain conditions exist before it can proceed. Both fungus and insects require sufficient oxygen, moisture, and food to do their work. The wood itself serves as the food; oxygen is always present in the air surrounding the wood; and the outdoors gets awfully wet from time to time.

The chemicals used to treat outdoor lumber prevent fungal decay and insect damage by poisoning the food source. As a result, treated lumber can maintain its integrity for many years. Estimates of the life of pressure-treated wood range from 40 up to 100 years, depending on the chemical, the type of wood, and how the wood will be used.

When you poison a board, it's important to poison the *entire* board, inside and out. This is why the lumber is pressure-treated. You can paint, stain, or even soak ordinary lumber in the same chemicals, but not get the same results. The protection will only extend a short distance into the surface of the wood. Prior to the widespread availability of pressure-treated lumber, some companies would 'incise' the lumber before treating it, in an attempt to make the wood more decay-resistant. They ran the stock between sharp-toothed rollers to separate the wood fibers and allow the preservative to penetrate more deeply. But these incisions still did not allow the preservative to soak in much beyond the depth of the cuts.

Commercial pressure-treating distributes the preservative throughout the wood. Treating mills typically dry the wood to about 20% moisture content, then stack the lumber in a huge 'retort'. After sealing the retort, they pump all the air out, creating a vacuum and extracting most of the remaining moisture.

Once the moisture falls to the desired level, the retort is flooded with preservative and pressurized to at least 175 pounds per inch. This pressure is kept up for hours, driving the preservative into every wood cell. After a prescribed time, the retort is drained and all the air pumped out, creating a second vacuum to remove any excess preservative or moisture. Finally, the wood is removed from the retort and stacked in the open air to complete the drying process.

Types of Outdoor Lumber

There are three types of pressure-treated lumber widely available today, and these are classified according to the chemicals they have been treated with: Creosote; Pentachlorophenol, and Chromated Copper Arsenate (CCA). Of these, the most common is CCA. The stacks of green lumber you see at many building supply centers are treated with chromated copper arsenate.

Creosote-treated lumber — Creosote, a coal tar distillate, is the oldest of the wood preservatives in use today. It is most commonly used in utility poles, railroad ties, and some landscape timbers. The creosote is applied under pressure with considerable heat to make the solution thin enough to fully penetrate the wood.

Creosoted lumber can be oily or dry, depending on the degree of treatment, and they all emit a strong odor. They cannot be painted, because neither oil or latex paint will bond well to a creosote-impregnated surface. While creosote is a cheap and effective preservative, it does not become chemically fixed in the wood. The preservative eventually 'leeches' out of the wood, especially during warm weather. This makes the wood harmful to plants. (You may have noticed the absence of plant life around the bases of utility poles. This is because the creosote has leeched out into the ground and killed the vegetation.) *Newly* creosoted timbers should not be used for gardens; although old railroad ties that have lost most of their preservative can be used without harming most flowers and shrubs. (See Figure 1.) Unfortunately, once the preservative has leeched out, the wood is once again vulnerable to decay.

Creosote can also be harmful to pets and people. The sticky residue that accumulates on your hands and arms as you work with the treated lumber can cause skin irritation. The fumes are poisonous. I remember as a boy watching my father brush a creosote solution on a wooden garage floor and being driven out of the building by overpowering fumes. In 1984, the Environmental Protection Agency (EPA) linked creosote with cancer.

Some of the dangers of creosote can be minimized by sealing the lumber with urethane, epoxy, or shellac. This helps to prevent the leeching. However, this adds a good deal more work and expense to your project, and there's no guarantee that the creosote won't eventually leech out anyway. Because the danger cannot be entirely eliminated, creosoted wood should never be used where it will come in contact with people, pets, food (both animal and human), garden plants, or even bees.

All these dangers notwithstanding, creosoted wood has enjoyed — and continues to enjoy — a busy career in appropriate applications such as piers, bridges, poles, ties, and landscape timbers.

Pentachlorophenol-treated lumber — Some outdoor lumber is treated with an EPA-registered pesticide containing the chemical pentachlorophenol, commonly referred to as 'penta'. Different forms of penta can be either water or oil soluble. Both forms are toxic (penta is chemically similar to the infamous 'Agent Orange' used in Vietnam), and neither forms bond permanently in the wood. This gives penta-treated lumber some of the same problems as lumber that has been treated with creosote.

The degree of protection that penta provides diminishes as the chemical leeches out of the wood. This leeching can be prevented with the application of urethane, shellac, or latex epoxy, but — as I mentioned before — this is extra work that will just have to be done all over again when the sealer begins to deteriorate. The only advantages that penta offers over creosote are that it is not as messy to work with, and it can be painted after it has set for some time in the weather.

Its toxicity and tendency to leech out of the wood make it dangerous to use where the wood might come in contact with people (particularly bare skin), animals, or food. It's best suited for remote structures where it will pose no serious environmental threat. Today's utility poles are generally treated with penta.

Chromated Copper Arsenate-treated lumber — The newest development in pressure-treated lumber is Chromated Copper Arsenate, or CCA. This is another EPA-registered pesticide, containing inorganic arsenic. CCA is water-soluble, so the wood doesn't have a greasy or sticky feel. There are no fumes, so it can be used for interior projects, if necessary. It also bonds permanently with the wood, and any leeching is negligible. And it can be painted. These factors make it the best choice for most homeowner outdoor projects.

Figure 1. Railroad ties and creosote-treated lumber should be used for garden landscaping only *after* it's weathered for many years. Newly creosoted timbers may be harmful to plants.

Even though CCA itself is toxic, when it's bonded in the wood, it's relatively harmless. Since it does not leech out, there will be little CCA residue on the surface of the wood or in the surrounding soil that could come in contact with people, pets, or plants. Some builders recommend that you hose down a structure built with CCA-treated wood or let it sit through several rainstorms before letting children and pets use it. This may be a wise precaution, since sawing the lumber may expose some CCA-saturated wood where the chemical hasn't completely bonded. But once the structure has been thoroughly 'washed', it's relatively safe. Nevertheless, CCA-treated lumber should never be used where it might come in contact with food or drinking water.

Treatment plants use CCA solutions of different strengths, depending on the intended end use of the lumber. The most common strength is .40 pounds of CCA per cubic foot of wood, after the pressure-treating is completed. (This number is referred to as the 'retention' figure.) Most manu-

facturers have found that a retention of .40 pounds provides an acceptable balance between the expected life of the wood and the cost of the chemical treatment.

Fence posts, small structural timbers (4 x 4's), landscape timbers — wood that will come in direct contact with the ground — is generally rated at .40 pounds. Most building supply stores will only carry .40-rated outdoor lumber. However, decking and timbers that don't touch the ground may not need quite so high a rating. If you can get lower-rated stock, you can save some money. If you're using larger timbers than 4 x 4's as structural members, you may need to put out the extra expense for a higher rating. Consult the chart included here to be sure of exactly what you need.

> **Tip ◆** The American Wood Preservers Bureau (AWPB) has a rating system that many manufacturers stamp on each board. LP-2 means the wood is rated at .25 pounds, and should *not* be used for ground contact. LP-22 signifies a rating of .40 pounds, and the wood may be used for ground contact. (See Figure 2.)

Uses of CCA-Treated Lumber

Retention Level	General Use	Specific Uses
.25	Above ground uses	Decking boards Fence boards Plates Sills Seating planks Railings Joists Headers Furring strips
.40	Soil or fresh water contact (non-structural)	Posts (round & square) Small timbers (4 x 4's) Landscape timbers Retaining walls Boardwalks Grape stakes Greenhouses
.60	Soil or fresh water contact (structural)	Foundations (wood) Building poles Decking/framing lumber Dock planks subject to salt water splash Bridge timbers
.80	Piles — Soil or fresh water contact (structural)	Piles Foundation piles, entirely buried
2.5	Salt water contact	Piling Timbers Framing lumber Bulkheads Retaining walls

Courtesy Osmose Wood Preserving Company

As I mentioned before, one of the big advantages of CCA-treated lumber is that it can be painted. However, unless the stock has been kiln-dried (which is unusual), the lumber should be allowed to air-dry for two to six months after you purchase it. This will help to make certain that most of the water is evaporated out and the paint will bond properly with the surface of the wood.

One additional note on CCA-treated lumber: When CCA first appeared, the chemical solutions contained impurities such as sulfate and sodium. These are called 'salt' solutions, and they would precipitate out of the wood to form a whitish or greenish-gray residue on the surface. This residue contained high levels of arsenic and would quickly corrode nails and fasteners.

Today, most manufacturers use a different type of CCA solution, called an 'oxide' solution. This produces clean, dry, well-preserved lumber, relatively free of any arsenic-tainted residue. You should not have any problem with lumber treated with this type of CCA. However, you should be on the lookout — don't purchase lumber that has a residue on the surface.

Precautions

Even though all pressure-treated lumber is *relatively* safe if used properly, it does contain potentially dangerous chemicals. Because of this, you should handle outdoor lumber with respect and take certain precautions when working with it.

Probably the most important precaution is to *never* burn the scraps in the open, in a fireplace, or in a stove. All types of outdoor lumber — creosote, penta, and CCA — produce poisonous gases when burned.

When you're done working, carefully clean up all the scraps and sawdust. Dispose of these in a local landfill or bury them yourself. (If your trash collection agency hauls off your garbage to an incinerator, *don't* put the scraps in the trash.) Be particularly careful to clean up if you've used this lumber on some project inside the home. You don't want the sawdust to find its way into your heating system — or your food.

If you're working with creosote- or penta-treated wood, avoid prolonged skin contact. Some builders also report getting an itchy rash when working with CCA-treated

Figure 2. Look for the AWBP stamp when buying CCA-treated lumber. A rating of LP-22 means the wood can be used in direct contact with the ground.

Figure 3. Use galvanized or stainless steel fasteners for outdoor building projects. If you don't, the metal may corrode and stain your project.

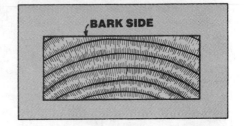

Figure 4. Nail decking lumber bark side up to help the wood shed water, and to keep it from cupping.

lumber, although this isn't common. To prevent any problems, wear 'impervious' (vinyl-coated) gloves, a long-sleeved shirt, and long pants when handling the stock. You may not be able to wear gloves all the time when you're working, but you can at least wear them when stacking or moving the lumber.

> **Tip ◆** Splinters from pressure-treated lumber will irritate more than the ordinary variety. Remove them as soon as possible.

Wear goggles and a respiration mask when sawing any type of treated lumber. This will help keep sawdust out of your eyes and lungs, where they can irritate sensitive membranes. All sawing should be done outdoors, so the dust in the air will blow away harmlessly.

Wash all exposed areas of your skin and hair before eating, drinking, or putting anything in your mouth. Launder the clothes you wore while working with pressure-treated lumber separately from other clothing.

Building Tips

When purchasing pressure-treated lumber, pay attention to what *species* of wood you're buying. East of the Mississippi, the predominant wood varieties used are Southern Yellow Pine, a good, hard conifer wood; and Red Pine, used mostly for fence posts and landscape timbers. West of the Big Muddy, Ponderosa Pine predominates. All three of these species are well suited for pressure-treating, and they have good structural integrity and dimensional stability.

Douglas Fir, Spruce, and White Pine, along with most common hardwoods, do not accept chemical preservatives very well. Douglas Fir will not accept chemicals even after incising. Consequently, you should avoid purchasing these species. As a rule, manufacturers will use the wood that is most cost effective for them to treat, and it just takes too much effort to get a good retention figure with anything other than Southern Yellow Pine, Red Pine, or Ponderosa Pine. So you won't often run into treated Douglas Fir. But it still behooves you to look.

> **Tip ◆** Don't buy anything labeled 'Southern Pine'. This is not Southern Yellow Pine, as the manufacturer would have you believe. It's just another name for White Pine.

When purchasing fasteners and hardware, look for hot-dipped, galvanized or stainless steel nails, screws, hinges, etc. These will resist corrosion, and they won't stain your project with rust streaks. (See Figure 3.) When nailing, drive nails at a slight angle through the top board into the receiving board.

Vary the angle back and forth. This will help 'hook' the lumber together, and lessen the chance of a board working loose. You may also want to use a nail set to avoid making hammer marks — 'smiles' — in the surface of the wood; and a drill to drill pilot holes to prevent narrow boards from splitting.

Nail the boards — especially decking or flooring boards — 'bark' side up. You can determine the bark side by looking at the end of a sawn board to see which way the annual rings curve. The bark side will always be above the crown of the rings. (See Figure 4.) By nailing the bark side up, the board will shed water better. This, in turn, helps inhibit the board's tendency to cup. And should some cupping occur, the board won't have raised edges that form 'toe-stubbers' and 'heel-catchers'.

While you're building, remember that the wood will still retain some moisture and will shrink after some months have passed. (In general, the wood may shrink about 1/8"-1/4" for every 6" of width.) Space your flooring and decking accordingly.

The original green color of most treated lumber will not remain forever, so don't fret if you dislike it. After six months of weathering, the green will begin to fade to a pleasant silver-grey color and remain that way. Some manufacturers use a CCA solution that's been tinted with a brown dye, to make the stock more visually pleasing. But this doesn't last either. Even these brown boards fade to silver-gray after a few months out in the weather. If you want some other color than gray, just wait a few months and paint or stain the wood to suit yourself.

Summing Up

Using pressure-treated lumber will prevent the ravages of insects and decay on your carefully planned, laboriously constructed outdoor project. However, to get the best results, you need to choose the materials that best suit the project; work with the materials as they are intended to be worked with; and, above all, follow a few simple precautions to keep you and your environment safe from the possible effects of toxic chemicals. If properly used, outdoor lumber will poison the bugs and the fungi — but nothing else.

Bending Wood in a Home Workshop

You don't need expensive equipment to bend wood, no matter how large the board — just the right technique.

A friend of mine — a fellow woodworker — and I were looking over a round pedestal table I had just finished. (The plans for this same table are in the **Projects** section of this book.) He traced the long curve of the aprons with his fingers. "Somewhere in this world," he said, jokingly, "there must be a tree farm where the foresters train the trees to grow in circles."

Actually, that's not such a farfetched thought. If you could afford to wait for twenty or thirty years, you could train a hardwood tree to grow in carefully planned patterns, then slice the lumber on a bandsaw. Unfortunately, most of us don't have the foresight — or the time. Instead, we have invented half a dozen ways to bend the wood *after* the tree has grown.

Large furniture companies have huge pressure chambers where the boards are bathed in either steam or ammonia. When the wood is removed from these chambers, it's as limp as a wet noodle. For the next 5-10 minutes, you can bend even the thickest, hardest boards into almost any shape you need.

'Pressure' bending is by far the easiest way to bend wood. Just let the wood cook for an hour or so, then slap it in a mold or tie it in knots. But it's dangerous — steam can scald and ammonia is poisonous. And it's expensive — high pressure chambers don't come cheap.

Most home woodworkers don't have the money, the shop space, or the training to own and safely use pressure bending equipment. Consequently, they avoid those projects that require bent wood. But there are several simple methods for bending wood in a home workshop that don't require special equipment or expertise. If you've been putting off a special project because it requires a few bent parts, you might try one of the techniques described here.

A Closer Look at the Wood

Before we discuss how to bend wood, it might be helpful if we all reviewed those properties of wood that allow it to be bent:

Living wood consists of long, slender cells, all oriented in the same direction. Some of these cells transport food (the phloem), others water (xylem). But all of them consist of the cell interior, filled with protoplasm, and the cell wall, which is made up of cellulose and some other non-living substances.

When the wood is cut and cured, the protoplasm dries up leaving the cellulose. This cellulose is a durable concoction of hydrogen, carbon, oxygen, and a few other trace elements thrown in to add some spice. Cellulose, left to its own devices, is springy and elastic. But when it's arranged in the honeycomb pattern of xylem and phloem, the cell walls reinforce each other like a steel truss on a bridge. Even though cellulose may be flexible, wood is rigid and hard.

If you want to bend a piece of wood without breaking it, there are three ways to do it:

◆ You can *reduce the thickness* of the wood. This has the same effect as removing spars from a bridge truss — the structure becomes weaker and more flexible.

◆ You can *heat* the wood. This softens the organic 'glue' between the cell walls so that they will slide over one another, allowing you to bend the wood. Going back to our bridge analogy, it's as if you removed a few strategic bolts from the truss so that you can rearrange the spars.

◆ You can *chemically treat* the wood to dissolve the bond between the cells. This accomplishes the same thing as heating the wood. Ammonia is the most commonly used solvent for this purpose.

Of these three methods, the only one that can't be performed in a home workshop is the last. Chemical bending requires pressure treatment so that you evenly disperse the chemical throughout the wood. As we've already discussed, this pressure equipment is expensive and dangerous.

However, there are several simple, safe techniques that use either heat or thinning out. By using one or a combination of these techniques, you can bend any size board.

Bending By Boiling

The easiest way to heat a board for bending is to boil it. (A large, oblong roast pan is ideal for this purpose.) Simply plunge the board in a bath of boiling water and leave it there for 30-45 minutes, depending on the thickness of the wood. (See Figure 1.)

Remove the wood with a pair of tongs and *quickly* place it in a mold. (See Figure 2.) Moving with all available speed, clamp the parts of the mold together, bending the wood. (See Figure 3.) It's important that you move as quickly as possible once you remove the wood from the boiling water bath. The wood will remain flexible only as long as it's hot — and it loses heat at an alarming rate.

There are two drawbacks to this technique: First of all, the size of board you can bend is limited by the size of the roast pan. And you have to let the wood dry in the mold for several weeks while the water evaporates. You may wonder why you can't simply bake the wood in your oven — most ovens are larger than roast pans and there's no water involved. Well, unfortunately baking dries the wood out and makes it too brittle to bend. You need the water to keep the wood fibers supple.

Figure 1. To heat the wood evenly, boil it. A roast pan makes a good boiler.

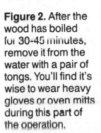

Figure 2. After the wood has boiled for 30-45 minutes, remove it from the water with a pair of tongs. You'll find it's wise to wear heavy gloves or oven mitts during this part of the operation.

Figure 3. When the boiled wood is in place, clamp the parts of the mold together. Do this quickly, before the wood cools.

Tip ◆ When you remove the wood from the mold after it has been sitting for several weeks, it will spring back slightly. Depending on the type of wood, it may lose 20%-30% of the bend. So it's wise to make the curves in your molds slightly more pronounced than you actually need.

Stovepipe Bending

If the boards you wish to bend are thin, like musical instrument stock, perhaps the easiest way to bend them is on a hot stovepipe — or a 'bending iron' that you can make. Of the two, the bending iron is the most convenient. You may not have a wood stove; and even if you do, you might not want to stoke it up on a hot day in August.

A bending iron is a round piece of pipe, 3″-4″ in diameter, brazed or welded to a flat sheet about the same size as a stove burner. (I use a copper pipe and sheet stock, because copper distributes the heat quickly and evenly.) This assembly clamps to your burner with two or more U-bolts, as shown in Figure 4.

Turn your stove burner on medium high heat to start with. Finding the proper heat setting will take some experimentation, but this is a good place to start. Wipe the area of the wood that you want to bend with a damp sponge, and hold it against the bending iron. (See Figure 4.) Push forward gently, as if you were trying to wrap the wood around the iron. Slowly roll the wood back and forth on the iron, so the area is heated evenly.

Eventually, you will feel the wood 'give' and begin to bend. As it bends, continue to roll it across the face of the iron, so that the bend is evenly distributed over the length of the board and doesn't occur in just one spot.

As you work, you must keep the wood damp and be careful not to get the wood so hot that it scorches. This takes some practice. At first it will seem that the water cools the wood down so that it never gets hot enough, and that if you don't let the wood burn slightly, it won't bend. But with a little

experimentation, you'll find the right combination of water and heat.

Getting the curve you're after also takes some experimentation. Keep a full-size drawing of the curve near the stove and compare the wood to it often. (See Figure 5.) The beauty of this technique is that, with a little patience, you can get *exactly* the curve you're after. If you bend the wood too far in one direction, simply heat the wood up again and take some of the bend out.

Bending by Lamination

If you plane a board down so that it's ⅛″ thick or less, you can bend it easily — but it won't *keep* the bend. Let it go and it will spring right back to its original shape. However, if you bend a second board with the first and laminate the two together, neither one of them will straighten after the glue is cured. The glue bond between the two holds the bend.

Bending in this manner takes quite a bit of pre-planning. First of all, you need to plane down a board and see if you can bend it far enough without breaking. If the board splinters, you may have to plane it down even further — then use more boards in the final lamination.

You'll also need to make a bending jig or a mold to keep the wood bent while the glue dries. If you're bending a long piece, a jig is easiest. Just insert pegs in a piece of particle board wherever you need them. (See Figure 6.) For small pieces, make a mold.

Once you've made the jig or mold, try a dry run before you actually laminate the wood. Cut all the strips, and clamp them together. Make sure that you have enough clamps or that your mold is properly dimensioned so that there are no

Figure 4. To use a bending iron, press the wood gently against the hot metal until it begins to 'give'. Be careful not to scorch the wood.

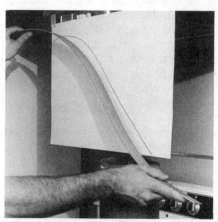

Figure 5. As you work, compare the wood you're bending to a full size drawing of the bend you want.

Figure 6. The first step in making a laminated bending is to make a bending jig. This can be nothing more than a few pegs in a sheet of plywood or particle board.

gaps between any of the strips. Once you're satisfied that you can bend all the strips and join them neatly, spread glue on the surfaces to be laminated. Then clamp them back in the jig or mold. (See Figure 7.) Clean off the excess glue with a wet rag.

> **Tip** ◆ Once you start spreading the glue, you'll need to work fast. Most wood glues begin to set up in fifteen minutes. After half an hour, you won't get a good bond. You may want to call in a few helpers once you get down to the actual lamination.

Let the glue cure for *at least* 24 hours before you remove the clamps. Then sand or plane all the strips of wood flush. The finished lamination will appear like a solid piece of bent wood.

The beauty of this technique is that you can glue up as large a piece as you need. And the finished lamination will be just as strong as a solid block of wood. In some cases, it may be stronger.

Kerf Bending

If you don't need the strength that lamination offers, you can bend large pieces of wood by sawing evenly spaced kerfs to thin out the wood at regular intervals. (See Figure 8.) This is the technique I used to bend the apron of the pedestal table. It allows you to bend the wood so that the *outside* appears to be a solid, curved board.

The only trick to this method is in figuring out how to space the kerfs. To do this, first figure out the radius on the bend. Let's say the radius is 5″. Put two marks, 5″ apart on a scrap board. Cut a single kerf at one mark. (If you're using ¾″ stock, make the kerf ⅝″ deep.) Clamp the board to your workbench at one end and lift the other end until either the kerf closes or the board begins to crack. Then measure the distance of the board off the workbench at the *second* mark. (See Figure 9.) If the distance is ¼″, space all your kerfs ¼″ apart.

If kerfing would weaken the board too much, you could try a variation of this method. Make one big kerf, or 'thin out' the board over the area you want to bend. Bend the wood and brace it so that it stays bent. Then carefully measure and cut a block to fill in the thinned out area behind the bend. (See Figure 10.) Glue this block in place to restore the strength of the board.

Combining Techniques

Depending on your project and your own needs, you can combine these methods, using two or more to get the effect you're after. For example, if you're bending a particularly tricky shape (like the side of a musical instrument), you might want to boil the boards and clamp them in a mold for a few weeks, then 'touch up' the bends on a hot stovepipe to get the precise shape you're after. You can also kerf two boards, then laminate the two kerfed surfaces together to get a single piece of bent wood with two good sides.

Whatever the type of project or the size of the piece needed, there's a simple way to bend the wood without the need for special skills or expensive equipment.

Figure 7. Glue the surfaces of the strips together in the jig. Use plenty of glue, and plenty of clamps — you don't want any gaps between the laminations.

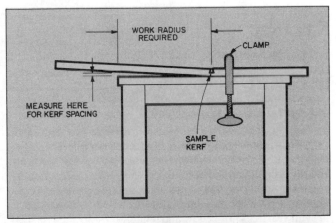

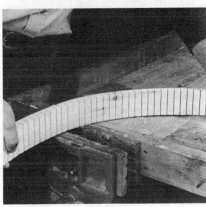

Figure 8. You can bend a thick board by cutting a series of kerfs in the side that won't show. These kerfs should be ¹⁄₁₆″-⅛″ shallower than the thickness of the board.

Figure 9. To find the proper spacing for a kerf, use the trick illustrated here.

Figure 10. To reinforce a board that's been thinned out and bent, carefully cut blocks to fill in behind the bent area.

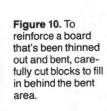

Jointer shavings magnified 25x.

Sawdust Collection and Control

Sawdust is something that woodworkers just have to live with — or is it?

"**B**rush off before you come in here," my better half calls. "You'll track sawdust everywhere."

I've been woodworking the better part of the morning, and my hair and clothes are loaded with sawdust. I'm already tracking wood dust and chips all across the great outdoors. The path between my shop and the wood storage shed is strewn with flecks of yellow and white. So I stop and brush off before I enter the house for lunch.

A cloud of white dust rises in the air as I flagellate myself with a whisk broom that my wife has put by the back door for just this purpose. Some of the sawdust falls in my face, and I begin to sneeze. Freelance — my collie — sniffs my pants cuffs and he sneezes.

When I'm thoroughly whisked, I go into the kitchen. As I sit down at the table, sawdust pours from my pockets onto the floor. Some of the chips left in my hair fall into the soup. My wife gives me a look that would cut a 2 x 4. "Didn't you hear me ask you to brush off?" she says acidly.

Does that sound like a familiar scene? Too many woodworkers — myself included — are plagued with sawdust problems. And these problems are rarely confined to the shop; the dust and wood chips seem to spread everywhere. After a while, you begin to doubt that there's anything you can do about the dust. Well, I've found there are many things you can do — but it takes more than a whisk broom.

Shopsmith has designed a sawdust collection system for their entire system, with the exception of the drilling, boring, and lathe modes for their multi-purpose tools. These collectors are 80%-95% efficient, depending on the tool or accessory you're using. With a little extra effort, you can collect most of the sawdust before it ever hits the floor while you're sawing, sanding, joining, planing, dadoing, shaping, routing, and molding.

The Danger of Sawdust

Before we talk about how to control sawdust, let's discuss the dangers that it presents to the woodworker — let's get to know the enemy. You'll find it's not just a simple housekeeping problem.

Sawdust and Health — Early in the 1980's, the Vermont Lung Association (a national research center for lung diseases) conducted a survey among professional woodworkers to determine the effects of sawdust on respiratory health. The results of that survey were not encouraging; researchers concluded that wood dust was a **possible** health hazard. The prevalence of "low pulmonary flow rates" (impaired breathing) among woodworkers exposed to medium amounts of dust were *two* to *four* times higher than among persons who were not exposed.

The part-time or 'hobby' woodworker does not incur the same health risk as a professional, perhaps, but there is still cause for concern. Many home shops are small and poorly ventilated. The air becomes saturated with sawdust quickly. In a few short hours, a part-time woodworker can inhale more dust than he would working all day in a larger shop. Dust masks and increased ventilation become extremely important under these circumstances.

Some woodworkers have medical problems that are aggravated by sawdust — emphysema, asthma, and allergic reactions. Furthermore, many types of sawdust are classified as *toxic* and may cause short-term but nonetheless dangerous reactions. Reactions to toxic wood dust generally fall into two categories — respiratory ailments and skin/eye allergies. Respiratory problems include bronchial disorders, asthma, rhinitis, and mucosal irritations. Skin and eye problems include dermatitis, conjunctivitis, itching, and rashes. Refer to the chart in this chapter to determine if a wood is toxic and what health problems it may cause.

Sawdust and Tools — It probably comes as no surprise to you that sawdust does your body no good. What may surprise you is that it does your tools no good either. Wood dust is particularly harmful to power tools.

Very fine sawdust can collect between an arbor and an oil-impregnated bushing, or even penetrate the seal of a 'permanently lubricated' bearing. The sawdust will absorb the lubrication like a sponge, cause the bushing or bearing to wear prematurely. Or the dust will mix with lubricating oil or grease, forming a thick, black goo that just 'gums up the works' and keeps the tool from operating smoothly. (See Figure 1.)

> **Tip** ◆ You can prevent some of these problems by using the *minimum* amount of lubrication recommended by Shopsmith — usually just one or two drops. Or use graphite powder instead of oil. (See Figure 2.) Keep the metal surfaces of the tool waxed *and* buffed so the dust won't stick to the tool and begin to accumulate.

Sawdust may also find its way into switches, motors, and other electrical parts of your tools, preventing a good connection. Without good current flow, the tools may overheat, fail to develop full power — or refuse to run at all.

Sawdust and Accuracy — As sawdust accumulates on your tools or workpieces, it can affect the quality of your work. If you use the bandsaw or jigsaw, you know that you must constantly remove sawdust in order to accurately follow the cutline on the workpiece. Wood chips build up between the work and the fence on the table saw and shaper, so the stock won't line up properly with the blade or cutter.

Sawdust and Safety — Finally, sawdust presents a threatening safety problem. If you allow it to accumulate underfoot, you might slip on the dust and wood chips into a running power tool. A spark from a power tool could ignite a pile of sawdust, starting a fire.

Picking a Shop Vacuum

I could spend a few paragraphs warning you about sweeping up your shop and encouraging you to wear a dust mask, but you've heard it all before. Masks and good housekeeping are important; they protect you against the many dangers of

Figure 1. If you over-lubricate your power tools, the sawdust will mix with the oil or grease, making a gummy black goo. This goo may prevent moving parts from operating properly.

Figure 2. Use graphite to lubricate sawdust-prone trouble spots. The threaded rods on the planer attract sawdust like a magnet. The graphite helps prevent that.

sawdust, but they fail to *control* the danger. To nip the problem in the bud, you need a good shop vacuum.

Most novice woodworkers think of a shop vacuum as nothing more than an automated broom. But this is only *one* of its many uses — and certainly not the most important use. Properly employed, a shop vac can be made to pick up sawdust *as you work* so that the level of wood dust in the air and on the floor never reaches dangerous proportions.

But not every good shop vac is engineered to do a good job of sawdust control. Small, underpowered units won't be much help, especially with the larger Shopsmith system of power tools. When you pick a shop vac, look for these features:

High Volume — The vacuum should draw at least 160 cubic feet of air per minute (CFM). Units rated at 80-90 CFM are not adequate.

Static Pressure — Volume isn't everything; you also need power. In a shop vacuum, static pressure (SP) is a good measure of the power of the unit. Look for a vacuum that draws 80 inches of water or better. Smaller units, with 10″ to 40″ SP, just won't pick up the sawdust as it falls.

Hose Diameter — Your vacuum should accept both 1¼″ and 2½″ hoses. Large (2½″) hoses are fine for general pick-up work, but there will be many times when you'll need to increase the air velocity in order to capture the dust or blow it away. The best way to increase the air velocity is to reduce the diameter of the hose. Also, there may be times when you want to pick up dust from more than one location on a tool. At these times, you'll find that two small hoses work better than two large ones.

Holding Capacity — You would be surprised to know just how many gallons of sawdust a jointer or a planer can generate in a very short time. A small vacuum, with less than 10 gallons holding capacity, might allow you to work for less than 30 minutes before you have to empty it. Get something with a capacity of 20 gallons or better.

The Shopsmith system includes two shop vacs that have all of these features. For smaller shops and weekend woodworkers, there's the 'Shopmate' dust collection system. This is a wet/dry vacuum with a 20-gallon tank and an assortment of both 1¼″ and 2½″ hoses. If you need a larger system, Shopsmith has recently developed a professional dust collector, the DC3300. This roll-around unit has a 30-gallon capacity and moves a good deal more air than smaller shop vacs. You can, in fact, collect sawdust from two or three separate tools *at the same time.* (See Figure 3.)

Sawdust Pick-Ups

Once you have an adequate shop vacuum or dust collector for your system, you can suck up 80%-95% of the sawdust you make *before* it ever reaches the floor — or your lungs. But in order to do this, you need to use the individual 'pick-ups' that Shopsmith has developed for each of their power tools and accessories.

These pick-ups are nothing more than specially-configured vacuum heads. Some of the tools in the Shopsmith system, such as the table saw and the belt sander, come with these vacuum heads built into the tool housing or guard. To collect sawdust as you work, just insert the vacuum hose in the proper port. Then turn on the power tool *and* the vacuum at the same time. (See Figures 4 and 5.) The vacuum will suck up the dust and chips as you work at the tool.

For other tools and accessories, you either have to install the dust pick-up (such as the bandsaw pick-up) or remember to use them when you're setting up the tools (such as the

shaper pick-up.) Here's a brief review of the available pick-ups:

Disc Sander/Dado/Molder Pick-Up — Sanders don't produce the *most* sawdust of any tool in your shop, but they produce the *finest* dust — and the most airborne particles. The lower sawguard is designed so that it will serve as a guard *and* a pick-up for a number of Shopsmith tools and accessories that attach to the arbor. After you mount the sanding disc and lower guard to the arbor, hook up a vacuum hose, just like you would if you were sawing. (See Figure 6.) This same pick-up also works for the molding head and the dado cutters.

Bandsaw Pick-Up — A bandsaw also generates an enormous amount of fine dust. Shopsmith has found that you can vacuum this dust right off the saw blade as it leaves the work and passes under the table. To attach the pick-up, cut a small hole in the plastic bandsaw cover, just under the table. Drill a few holes, and bolt the pick-up to the cover. Insert a vacuum hose in the pick-up, and you're in business. (See Figure 7.)

Router/Shaper Pick-Up — Both the Shopsmith shaper and router accessories use the same pick-up. This fits under the table, and catches the chips as they fall down through the

Figure 5. The rear housing on the belt sander has a port so that you can vacuum up the sawdust as you work.

Figure 3. The new DC3300 will collect sawdust from up to three tools at a time.

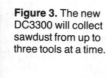

Figure 4. The lower sawguard on the Shopsmith Mark V and Model 510 incorporates a sawdust chute so that you can collect the waste as you work.

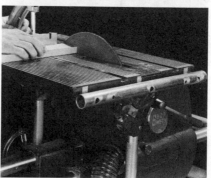

Figure 6. The same lower guard that you use to collect sawdust while you're sawing can also be used while you're disc sanding, molding, and dadoing.

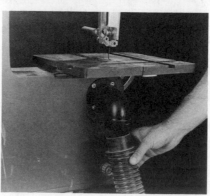

Figure 7. This bandsaw pick-up was attached by cutting a hole in the bandsaw cover, just under the table.

round hole in the table insert. Then they're whisked away by the vacuum. (See Figure 8.)

Jointer Pick-Up — The Shopsmith jointer pick-up fastens to the bottom of the jointer, and doubles as a safety guard. The chips fall down through the opening in the bottom of the jointer, then are channeled into the vacuum pick-up. (See Figure 9.) The pick-up is so designed that you don't absolutely have to use a vacuum with it. Just put a small waste can nearby and most of the chips will fall into the can. However, it works much better with the vacuum attached.

Planer Pick-Up — Of all the tools in the system, the Shopsmith planer probably generates the most sawdust. To help contain the mess, you can purchase a pick-up that fits under the outfeed housing. (See Figure 10.) Because the pick-up is positioned so close to the knives, it's extremely efficient. If you use it with a reasonably powerful vacuum, less than 5% of the chips will escape.

Improvising Your Own Pick-Ups

Shopsmith doesn't make pick-ups for every tool and accessory in its system — yet. On tools like the drill press and the lathe, a pick-up might interfere with the safe operation of the tool. However, you may be able to improvise a sawdust

Figure 8. Both the shaper and the router accessories use the same pick-up. The pick-up bolts under the worktable.

Figure 9. The jointer pick-up also serves as a safety guard. It will work with or without a vacuum attached — but it's better with.

Figure 10. The planer pick-up fits under the outfeed housing, and the vacuum port comes up through the housing.

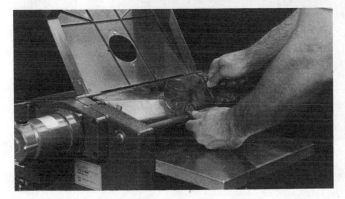

Toxic Woods

There is evidence to show that prolonged exposure to **all** types of sawdust can be harmful, but certain types of woods are known to cause health problems after a relatively short exposure. These woods are classified as 'toxic'.

Toxic woods cause two types of unhealthy reactions — "respiratory ailments" and "skin and eye allergies". Respiratory ailments include bronchial disorders, asthma, rhinitis and muscosal irritations. Skin and eye allergies include dermatitis, conjunctivitis, itching and rashes.

For your safety, here's a list of toxic woods and the reactions they may cause:

Wood	Respiratory Ailments	Skin and Eye Allergies
Arborvitae	x	
Ayan		x
Blackwood, African		x
Boxwood	x	x
Cashew		x
Cedar, Western Red	x	x
Cocobolo		x
Cocus		x
Dahoma	x	
Ebony	x	x
Greenheart	x	x
Guarea	x	
Ipe (Iapacho)	x	x
Iroko	x	x
Katon	x	
Mahogany, African	x	x
Mahogany, American		x
Makore	x	x
Mansonia	x	x
Obeche	x	x
Opepe	x	x
Peroba Rosa	x	x
Peroba, White	x	x
Ramin		x
Rosewood, Brazilian		x
Rosewood, East Indian		x
Satinwood, Ceylon		x
Satinwood, West Indian		x
Sequoia Redwood	x	
Sneezewood	x	
Stavewood	x	
Sucupira		x
Teak		x
Wenge	x	x

*List of toxic woods courtesy **Fine Woodworking** Magazine.*

collector to catch most of the waste so that it can be disposed of easily.

For example, an ordinary cardboard box, set under the lathe while you work, will catch a great deal of sawdust. If you've been collecting your back issues of *Hands On!*, there's a plan for a "Clutter Collector" in the May/June 1981 issue. This plywood trough attaches to the lower way tubes of your Mark V or Model 510, and will catch the sawdust when you're turning or boring.

You may also be able to clamp one of the vacuum heads near your work to suck up the sawdust as you make it. For example, you can easily clamp the DC3300's small floor pick-up between the upper way tubes of the Mark V or Model 510 while you're using the new Shopsmith pneumatic drum sander. (See Figure 11.) This isn't as efficient as a collector that someone might design especially for the sander, but it still collects a great deal of sawdust before it gets to the floor — or your lungs.

If you make or improvise your own pick-ups, be very careful that they do not interfere with the work. Go through a 'dry run' first, without turning the machine on, to see if there are any problems. Then try out the pick-up while working with scrap wood, before you start in on the good stuff.

Figure 11. To improvise your own pick-up, clamp a vacuum head near the work. Just make sure it doesn't interfere with the action of the tool or the movement of the stock.

Keep Your Whisk Broom

If you use your shop vac and pick-ups religiously, you'll find that the dust problem in your shop will decrease noticeably. As I mentioned before, the Shopsmith pick-ups are designed and positioned to suck up over 80% of the waste generated by a tool. This is great news for you and your spouse, but remember that as much as 20% of the sawdust still escapes. Continue to wear your dust mask, clean up your shop regularly — and don't throw away your whisk broom.

TIPS
SAWDUST CONTROL

Accessory Caddy

It goes without saying that to be truly useful, a shop vacuum must also be portable. Unless you have the money and the space for several vacuum units, your one unit has to be carried or wheeled around to each tool as you use them. This is rarely a problem; both the Shopsmith Shopmate and DC3300 come with wheels or dollies.

However, it becomes a problem when you need to constantly mount and remount different size hoses and nozzles on your vacuum. If you store these accessories in a stationary location, you'll find yourself crisscrossing the shop needlessly.

◆ You can make *both* the shop vacuum and its accessories portable by making a 'caddy' that hangs on the side of the vacuum tank or dust collector frame. The caddy shown here has room to store extension wands and several different nozzles.

Figure A. A 'caddy' mounted on your shop vacuum keeps your vacuum accessories handy.

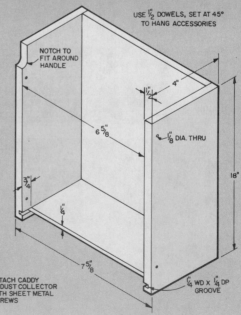

USE ½" DOWELS, SET AT 45° TO HANG ACCESSORIES

NOTCH TO FIT AROUND HANDLE

4"

½"

6 ⅝"

1⅛" DIA. THRU

18"

¾"

¼"

ATTACH CADDY TO DUST COLLECTOR WITH SHEET METAL SCREWS

7 ⅝"

¼" WD X ¼" DP GROOVE

Index